DAVID O. MCKAY LIBRARY

P9-DVD-918

THE PROFANE,
THE CIVIL,
&
THE GODLY

JUN - 1 2004

PROPERTY OF:
DAVID O. McKAY LIBRARY
BYU-IDAHO
REXBURG ID 83460-0405

The Kenneth Scott Latourette Prize
in Religion and Modern History

The Conference on Faith and History, an organization of more than 600 scholars devoted to exploring the relationship of faith to historical study, sponsors a series of historical monographs that assess religion's role in modern culture. These books are the prize winners of an annual manuscript competition conducted by the Conference.

With this series, we honor the memory of a founding member of the Conference on Faith and History, Kenneth Scott Latourette (1884–1968). Latourette was Sterling Professor of Missions and Oriental History at Yale University and the author of more than a score of books on Asian history and on the history of Christianity. Recognized as a preeminent authority on the history of Christianity, of its development in non-Western cultures, and of the history of East Asia, Professor Latourette served as President of the American Historical Association, the Association of Asian Studies, and the American Society of Church History. His deep interest in the study of modern religious and cultural history, his gracious example as a Christian historian, and his outstanding scholarly accomplishments make him our obvious choice for naming this prize.

Religious and cultural history, as Professor Latourette demonstrated throughout his work, is much broader than church history. Indeed, the unifying theme for this competition is the historical study of religion's interplay with other elements of modern culture. The period of history since 1500 has brought a complex of social and cultural developments that provide the common reference point for this series. Religion provides another, for this series will focus on the profoundly human propensity to ground one's identity and life's meaning in a transcendent purpose or force. A historical approach is a fitting way to explore the interaction of religion and modern culture since it allows scholars to address the element so characteristic of modernity, namely, change.

It is the Conference on Faith and History's hope that these books will stimulate further scholarly interest in a field that has already produced path-breaking work, and that they will provide exciting and worthwhile insights for anyone interested in the complex dynamics of religion and modern culture.

THE PROFANE,
THE CIVIL,
&
THE GODLY

The Reformation of Manners in
Orthodox New England,
1679-1749

Richard P. Gildrie

THE PENNSYLVANIA STATE UNIVERSITY PRESS
University Park, Pennsylvania

Library of Congress Cataloging-in-Publication Data

Gildrie, Richard P.
    The profane, the civil, and the godly : the reformation of manners
in orthodox New England, 1679–1749 / Richard P. Gildrie.
        p.   cm.
    Includes bibliographical references and index.
    ISBN 0-271-01065-7. — ISBN 0-271-01068-1 (pbk.)
    1. Puritans—New England—History—17th century.   2. Puritans—New
England—History—18th century.   3. New England—Church
history—17th century.   4. New England—Church history—18th
century.   5. New England—Social life and customs—To 1775.
I.   Title.
BX9355.N35G54   1994
285′.9′0974—dc20   92-46614
                                                                                          CIP

Copyright © 1994 The Pennsylvania State University
All rights reserved
Printed in the United States of America

Published by The Pennsylvania State University Press,
Barbara Building, Suite C, University Park, PA 16802-1003

It is the policy of The Pennsylvania State University Press to use acid-free paper for the first
printing of all clothbound books. Publications on uncoated stock satisfy the minimum
requirements of American National Standard for Information Sciences—Permanence of
Paper for Printed Library Materials, ANSI Z39.48–1984.

To Meredith, Elizabeth, and Evelyn

Contents

Acknowledgments

Scholarship, as in much else in life, is really an extended conversation. Those who have read and commented extensively on various parts of the argument in this work include T. H. Breen, Charles W. Calhoun, Jonathan Chu, Jack P. Greene, Joan Kamensky, Gloria Main, Malcolm Muir, Stephen Nissenbaum, Bernard Rosenthal, George Selement, Charles Sorensen, Kerry Trask, and James Walsh. Four persons—Frank Bremer, William T. Gilmore, Laurel T. Ulrich, and T. Howard Winn—have read and criticized the whole manuscript, sometimes more than once. To all these scholars, and particularly the last four, my debts and appreciation are great. Scholarship, again like life, is replete with sins of omission and commission. The blame for those remaining in this work, despite the best efforts of the persons named above, are mine alone.

I am also heavily indebted to several institutions and libraries. Much of the research in primary sources was done at the American Antiquarian Society while I was a Peterson Fellow in 1983. The Essex Institute, Alderman Library of the University of Virginia, Eisenhower Library at Johns Hopkins University, and Woodward Library at Austin Peay State University were also unfailingly helpful. Many of the questions were formulated at summer seminars sponsored by the National Endowment for the Humanities and taught by T. H. Breen at Northwestern in 1975 and by Jack P. Greene at Johns Hopkins in 1982. I have also received financial assistance from the Tower Fund and Faculty Development Fund of Austin Peay State University over the years and was granted six months free of teaching responsibilities in 1989 to prepare a rough draft through Austin Peay's Faculty Professional Development Assignment Committee. I also want to thank the Institute for the Study of American Evangelicals, headed by Darryl Hart, for awarding the Kenneth Latourette Prize to this manuscript and seeing it into the hands of an energetic, talented editor, Peter J. Potter of the Penn State Press. Word-processing assistance was given by Colleen Watt and Nancy Profitt, without whom the manuscript might very well have died aborning.

It is a pleasure to acknowledge these persons and institutions, because for me they have constituted over the years a scholarly community that has been the source of great joy and inspiration. Finally, this work is dedicated to my wife and daughters—Meredith, Elizabeth, and Evelyn—who form another joyous community, a "well-ordered family."

List of Abbreviations

AAS — American Antiquarian Society

Assistants Recs. — John Noble, ed., *Records of the Court of Assistants of the Colony of Massachusetts Bay,* 3 vols., Boston, 1901–28.

EIHC — *Essex Institute Historical Collections*

Essex Recs. — George F. Dow and Mary Thrasher, eds., *Records and Files of the Quarterly Court of Essex County, Massachusetts, 1636–1691,* 9 vols., Salem, Mass., 1911–21, 1975.

Hampshire Recs. — Hampshire Quarterly Court Records, AAS

Mass. Recs. — Nathaniel B. Shurtleff, ed., *Records of the Governor and Company of Massachusetts Bay in New England,* 5 vols. in 6, Boston, 1853–54.

"Mather Correspondence" — *Massachusetts Historical Society Collections,* 4th ser., VIII (1868).

NEHGR — *New England Historical and Genealogical Register*

NEQ — *New England Quarterly*

Plymouth Recs. — Nathaniel B. Shurtleff and David Pulsifer, eds., *Records of the Colony of New Plymouth,* 12 vols., Boston, 1855–61.

Pynchon Recs.

Joseph Smith, ed., *Colonial Justice in Western Massachusetts, 1639–1702: The Pynchon Court Record,* Cambridge, Mass., 1961.

Suffolk Recs.

Samuel E. Morison, ed., *Records of the Suffolk County Court, 1671–1680,* Colonial Society of Massachusetts *Publications* 29–30 (1933).

WMQ

William and Mary Quarterly

Prologue

Deep into a Sabbath night in 1686, as the moon shone over a crisp February snow covering Ipswich, Massachusetts, Richard Walker, a stolid farmer near the age of fifty, "heard a great noise of dogs barking" after the family was abed "by which his wife was much disturbed, thinking that wolves were about."[1] Two hours before dawn, Walker arose and "lookt out of dores" into "a still night." Then sometime later as he warmed himself by the fireside, he heard voices, "crackling & Ratling," and "a great Rending & spliting of boards." As he walked out to the "roadway" in the gathering dawn his suspicions were confirmed. A band of six to ten of his neighbors "mischievously tore in pieces and threw down a house" and were loading the boards and timber onto a horse-drawn sled.

What was afoot was an extralegal step in a property dispute between two farmers that stretched back over two years. The leader of the demolition crew was Edmund Potter, who had bought fifteen acres, including the land on which the house stood, from Sam Lummas in December 1683. The two men agreed in January 1684 that Lummas could continue to "improve" three of those acres for a year and then had "liberty to carry off the house, barn, apple trees, and most fence" on the lot. But when the year was up Lummas reneged, claiming that Potter had not paid him for a herd of swine. The pigs could not be attached because they were "found cruelly abused and dead" before the warrant could be served. Lummas kept the property and in April 1685 sold off the foundation stones of the barn, bragging that he had the best of Potter. Believing that he had been both swindled and publicly humiliated, Potter bided his time until Lummas moved out of the house.

Goodman Potter was determined to reclaim his honor and as much of his property as possible in a thorough and public manner. As his band gathered at his home to prepare for the removal of the disputed house, he and his wife prevailed upon Thomas Manning, trumpeter for the local militia band, to join the company. Manning was "to sound his trumpet both morning and evening" to ensure that no one in the vicinity would miss the event. And so

1. *Essex Recs.* IX, 580–83, for the case.

at dawn as the sled was being loaded Manning blew a call, tumbling neighbors John Colborne and Goodman Tilton out into the road with Richard Walker. As intended, the uproar also brought Sam Lummas. As the four men walked toward the lot a respectable older fellow called out, apparently taunting Lummas, "you Rogue, you Rogue, you are gon, you are gon."

They then encountered Potter on horseback, and when Lummas asked "whether those Ruines were by his order, Potter answered that he had set them on the worke and warned Lummas of [f] his ground." When Lummas lamely countered that he was on the snow, not the ground, one of Potter's companions claimed that the snow was his, implying that he would defend the right. With the threat of violence in the chill air, Lummas and his friends withdrew. As they left, a young man carrying timber to the sled called after them "in a scoffing way . . . , saying stay & take a dram." To add to Lummas's discomfiture, Potter drove the burdened rig out of his way past his rival's new house with the trumpet sounding, punctuated by gunfire and the shouts of a bystander, "hah Brave boyes, ha brave boyes, ha brave boyes." The festive trumpet-calls and gunfire were repeated at Potter's home lot. Presumably dinner and more drinking followed at Goodman Potter's expense.

Edmund Potter and his compatriots were using a traditional ritual comprehensible throughout the early modern Western world: the *charivari* or "rough music." Combining both penal and festal purposes, these crucial ceremonies of European popular culture allowed common folk to enforce their sense of moral order and to rectify wrongs without recourse to courts or higher authorities. Although their size and degree of elaboration varied considerably, they all involved some central elements expressing folk attitudes and style. There had to be clear targets, and the actions against them must have unmistakable connections, however symbolic, to the faults being punished. Other essential elements included loud and dissonant noises, processions of armed men, derisive and mocking insults widely broadcast, violence or the threat of it, and a celebratory tone, usually involving liquor.[2]

Agents and defenders of the newly emerging nation-states and of the churches of the Reformation and Counter-Reformation were suspicious of, and often hostile to, such customs as threats to public order. Even when not so intended, "rough music" inflicted by the populace undermined the new

2. André Burguière, "The Charivari and Religious Repression in France during the Ancient Regime," in Robert Wheaton and Tamara K. Hareven, eds., *Family and Sexuality in French History* (Philadelphia, 1980), 84–110, esp. 93; Martin Ingram, "Ridings, Rough Music, and the 'Reform of Popular Culture' in Early Modern England," *Past and Present* 105 (1984): 79–113.

governments' and churches' claims to a monopoly on legal and moral enforcement. Other criticisms included the danger to property, unjustifiable violence or excessive humiliation, possible injustice arising from malice and lies untested in a rational legal proceeding, and the opportunity and cover given to vicious persons to subvert rather than defend community rights and standards. Obviously these criticisms were not restricted to "elites." By the late seventeenth century the custom, although rarely directly or forcibly suppressed, was clearly falling out of favor in both England and France.

The orthodox Puritan leaders in Massachusetts, with their emphasis on equitable law and broad popular access to official justice, understandably took a dim view of such conduct. Consequently, when Samuel Lummas hauled Edmund Potter before the Ipswich magistrate, Samuel Appleton, Goodman Potter's defense was, first, that he legally owned the house according to the deed and, second, that his actions were "not done in a riotous manner." He downplayed the element of threat to public order by asserting that "no unlawful weapons were used, only such tools as were proper for the work." Nonetheless, Appleton found Potter liable for damages. Potter appealed to the Essex Quarterly Court, which gathered depositions late into March, but in the end the case was "nonsuited" for unspecified reasons.

This story suggests that some of the more indecorous and rowdy elements of traditional European popular culture had made their way across the ocean to provincial Massachusetts and that these ideas and customs were embraced by respectable, solid citizens. Goodman Potter and his friends were not mariners or servants or youths or recent immigrants unaccustomed to Puritan rule. Nor were they poor, communal-minded "peasants" resisting the encroachment of market-oriented individualism. Edmund Potter, a substantial profit-seeking farmer, used a traditional custom to protect his economic interests and to vindicate his honor before his peers. Although the device was ancient, the fact that he chose to rely on himself and his friends rather than on the official institutions of his society suggests not only his orientation to a European village tradition but also to a future that would enshrine the "independent yeoman farmer" as the backbone of a free society.

INTRODUCTION

Puritanism, Popular Culture, and the Reform Tradition

A major goal of the Puritan movement in England and America was a "Reformation of Manners," an effort to recast public and private conduct toward self-control, prudence, orderliness, diligence, and piety. In this ambition Puritanism was not unique, for prolonged campaigns for moral reform are a recurrent feature of Western civilization. During the early modern era, English Puritanism was one of several movements, growing out of the Reformation and Counter-Reformation, bent on what has been called "The Triumph of Lent."[1]

That orthodox New England—those settlements that coalesced in the seventeenth century to form the colonies of Massachusetts and Connecticut—also vigorously pursued the Reformation of Manners late in that century may seem odd or even excessive, given the success of the Puritan movement in creating and shaping the region's distinctive society and culture. If "Lent" had triumphed anywhere in the Atlantic world, it would seem to have been Puritan New England. Yet a reinvigorated moral and social reform movement flourished amid the crises that gripped the region from King Philip's War through the Great Awakening. Orthodox New England too participated in what Jon Butler has insightfully termed a "renewal of Christian authority," which swept the colonial world from the 1680s to the mid-eighteenth century.[2]

---

1. Peter Burke, *Popular Culture in Early Modern Europe* (New York, 1978), 207–43; Bruce Lenman, "The Limits of Godly Discipline with Particular Reference to England and Scotland," in Kaspar von Greyerz, ed., *Religion and Society in Early Modern Europe, 1500–1800* (London, 1984), 124–25.

2. Jon Butler, *Awash in a Sea of Faith: Christianizing the American People* (Cambridge, Mass., 1990), 98–128, esp. 98–99.

Beginning with the Massachusetts Reforming Synod of 1679, this study seeks to understand not only the fears and aspirations of the reformers but also the customs and attitudes they sought to transform. That Anglo-American Puritanism embodied a coherent but supple social ethic stressing communal order, the "spiritualized household," and personal sobriety is beyond dispute. In England and America, Puritan moralists denounced those vices and crimes, such as gambling, drunkenness, violence, and adultery, that contradicted their vision of the good society. They also sought to suppress or regulate alehouses and such customs as harvest revels and the traditional Christmas, which, they believed, bred vice and disorder.[3]

In their view, these evils were not random but rather expressions of alternative modes of life and thought. A major theme of this study is that their analysis was essentially correct, even in orthodox New England. The Reformation of Manners was a struggle among competing but, as we shall see, overlapping visions of the good life. The alternative views were less coherent than Puritan orthodoxy but still had sufficient moral and intellectual integrity to make the contest something more than a prudish campaign to suppress the quaint customs of old England or to cure the ills to which all flesh is prone. Indeed, in the struggle, American Puritanism and its alternatives were changed. New definitions of liberty and social responsibility emerged, laying the foundations for eighteenth-century New England's peculiar "compound of republican and liberal ideals," to quote John L. Brooke.[4]

By the 1680s Puritan moralists commonly referred to these varying ways of life as "conversations." In 1684, for instance, William Hubbard, then pastor at Hingham, Massachusetts, explained "that according to the Original word, nothing is intended therein, but the way or course of a mans life, according to the Metaphor usual in the Scriptures, where a mans works or the course and frame of his life is compared to a way or path that leads from one place to another."[5] Hubbard and his colleagues understood the "course and frame" of a person's life not only as a direction but also a mode of

3. Margo Todd, *Christian Humanism and the Puritan Social Order* (New York, 1987), 16–19; William Hunt, *The Puritan Moment: The Coming of Revolution in an English Country* (Cambridge, Mass., 1983), 79–81; Stephen Foster, *Their Solitary Way: The Puritan Social Ethic in the First Century of New England* (New Haven, 1971); David D. Hall, *Worlds of Wonder, Days of Judgment: Popular Religious Belief in Early New England* (New York, 1989), esp. 240.

4. John L. Brooke, *The Heart of the Commonwealth: Society and Political Culture in Worcester County, Massachusetts, 1713–1861* (New York, 1989), xiv–xv.

5. William Hubbard, *The Benefit of a Well-Ordered Conversation* (Boston, 1684), 3–4.

communication, which, by its very nature, must have both social and cultural meaning.

Although "in this lower world . . . , there are many paths or wayes," Hubbard and other Puritan thinkers generally classified these moral styles as "profane," "civil," or "godly."[6] Described as "disorderly," "idle," and "intemperate," the profane were self-centered and self-indulgent persons indifferent to their obligations to God or to the society at large. At the opposite extreme, of course, was godliness, the proper ordering of one's spiritual and social life so as to honor God and serve humanity. In between were the civil, those who embraced order, decency, and generally the same "outward" standards of conduct as the godly but from self-seeking, prudential motives. Increase Mather in 1682 denounced "only civil moral men" as "hypocrites" who, animated by the "lust of the flesh, the lust of the eyes, and pride of life," sought "worldly profits, pleasures, preferments" through the "external performance of duty." In his view, both the civil and profane were "vain persons" because, whatever their outward differences in conduct, they were self-absorbed. There was no assurance that the merely civil would not readily transgress the rules of good conduct if that suited their immediate interests, for they had no grounding in "true godliness." Their "conversation," like that of the profane, could lead to disorder in this world and damnation in the next. Hence there was great social as well as religious significance in conversion. As Mather preached, "True conversion implieth not only a marvellous change as to man's outward actions, causing him to walk in new ways, which once he was a stranger unto, but as to his nature, and inward disposition and inclinations."

Yet there was ambiguity even in Mather's strict interpretation of the distinctions between godliness and civility. From a social as opposed to a religious perspective, even he did not doubt that the civil were clearly preferable to the profane. As he once observed, "There is a Moral Sobriety which is not saving, and yet even that is lovely and commendable."[7] Any government, including "heathenish" ones, could and should enforce civility, while godliness, in the "saving" sense, came solely by the grace of God and was found only in the "true, reformed Churches of Christ." At other times Mather and his allies spoke as though even godliness could be taught and learned. As many scholars have noted, this apparent contradiction was inherent in Cal-

---

6. For instance, Hubbard, *Benefit of a Well-Ordered Conversation*, 36–40; Increase Mather, *Practical Truths Tending to Promote the Power of Godliness* (Boston, 1682), 81, 172–78.

7. Increase Mather, *Wo to Drunkards* (Boston, 1673), 15.

vinism, and efforts to reconcile it were crucial to Calvinism's development. Thus the relationship between piety and civility in the Reformation of Manners, which sought to instill good conduct while encouraging a godliness that established the spiritual context and underpinning of that civility, was close but not unambivalent.[8]

For the reformers the terms "godly, civil, and profane" did not refer to social or economic classes, although the pursuit of each had obvious social and economic consequences. Rather, they represented modes of conduct, together with the "inward dispositions" or attitudes that guided them. Thus, the profane included not only the bawdy and idle among the poor but also those wealthier traders who sought "Commodities to make fuel for Lust, and called young persons not to the temple of the Lords House, but to our own private recesses to offer sacrifices to Bacchus and Venus."[9] Each term also implied characteristic institutions and rituals. For example, illicit alehouses, "rough ridings," and Maypole dances were profane. Meetinghouses and religious services were associated with godliness, while pursuing one's interests in court rather than seeking mediation in "a church way" was "merely civil." Nor did the reformers hold that individuals were necessarily bound exclusively to one mode. They knew that the godly could lapse into "profane conversation" and that the profane could experience civil or even godly impulses. Indeed, that very mutability provided the opportunity for conversion and the rationale for the Reformation of Manners.

In modern terms, the reformers were analysts of and partisans in an extended conflict over what Clifford Geertz has called "moral imagination." He described the "social history of moral imagination" rather jargonistically as "the construction and deconstruction of symbolic systems as individuals and groups of individuals try to make sense of the profusion of things that happen to them." Geertz's argument is that the formation and conflicted histories of these moral visions provide the unifying principles of cultures, which otherwise would be little more than hodgepodges of notions, artifacts, styles, and customs. As a recent historian has argued, "The core of culture lies in how people conceptualize their relations to each other—the claims people

---

8. Todd, *Christian Humanism,* 178, 193, 203–4; Richard P. Gildrie, "Civility, Piety, and the Reformation of Manners in Augustan New England," *Studies in Puritan American Spirituality* 2 (1991): 107–28; Norman Pettit, *The Heart Prepared: Grace and Conversion in Puritan Spiritual Life* (New Haven, 1966); John Morgan, *Godly Learning: Puritan Attitudes towards Reason, Learning, and Education, 1560–1640* (New York, 1986), esp. 23–40; Harry S. Scout, *The New England Soul: Preaching and Religious Culture in Colonial New England* (New York, 1986), esp. 32–47.

9. Hubbard, *Benefit of a Well-Ordered Conversation,* 97–98.

make on each other, the deference toward each others' claims, and the concerns and caring people have for one another."[10] Each of the conversations described by William Hubbard, Increase Mather, and other reformers was an exercise in "moral imagination," a comprehensible pattern of thought and conduct, and their complex interaction was central to the social and intellectual history of New England, certainly from the 1680s through the 1740s.[11]

In light of current scholarship on popular and learned cultures of the early modern era, an obvious question is how or even whether this pattern of profane, civil, and godly conversations fits within that broader framework.[12] The problem is difficult. Yet, as the works of David D. Hall among others demonstrate, it is possible to use terms like "popular culture" or "popular religion" in Puritan American studies without becoming embroiled in simplistic dualisms or social and economic determinism.[13] Further, it is essential to try to reconcile these quite different forms of analysis for two reasons. First is a need for comparative perspective. The New England Reformation of Manners after 1679 was a phase not only of a longer, more geographically encompassing Anglo-American Puritanism but also of even broader reform currents stretching from the Reformation and Counter-Reformation through the Enlightenment. The scholarship on these movements is almost invariably written in terms of the learned-popular paradigm.[14] The second reason is that this modern historiography, although fraught with confusion and distracting controversy, is lush with insights and suggestions. For instance, some of these studies provide ways to translate the reformers' terminology into concepts that

10. Clifford Geertz, "Found in Translation: Social History of Moral Imagination," in his *Local Knowledge: Further Essays in Interpretive Anthropology* (New York, 1983), 36–54, 119; Gerald M. Sider, "The Ties That Bind: Culture and Agriculture, Property and Propriety in the Newfoundland Village Fishery," *Social History* 5 (1980): 21.

11. Philip F. Gura, *A Glimpse of Sion's Glory: Puritan Radicalism in New England, 1620–1660* (Middletown, Conn., 1984), makes a similar argument, albeit in different terms, to explain the earlier development of the New England Way.

12. A wise friend suggested that this issue not be raised and that only the language of the contemporary advocates of the Reformation of Manners be used because the contemporary concepts are more supple, immediately relevant to the participants, and free of the ideological baggage and accumulated confusions of recent scholarship.

13. Good examples include Hall, *Worlds of Wonder,* 3–20; George Selement, "The Meeting of Elite and Popular Minds at Cambridge, New England, 1638–1645," *WMQ* 61 (1984): 32–48.

14. For commentaries, see Stuart Clark, "French Historians and Early Modern Popular Culture," *Past and Present* 100 (1983): 62–99; Natalie Zemon Davis, "From 'Popular Religion' to Religious Cultures," in Steven E. Ozment, ed., *Reformation Europe: A Guide to Research* (St. Louis, 1982), 321–44; Peter Burke, "Popular Culture between History and Ethnology," *Ethnologia Europaea* 14 (1984): 5–13.

at least seem more comprehensible and less pejorative to modern understanding. In this reconciliation of perspectives, however, the reformers' model of conflicting conversations has priority, and recent analyses will be used mainly to clarify their sense of the attitudes and conduct of all sides engaged in the Reformation of Manners.

An important strain among current interpretations of popular and learned cultures conceives of them as patterns of discourse, styles of communication including not only verbal expressions but also rituals, customs, and characteristic forms of conduct.[15] Because these systems were taught and learned, it was possible for persons to move from one mode to another, depending upon their degree of exposure to and understanding of their options. This general theory of culture is congruent with the reformers' sense of moral conversations. In a combined view, traditional English popular culture is that broad pattern of discourse, or conversation, which virtually all English folk, regardless of status or learning, understood. To understand, of course, is not necessarily to approve. Also, if cultures are analogous to conversations and not to syllogisms, then they should contain contradictions and confusions that animate the discourse, shaping them over time. We expect to see that process in learned discourses, as in theology, formal philosophy, and even classical music. There is no reason, according to these theories, to believe that popular cultures do not involve similar internal dynamics.

Finally, popular and learned discourses often influence each other. There are always persons conversant with at least elements of both who then are "brokers" applying ideas or styles from one to the other. This process is not invariably one-way, leading to some form of "cultural hegemony" of learned or "elite" over popular or "folk" discourse.[16] The clerics of the Reformation of Manners were such "brokers," expressing a moral vision developed largely out of their superior education and status and seeking to influence a popular culture that, in turn, had helped to shape not only their daily experience but also the learned culture out of which they spoke.

15. Rhys Isaac, "A Discourse on Method: Action, Structure, and Meaning," in his *Transformation of Virginia, 1740–1790* (Chapel Hill, 1982), 323–57; Fred Mathews, "'Hobbesian Populism': Interpretive Paradigms and Moral Vision in American Historiography," *Journal of American History* 72 (1985): 92–115; David D. Hall, "Introduction," in Steven L. Kaplan, ed., *Understanding Popular Culture: Europe from the Middle Ages to the Nineteenth Century* (Berlin, 1984), 5–18. For a thoughtful critique, see John E. Toews, "Intellectual History after the Linguistic Turn: The Autonomy of Meaning and the Irreducibility of Experience," *American Historical Review* 92 (1987): 879–907.

16. T. J. Jackson Lears, "The Concept of Cultural Hegemony: Problems and Possibilities," *American Historical Review* 90 (1985): 567–93.

Although the reformers' concept of conversation is congruent with the stress on discourse among many recent scholars, it is more difficult but still possible to reconcile the reformers' sense of the profane, civil, and godly with the modern popular-learned model. There are no exact equivalences. The profane conversation was not identical to popular culture. Nor was godliness restricted to the learned. After all, in the eyes of these Anglo-American moralists much of the philosophy and literature of the ancient world, familiar in their original languages only to the very learned, was profane indeed. Also, much that was popular, meaning part of the broadest folk culture, encouraged godly conversation. In other words, "popular" is certainly not to be used as a synonym for "secular" or "pagan," another favorite term of the reformers. Despite some scholars' suggestions to the contrary it is hard to imagine, as one recent historian has observed, that Christianity and English folk culture could coexist for a thousand years without changing and without profoundly influencing each other.[17]

The connections are closer but not exactly equivalent at the levels of "inward disposition," as the reformers put it, or "moral imagination." Increase Mather and his colleagues were convinced that persons who remained bound by either or both of the profane and civil conversations were "unregenerate." He lumped them together in the aftermath of the Reforming Synod of 1679 as "vain persons," where "vain" implied both ultimately futile in their attempts to shape a good or meaningful life and proud or self-seeking in those efforts.[18] In modern terms, what the profane and civil seem to share is a commitment to individualism, a vision of society as a competitive arena. Godliness, in contrast, stressed cooperation and mutuality among persons. Individualism was at the core of the moral imagination shaping traditional English popular culture, and it was what they took to be its more excessive expressions that most offended the advocates of the Reformation of Manners.

In noting the extremes of this temperament, Michael Zuckerman has described English colonists who "were impatient of conventional social ties and inclined to set their own advantage before the public good. In Massachusetts, as much as in Virginia and Carolina, authorities had to contend with 'self-love' that 'forgot all duty' and with men who 'neither feared God nor man.'" As Zuckerman implied, such individualism is not to be identified simply with acquisitiveness. It was a much broader attitude. At its core was

17. Richard Godbeer, *The Devil's Dominion: Magic and Religion in Early New England* (New York, 1992), 25–30.
18. Mather, *Practical Truths Tending to Promote the Power of Godliness,* esp. 160–67, 172.

the assertion of a personal sense of worth and autonomy, even at the expense of communal interests, which nonetheless demanded respect or affirmation from others. In seventeenth-century terms, personal "honor and dignity" included both self-esteem and public recognition. Hence, individualism was a type of social relations. Naturally such individual "honor and dignity" was often tenuous, particularly in hierarchical societies, and was frequently expressed aggressively.[19]

In a fairly typical incident in 1705, several substantial farmers, driving carts loaded with firewood for sale in Boston, met the governor, Joseph Dudley, and his entourage on a narrow, snowy road. Upon being commanded to allow the governor's carriage free passage, one farmer shouted, "I am as good flesh and blood as you; I will not give way; you may goe out of the way," and prepared to defend himself. The governor, sword in hand, advanced on him, but the farmer "layd hold of the Govr. and broke the sword in his hand." The farmer had his way, forcing the furious governor to wait. The personal honor of both the farmer and the governor were immediately at hazard, and both responded violently.

The assertion by personal pronoun that "I am as good flesh and blood as you" was a common challenge. In 1699 Cotton Mather reported a servant who "would utter such words as these, I am Flesh and Blood, as well as my Master, and therefore know no Reason why my Master should not obey me as well as I obey him!"[20] Also, the frequent reference to "flesh and blood" in such assertions, echoing the imagery of the sacraments, gave the claim to egalitarian individualism a certain sanctity.

Such attitudes were quite widespread. Describing the people of seventeenth-century Springfield, Massachusetts, Stephen Innes wrote, "In their social conduct, as in their economic activities, the inhabitants behaved as self-assertive individuals, not as other-directed communitarians." In that trait, the people of Springfield were hardly unique. More generally in colonial New England, according to another recent scholar, "a dramatic and poignant struggle took place between community-oriented values and antinomian

---

19. Michael Zuckerman, "Identity in British America: Unease in Eden," in Nicholas Canny and Anthony Pagden, eds., *Colonial Identity in the Atlantic World, 1500–1800* (Princeton, 1987), 132; Keith Thomas, "The Social Origins of Hobbes's Political Thought," in K. C. Brown, ed., *Hobbes Studies* (Cambridge, Mass., 1965), 185–236, esp. 189–90; Alan Macfarlane, *The Origins of English Individualism: The Family, Property, and Social Transition* (New York, 1978, 1979).

20. M. Halsey Thomas, ed., *Diary of Samuel Sewall, 1674–1719* (New York, 1973), 1:532–37; Cotton Mather, *Pillars of Salt: A History of Some Criminals Executed in This Land* (Boston, 1699), 68–69.

individualism."[21] This conflict was central to the cultural and social development of the region.

It is a mistake, however, to regard the relationship between individualism and communalism as a simple dichotomy. As J. E. Crowley observed, "In the right conditions, individualism and devotion to community were complementary." The problem for orthodox New England was to discover those conditions, to find ways to affirm and embody elements of both communal and individualist spirits.[22] In fact, one finding of this study is that the dialogue between the reformers and the profane eventuated for many New Englanders in a tamed, disciplined individualism dwelling within a libertarian communalism. That dialogue and result are at the core of orthodox New England's experience from the Reforming Synod through the Great Awakening.

But this quest for personal autonomy was not a simple impulse finding only one mode of expression. The individualism ingrained in traditional English, and perhaps even Western European, popular culture took at least three occasionally contradictory forms: hedonistic, possessive, and pietist. The interplay of these three constituted much of the conversation or dialectic shaping popular culture in Old and New England. As brokers operating largely from a learned and godly perspective, the reformers joined that conversation and used the contradictions in their efforts to recast popular culture. In New England they succeeded to a remarkable extent. Yet in the process their attitudes and tactics were also changed. As Peter Burke has noted in a wider context, "The history of European popular culture shows that it is extremely resilient, that ordinary people have often been able to resist attempts to reform them. In order to reduce such resistance it has been traditional for missionaries to 'accommodate' their ideas to their audience—a process which sometimes leaves one wondering who was converting whom."[23] These complex dynamics were at the heart of the Reformation of Manners.

The reformers were most appalled by hedonistic individualism, which was the "inward disposition" of the profane. It found expression through preference for leisure or "idleness" over work, for consumption over saving, and for spontaneity in general over calculation. Deep drinking, gambling, and

---

21. Stephen Innes, *Labor in a New Land: Economy and Society in Seventeenth-Century Springfield* (Princeton, 1983), xviii; Patrice Higonnet, *Sister Republics: The Origins of French and American Republicanism* (Cambridge, Mass., 1988), 15.

22. J. E. Crowley, *This Sheba, Self: The Conceptualization of Economic Life in Eighteenth-Century America* (Baltimore, 1974), 31. See also David D. Hall, "Religion and Society: Problems and Reconsiderations," in Jack P. Greene and J. R. Pole, eds., *Colonial British America: Essays in the New History of the Early Modern Era* (Baltimore, 1984), 335–36.

23. Burke, "Popular Culture between History and Ethnology," 7.

other diversions deemed "wasteful" or "dangerous" by censorious reformers grew out of this outlook, along with a marked tolerance for disorder and an often cavalier attitude toward the interests, feelings, and property of others. Although profane conduct often appeared merely impetuous or random, it in fact had a pattern with its own rituals and principles. It was an assertion of personal autonomy, impatient of control by civil or religious authority. Yet the profane also sought respect from their peers through such devices as wrestling matches and competitive consumption in feasting, drinking, impulsive generosity, and wagering. There was an inherent egalitarianism in this mode of life that many in England and America thought incompatible with social order, an attitude not restricted to the advocates of the Reformation of Manners.[24]

Possessive individualism, to use C. B. Macpherson's famous term, was a drive to acquire property and improve economic security for oneself or one's family.[25] To the reformers, this desire was an essential motive or "inward disposition" of the merely civil. Although modern scholars restrict this concept to economic goals, the reformers, while mentioning the economic aspect most frequently, also included other self-seeking benefits such as social respectability or political influence to be gained by prudential or "hypocritical" obedience to the rules of propriety. As this form of individual self-expression required a commitment to prudence, labor, calculation, and self-discipline of passions, it conflicted with hedonistic conduct, even though both shared a stress on competition. Because its virtues overlapped with godliness, despite the differences in motive and social vision, the reformers tended over the long haul to compromise with the civil in order to control the profane.[26]

Pietistic individualism was an intense commitment to personal religious experience, often in preference to or even in defiance of the theology, rituals,

24. Christopher Hill, "The Many-Headed Monster," in his *Change and Continuity in Seventeenth-Century England* (Cambridge, Mass., 1975), 101–204; Edmund Leites, *The Puritan Conscience and Modern Sexuality* (New Haven, 1986), esp. 5; John Addy, *Sin and Society in the Seventeenth Century* (London, 1989), 103–58.

25. C. B. Macpherson, *The Political Theory of Possessive Individualism: Hobbes to Locke* (Oxford, 1962). Alan Macfarlane, in his *Origins of English Individualism* and *The Culture of Capitalism* (London, 1987), argues that this learned philosophy of "liberalism" was grounded in "peasant" or folk conduct and attitudes in England reaching back at least into the thirteenth century and was thus an essential element of traditional English popular culture.

26. Arthur Mitzman, "The Civilizing Offensive: Mentalities, High Culture, and Individual Psyches," *Journal of Social History* 29 (1987): 663–87; R. L. Entzminger, "Courtesy: The Cultural Imperative," *Philological Quarterly* 54 (1974): 389–400; Crowley, *This Sheba, Self;* Ralph Lerner, "Commerce and Character: Anglo-American as a New Model Man," *WMQ* 36 (1979): 2–26.

and institutions of orthodoxy. This "individual quest for God," in the words of a recent French historian, "was probably the dominant theme in popular religion, perhaps in all religion from the fourteenth to the eighteenth century."[27] In its indifference to fine distinctions, popular religion tended to be simpler and more eclectic than the preferred clerical standards. For instance, popular religion in New England and elsewhere in the English world exhibited greater tolerance for occult or magical practices than the strict Protestant orthodoxy of the reformers.[28]

In the reformers' view the amorphousness and eclecticism of popular religion were important problems, but even more fundamentally they were symptoms of a lack of spiritual and intellectual discipline reflecting a tendency toward excessive individualism. Pietism, a strong commitment to personal religious experience, was, of course, a vital element of Puritan orthodoxy, along with moralism and what Theodore Dwight Bozeman has called "biblicist primitivism" or a marked preference for scriptural interpretation over patristic or medieval theological tradition as a source of religious authority.[29] The reformers' worry was that personal pietism, unbounded by moral definition or biblical authority, was a prolific source of heresy and social disorder. To them, such movements as antinomianism, radical separatism, "enthusiasm," and Quakerism shared an undisciplined and hence arrogant spirituality. This spiritual pride found competitive expression as persons compared and debated their religious ideas and experiences. Such personal piety in popular religion became over time a form of spiritual athleticism in which the more skilled and flamboyant won laurels from God and their peers while the losers were cast into outer darkness. Pietistic individualism, then, was an element of popular culture that seemed to the reformers to be a self-seeking parody of godliness.[30]

These three strands of English popular culture—hedonistic, possessive, and pietistic individualism—together with the attitudes and conduct to which they gave rise do not exhaust the possibilities, complexities, and nuances of

27. Ranum Orest, "The Refuges of Intimacy," in Roger Chartier, ed., *A History of Private Life,* vol. 3, *Passions of the Renaissance,* trans. Arthur Goldhammer (Cambridge, Mass., 1989), 236.

28. Godbeer, *Devil's Dominion,* 16–17, 25, 41, 46–53; Hall, *Worlds of Wonder,* 71–116; Butler, *Awash in a Sea of Faith,* 67–97; Barry Reay, "Popular Religion," in his *Popular Culture in Seventeenth-Century England* (London, 1985, 1988), esp. 111.

29. Theodore Dwight Bozeman, *To Live Ancient Lives: The Primitivist Dimension in Puritanism* (Chapel Hill, 1988), 9–12.

30. David S. Lovejoy, *Religious Enthusiasm in the New World: Heresy to Revolution* (Cambridge, Mass., 1985), 1–3, 22–134.

that ancient tradition as it developed in Old and New England. Yet they were the forms of moral imagination or social vision of deepest concern to the advocates of the Reformation of Manners. The dynamism within popular culture itself, the pressures of individualism in various forms, and the interplay of the profane, the civil, and the godly all helped to shape the history of Puritanism and the people it was meant to serve and reform.

With this overall pattern in mind, we can posit phases of the cultural development of early New England, particularly the interaction of Puritan standards and popular traditions. Before 1660 those elements of folk culture most distinct from Puritanism were present, but usually in attenuated forms. In England the ritualistic details of "ridings," carnival, and harvest festival, for instance, were customary and local. In earliest New England, with settlers from various parts of England, establishing new patterns was difficult. Meanwhile, Puritan orthodoxy—based more directly on written prescription than on custom and centered on meetinghouse and town meeting—became strongly established and opposed vehemently the more flamboyant expressions of popular mores, particularly those related to hedonist conduct. Those portions of popular tradition most congruent with Puritanism, such as strong personal piety and the ambition to place families on the land, flourished. The anticlerical, antiauthoritarian impulses were often channeled into congregational autonomy, heresies such as antinomianism and Quakerism, and occasional squabbles over political and property rights.[31]

By 1660 a fairly coherent provincial variant of English popular culture emerged in New England. Gradually the populace grafted the themes of traditional rituals onto the official Puritan system of civic and religious observances. This process paralleled the development of standardized agricultural and governmental practices, which also took time. As the population became denser, it was easier to reproduce such things as the tavern culture, so crucial to English daily life.[32] Thus, by 1660 elements of popular culture not directly related to Puritan forms appeared, including even the celebration

31. Richard L. Bushman, "American High-Style and Vernacular Cultures," in Greene and Pole, eds., *Colonial British America*, 370–72; Gura, *Glimpse of Sion's Glory;* Michael Zuckerman, "Pilgrims and the Wilderness: Community, Modernity, and the Maypole at Merrymount," *NEQ* 50 (1977): 255–77; John Demos, "Notes on Life in Plymouth Colony," *WMQ* 12 (1965): 264–86; James T. Lemon, "Spatial Order: Householders in Local Communities and Regions," in Greene and Pole, eds., *Colonial British America*, 100–101.

32. Richard P. Gildrie, "The Ceremonial Puritan: Days of Humiliation and Thanksgiving," *NEHGR* 136 (1982): 3–16; David Grayson Allen, *In English Ways: The Movement and Transferal of English Local Law and Custom to Massachusetts Bay in the Seventeenth Century* (Chapel Hill, 1981); Peter Clark, *The English Alehouse: A Social History, 1200–1830* (London, 1983), 145–249.

of Christmas. What apparently did not flourish, except perhaps among mariners, was the rich vocational subcultures of England, for there were too few artisans of any one trade to support those customs and festivals until the eighteenth century. For the same reason markets and fairs, while they had recreational uses, seem more strictly economic in function in early New England.

In the aftermath of King Philip's War (1675–76), stimulated by frontier and imperial pressures, the pace of social, political, and ideological conflict increased markedly.[33] The clerics of Massachusetts Bay responded with a renewed effort at moral and social reform, a campaign officially opened at the Reforming Synod of 1679 and concentrating on such fundamental issues as "family government," the "rising generation," economic ethics, and tavern mores. Although, as one scholar has remarked, "it is a bad habit in historians to take at their face value the hysterical exaggerations of the pulpit,"[34] it seems equally unwise to ignore their analyses and the possible impact of their efforts. The fact that there were simultaneous eruptions of reform in England and Virginia should indicate a significance beyond a local New England purgation of conscience or a cynical attempt by ministers to regain lost influence.[35]

The crisis over the Dominion of New England (1685–93), including the Salem witchcraft trials, marked a turning point and opened a phase of Augustan civility corresponding rather closely to developments in moral thought and reform in early eighteenth-century Britain. These decades saw an emphasis on the "anglicization" of the institutions and mores of orthodox New England. Prior to the American Revolution, this latter phase of moral and social reform was related to the Great Awakening. Out of this long sequence there emerged in New England, in parallel with other parts of the English-speaking world, a sort of "tamed individualism," a temporary reconciliation of reformed standards and popular traditional aspirations and mores that helped establish a moral basis for a new republic.[36]

33. T. H. Breen, "War, Taxes, and Political Brokers: The Ordeal of Massachusetts Bay, 1675–1692," in his *Puritans and Adventurers: Change and Persistence in Early America* (New York, 1980), 81–105.

34. Ronald A. Knox, *Enthusiasm: A Chapter in the History of Religion, with Special Reference to the Seventeenth and Eighteenth Centuries* (New York, 1961), 396.

35. Harry Grant Plum, *Restoration Puritanism: A Study in the Growth of English Liberty* (Chapel Hill, 1943), 13–14, 44–45, 56; Paton Yoder, "Tavern Regulation in Virginia: Rationale and Reality," *Virginia Magazine of History and Biography* 87 (1979): 259–78.

36. Richard L. Bushman, "'This New Man': Dependence and Independence, 1776," in his *Uprooted Americans: Essays to Honor Oscar Handlin* (Boston, 1979), 77–96. See also Crowley, *This Sheba, Self.*

In 1738 Jonathan Edwards, the finest mind of New England's Awakening, expressed what had become the common sense of his time and people about the pursuit of happiness.

> Some, although they love their own happiness, do not place that happiness in their own confined good, or in that good which is limited to themselves but more in the common good—in that which is the good of others, or in the good to be enjoyed in and by others. A man's love of his own happiness, when it runs in this last channel, is not what is called selfishness, but is the very opposite of it.[37]

Here the Puritan voice reconciled the drive to individual autonomy central to popular tradition with the civic humanist claim that the full dignity of persons requires responsible participation in civil life, as well as with the century's definition of "virtue" as a willingness to promote the public welfare over private interest. The most profound contribution of popular culture to this pattern of republican thought in America was the insistence that the true ground of this uneasy synthesis lay not in obligation to God or state or even in mutual dependence but in the right of self-assertion in all realms. It is that right upon which human dignity most depends, and it is that right and its concomitants that make a virtuous republic even conceivable. Hence the state, the economy, and social life in general exist only to protect, express, and respond to that essential human right. Indeed, it is that definition of human dignity that not only justified and connected capitalism and popular sovereignty in America, but also limited permissible conduct pursued in their names.[38]

Of course it should be remembered that this perennial attempt to reconcile freedom and order, in which the Reformation of Manners played an important role, had implications beyond political thought and economic ethics. It also concerned daily mores, family life, gender relations, and the themes of literature and art. In short, what we are endeavoring to explore is a portion of that large, old-fashioned realm of social and intellectual history,

---

37. Jonathan Edwards, *Charity and Its Fruits [1738]* (1852; Carlisle, Pa., 1969), 164.

38. Thomas L. Prangle, *The Spirit of Modern Republicanism: The Moral Vision of the American Founders and the Philosophy of John Locke* (Chicago, 1988), 127; Ralph Lerner, "Commerce and Character: The Anglo-American as a New Model Man," *WMQ* 6 (1979): 2–26; J.G.A. Pocock, "Virtues, Rights, and Manners: A Model for Historians of Political Thought," in his *Virtue, Commerce, and History: Essays on Political Thought and History, Chiefly in the Eighteenth Century* (Cambridge, 1985), 37–50; Joyce Appleby, "Republicanism in Old and New Contexts," *WMQ* 43 (1986): 20–34.

"manners and morals," seen in a wide cultural context. In pursuing this "social history of moral imagination" in provincial New England,[39] we seek to understand the profane, the civil, and the godly in their struggles to comprehend and express their conflicting versions of the good life. We do this because those of that era who were on this quest not only acted in their time and place but also influenced the traditions we inherit. Their story is in large part our story as well.

To better understand those moral imaginings and the rich texture of experience out of which they came and which they helped to form, this study is restricted largely to provincial Massachusetts, Plymouth, and Connecticut from the Massachusetts Reforming Synod of 1679, which most clearly defined the problem, to the end of the Great Awakening. It is organized into three sections. The first, including a chapter on the synod and one on the moral imagination of the profane, is a description of the antagonists' points of view and general conduct. The next five chapters, grouped under the heading "Arenas of Conflict," concern particular issues and tensions as the Reformation of Manners proceeded through the end of the seventeenth century. The third section, "The Measure of Civility," concentrates on a redefinition of civility during the early eighteenth century. A major strand of the argument is that the unique social and cultural development of orthodox New England cannot be attributed, in whole or in part, to an anomalous absence of a traditional popular culture found everywhere else in the English-speaking world. Rather, the colony evolved largely out of a dialectic encounter that changed both Puritanism and popular culture within that specific geographic and historical setting.

Nor were the ideas and pressures shaping the region purely local. Both Puritanism and popular culture were, after all, English and continued to be influenced by English events, persons, and styles. Indeed, in the early eighteenth century closer political, social, and economic ties to the homeland virtually raised a "gentrified" royalist anglicization to the status of a fourth "voice" in New England's life and thought. In short, dynamism, not stagnation, marked the moral and intellectual heritage of orthodox New England and thus better accounts for the remarkable creativity of the region throughout American history.

39. Geertz, "Found in Translation," 36–54.

THE REFORMATION OF MANNERS

ONE

The Reforming Synod of 1679

Increase Mather, pastor of Boston's North Church for nearly twenty years, had reason to be pleased as he walked through a September morning to the first session of what was to be the Reforming Synod of 1679. The meetings, which he had worked toward for over five years and which he would nearly dominate, ratified his position as one of the most important intellectual and political leaders of his generation of New England clerics.[1] More important, the synod marked a crucial moment in redefining or clarifying the American Puritan mission in the aftermath of the Restoration of Charles II that ended the Puritan Revolution in England.

The Reforming Synod reinvigorated the Reformation of Manners in Massachusetts and, to some extent, throughout orthodox New England. To understand the origins of the meeting, the nature of the debates among participants and observers, and the immediate reactions of the Bay Colony's religious and political leaders is essential to grasping the point of view of the reformers during the last decades of the seventeenth century.

Such synods were both unusual and pivotal in the development of American Puritanism. An official call from the Massachusetts General Court for a gathering of representatives, lay and clerical, of the colony's churches was required. There were only three under the Old Charter, the Reforming Synod being the last. Their rarity enhanced their significance.[2] The first in 1648 produced the Cambridge Platform standardizing the institutional forms of

1. Michael G. Hall, *The Last American Puritan: The Life of Increase Mather, 1639–1723* (Middletown, Conn., 1988), 153–54.
2. David D. Hall, *The Faithful Shepherd: A History of the New England Ministry in the Seventeenth Century* (Chapel Hill, 1972), esp. 128–29, 200, 209, 244; Robert G. Pope, *The Half-Way Covenant: Church Membership in Puritan New England* (Princeton, 1969); Francis Bremer, *The Puritan Experiment: New England Society from Bradford to Edwards* (New York, 1976), 150–51.

Massachusetts Congregationalism. The second in 1662 wrestled with the rights of those baptized but unable to demonstrate conversion and resulted in the Half-Way Covenant debates still raging in the 1670s. In the aftermath of King Philip's War (1675–76), as the colony endured serious fires in Boston, depressed trade, English imperial pressure, and a string of poor harvests, the new synod was called to answer two questions formulated by Mather and formally asked by the colony's legislature: "What are the evils that have provoked the Lord to bring his judgment on New England?" and "What is to be done so that those evils may be reformed?" Thus the result was to be not only an analysis of New England's problems but also a plan of reform that would rectify them. This was an ambitious program of potentially surpassing importance to everyone in New England.

For Mather the road to the 1679 synod had been long and tortuous. Shortly after his return from England in 1661 the young minister found himself in the minority at the Half-Way Synod arguing, even against his august father, in favor of maintaining tighter requirements for full admission to the sacraments. Having witnessed the collapse of Puritan rule in England firsthand, he was unwilling to concur in anything he interpreted as New Englanders "forsaking their first love & principles." He was in an awkward position. His own brother-in-law, Seaborn Cotton, chastised him privately for acting "disorderly in opposing the synod & that being disorderly was as bad as drunkenness or scandal." He even hinted that Mather might be deprived of formal ordination into the North Church. Understandably self-pitying, Mather muttered in his diary about returning to England so as to "suffer there more under prelacy than to stay in N.E. to suffer under them that [are] looked upon as godly." However, he remained to continue to debate his colleagues "about the sins of N.E." "Alas," he confided to his diary in July 1666 about one such session, "there was not that agreement which is desirable."[3]

Mather was determined to promote a renewed, more thorough commitment to "reformation" so as to live up to New England's high calling envisioned by the founding generation and to fend off the judgment of God, which was the penalty of failure. In this view, of course, he was not without support. Although the details of analysis and prescription varied among practitioners, several of the ministers had been developing jeremiad sermonic themes similar to Mather's at least since John Higginson of Salem delivered his 1663 election sermon, *The Cause of God and His People in New England.* The jeremiad form became standardized in the early 1670s as a drama of moral

3. Increase Mather Diary, Mather Family Papers, AAS, box 3, folder 1, 21 June 1664, 22 June 1664, 5 July 1666, 17 July 1666.

and social regeneration in three parts: a restatement of New England's mission on the pattern of the Exodus, an account of the faults together with recommended reforms, and, finally, a vision of a redeemed future, coupled with dire warnings in case of failure. The jeremiad sermons interpreted the crises of the era not only as signs of God's displeasure but also as tokens of his continuing concern. There was, in short, an ironic cathartic element to them.[4]

The jeremiad tradition, however, was something more than a local psychodrama or, as Perry Miller put it, "a way of conceiving of the inconceivable, of making intelligible order out of the transition from European to American experience." In England too, amid a major depression and in the wake of the collapse of the Puritan Revolution, the passage of the Conventicle Acts (1664, 1670), the humiliations of the Second Dutch War, and the Great London Fire of 1666, the jeremiad became also an English "way of conceiving of the inconceivable"—the notion that theirs too might not be the chosen people. Reform-minded Anglicans joined with Nonconformists in producing pamphlets and sermons denouncing such evils as swearing, intemperance, and oppression of the poor and stressing Sabbatarianism, increased attention to individual piety, and general moral and political reform. Increase Mather and other New England ministers were keenly aware of these trends, including the rapprochement between Low Churchmen and Nonconformists in the interest of social regeneration. Realizing the transatlantic character of the campaign, Thomas Shepard, Jr., minister of Charlestown, Massachusetts, insisted in one of the more famous jeremiads, *Eye-Salve* (1672), that his listeners and readers "Remember that a main design of God's People's adventuring into this wilderness was for progress in the work of Reformation," but that the task must be seen "in the way of brotherly communion with the reformed churches of Christ in other parts of the world."[5]

Also underlying the apparently random denunciations and prescriptions was a coherent moral theology that shared with contemporary philosophy "an

4. Perry Miller, *The New England Mind: From Colony to Province* (Boston, 1953, 1961), 27–39, esp. 30–31; Sacvan Bercovitch, *The American Jeremiad* (Madison, Wis., 1978), esp. 52–53, 62; Sacvan Bercovitch, "New England's Errand Reappraised," in John Higham and Paul K. Conkin, eds., *New Directions in American Intellectual History* (Baltimore, 1979), 85–104, esp. 91.

5. Miller, *New England Mind,* 31; Harry Grant Plum, *Restoration Puritanism: A Study in the Growth of English Liberty* (Chapel Hill, 1943), 35–36, 44–45; Francis J. Bremer, "Increase Mather's Friends: The Trans-Atlantic Congregational Network of the Seventeenth Century," AAS *Proceedings* 94, pt. 1 (1984): 59–96; excerpts from Thomas Shepard, Jr., *Eye-Salve: or a Watch-Word from Our Lord Jesus Christ unto His Churches in New England* (Boston, 1672), in Alan Heimert and Andrew Delbanco, eds., *The Puritans in America: A Narrative Anthology* (Cambridge, Mass., 1985), 258.

emphasis on doctrines of living, the formulation of a synthetic practical faith in a world of cosmological and religious uncertainty," to quote Norman Fiering. Much of this writing was avowedly popular, aimed at a literate general public, and sought to shape both thought and conduct. As developed by both Puritan and Anglican thinkers, this system rested on a Thomist theory of a two-part rational conscience: an ability to grasp general moral principles and to apply them to specific cases. These capacities were partly innate but, although impaired by Original Sin, could be improved. Thus morality was largely a matter of habit, a product of instruction and training. The "Law," in both the theological and the civic sense, was not seen as an external, arbitrarily imposed code but as a pattern of conduct intrinsic to human nature and to the natural and social order as God created them.[6] Conversely, the sins cataloged in the jeremiad tradition were not merely evils in and of themselves but also symptoms of flawed individual character and of the failure of institutions (family, church, government) to inculcate proper habits and suppress evil ones.

It is within this context of evangelical Christianity that the reformers developed in their popular preaching the three-tiered classification of the moral habits of persons and societies as godly, civil, and profane. This language became particularly prominent in Massachusetts in the 1680s after the synod and also appeared in the works of the popular English evangelical John Flavel at about the same time.[7] In effect, the reformers were reasserting the Puritan truism that continual reform of both individual conduct and the institutions and customs that shaped it were essential to the very definition of a good society.[8] They were also convinced, on both sides of the Atlantic, that failure entailed gruesome practical and spiritual consequences.

Despite these points of commonality there was a major difference after 1660: Puritan rule had ended in England but not in Massachusetts. English Nonconformists and their Low Church sympathizers increasingly

6. Norman Fiering, *Moral Philosophy at Seventeenth-Century Harvard: A Discipline in Transition* (Chapel Hill, 1981), 51; H. R. McAdoo, *The Structure of Caroline Moral Theology: An Investigation of Principles* (London, 1949), 9–16, 66–69. The author is indebted to Thomas Kennedy, Philosophy Department, Valparaiso University, for the latter reference.

7. Increase Mather, *Practical Truths Tending to Promote the Power of Godliness* (Boston, 1682), esp. 177–78; William Hubbard, *The Benefit of a Well-Ordered Conversation* (Boston, 1684), 36–40; John Flavel, *The Reasonableness of Personal Reformation and the Necessity of Conversion* (London, 1691; reprint, Boston, 1725), 130–31.

8. David Cressy, *Coming Over: Migration and Communication between England and New England in the Seventeenth Century* (New York, 1987), 101–3.

argued for religious toleration as an element of reform. New England clerics such as Thomas Shepard, Jr., seizing on this element of uniqueness, asserted that New England's mission "was for Reformation, then, not for toleration of all religions." One reason was that these ministers were convinced that uniformity on what they took to be the pattern of primitive Christianity was essential to success. As Samuel Torrey of Weymouth claimed in 1674, "If ever we do hope, or intend to make thorough work in *Reformation*, we must recover Order, the Beauty, the Harmony, the Peace and Tranquillity, the Regularity, the Purity and Simplicity, the Power and Efficacy, Life and Spirit of Order, Gospel-Order."[9] Another was the hope that the "godly magistracy" of Massachusetts would assist the churches in furthering reform.

The clergy, however, proved easier to mobilize than the magistrates. By 1674 a consensus had emerged among the former on the main elements of reform, if not on the Half-Way Covenant. Mather established himself as its most prominent explicator in two sermons published as *The Day of Trouble Is Near* (1674), "warning of judgment near at hand" because of "the sins of the Countrey, and the Symptoms of divine displeasure." Typically, he denounced "Spiritual Pride" as reflected in such conduct as pursuit of fashion; "Disobedience" in families, churches, and the commonwealth; and those who "grind the faces of the poor." This depiction of sins well fits the moral theology of the times and was so recognized. Remarking that "Professors of Religion [church members and clergy] fashion themselves according to the world," Mather was also noticing that by his generation the church was broadly representative of society and was in danger of losing its prophetic role. He blamed such things as the Half-Way Covenant for this condition. In order to reestablish the church's spiritual, critical function, ministers and pious laity had first to reform themselves and then the society around them.[10] The churches (or at least the clergy) were responding to his call, but the colonial government was another matter.

Disagreeing among themselves about how best to cope with increasing pressures toward conformity with the evolving English imperial system and

---

9. Stephen Foster, "English Puritanism and the Progress of New England Institutions, 1630–1660," in David D. Hall et al., eds., *Saints and Revolutionaries: Essays in Early American History* (New York, 1984), 3–37, esp. 36; Shepard, *Eye-Salve*, 258; Torrey quoted in Norman Fiering, *Jonathan Edwards's Moral Thought and Its British Context* (Chapel Hill, 1981), 111.

10. M. Hall, *Last American Puritan*, 98–99; Michael G. Hall, ed., "The Autobiography of Increase Mather," AAS *Proceedings* 71 (1961): 301–2; D. Hall, *Faithful Shepherd*, 249.

remembering the futile and embarrassing attempt to suppress the Quakers in the early 1660s, the political leaders of Massachusetts were reluctant to embark on anything likely to encourage more division among the colonists or to provoke more hostile interest from London. However, the shock of King Philip's War, which began in June 1675, seemed to bear out the warnings of Mather and his allies and forced a shift in the political atmosphere. In October Mather was invited to address the General Court and to meet with a legislative committee "to consider about Reformation of those evils which provoke the Lord against N.E."[11]

The result was the famous Provoking Evils Law, passed on 3 November 1675, which officially recognized the war as God's judgment "so as to be effectually humbled for our sinns to repent of them, and amend our wayes." In essence, the law was a compendium and restatement of earlier prohibitions and exhortations including such perennial themes of the European and English reform tradition as "contempt of authority," "idleness," violations of sumptuary standards, swearing and cursing, excessive drinking, "profane-[ness]" during religious services, and economic "oppression" by merchants and laborers. There was also a denunciation of continued Quaker meetings and an exhortation to the churches to improve catechizing, another perennial reform issue. Directly related to the war, the General Court admonished towns to maintain proper flints and denounced "disorders" in the Indian trade, which helped to cause the war.

Upon passage of the law Mather and other clergymen met at Cambridge "to discourse of Reformation" and to decide upon further courses of action. The whole effort seemed blessed by Providence when a "ship laden with provisions" from Irish sympathizers arrived in time to prevent "a famine at least among the poorer sort of people," largely refugees generated by frontier desolation. Also arriving were one hundred pounds sterling and several loads of clothing from England "to be distributed amongst the poor people in this land."

Mather's satisfaction, however, was short-lived. In preparation for a Day of Humiliation in January 1676 Mather groused to his diary that "Reformation doth not go forward. Magistrates too slow in that matter." Given the press of time and battle, this lack of action is understandable. Even in the longer term, the only thing apparently arising out of the law was some desultory harassment of Quakers. This provoked the now standard acts of

---

11. Increase Mather Diary, 14 October, 18 October, 17 November 1675; *Mass. Recs.* V, 59–64; M. Hall, ed., "Autobiography," 302, for this and subsequent two paragraphs.

defiance and protests to the Crown—just the sort of thing most likely to unnerve cautious legislators and merchants, particularly since many Quakers in the northern areas of the colony, were respectable, influential folk.[12] Further complicating the magistrates' response was the fact that the Provoking Evils Law contained no specific regulations, such as wage and price controls or limitations on the number of tavern licenses, that could be readily enforced. Indeed, the whole question of enforcement was simply recommended to the county quarterly courts for their discretion. There was also a tendency to view laws as statements of what is intrinsically true and right rather than as codes to be strictly enforced even where such a possibility existed. In short, most magistrates seem to have regarded the Provoking Evils Law as hortatory rather than regulatory.

Mather's building frustration erupted at a dinner party with the governor, John Leverett, and other magistrates. The governor, who had spent as much time in England as Mather had, tweaked the minister for claiming during his lecture that day "that strangers said that they had seen more drunkenness in N.E. in half a year than in England in all their lives." That gross exaggeration aside, Leverett also opined that "there was more drunkenness in N.E. many years ago than there is now," a mild slap at the jeremiad myth about the superior virtue of the founding generation. William Stoughton, the deputy governor, interceded "pleasantly" that perhaps Mather might "preach a Recantation sermon." Armed with militant righteousness, Mather "told him, no, but if men would not accept my Labors God will." Leverett, with his liberal policy of tavern licensing occasionally over the objections of local selectmen, was for Mather "the principal Author of the multitude of ordinaries which be in Boston." Mather could not forbear the pun, "No wonder that N.E. is visited, when the Head is so spirited." In the drive for further assistance from the colonial government there would be no practical success until John Leverett's death in March 1679.[13]

Such political resistance did not deter Mather and his allies from continuing to pressure the government, mobilize the churches, and instruct the citizenry. In an effort to "quicken sedulous endeavours towards the Reformation of provoking evils," Mather issued a particularly clear explication of the new law in *An Earnest Exhortation to the Inhabitants of New England* (Boston, 1676).

12. Increase Mather Diary, 3 January 1676; Christine Leigh Heyrman, "Specters of Subversion, Societies of Friends: Dissent and the Devil in Provincial Essex County, Massachusetts," in D. Hall et al., eds., *Saints and Revolutionaries,* 39; Jonathan Chu, "The Social Context of Religious Heterodoxy: The Challenge of Seventeenth-Century Quakerism to Orthodoxy in Massachusetts," *EIHC* 118 (1982): 119–50.

13. Increase Mather Diary, 27 January 1676; M. Hall, *Last American Puritan,* 147.

The first section was a catalog of the sins in which he stressed "Inordinate Affection to the World" (possessive individualism), which led people to "prefer their Farms and Merchandize above the Gospel." Because "plenty . . . hath been abused unto great sensuality," even by church members, it did not surprise him that God was allowing so much property damage by Indian warriors.

Most interesting, however, was the last and longer section in which he outlined the comprehensive strategy he would continue to urge and pursue over the next several years. First and foremost, "wholesome laws" must be enforced. Second, he recommended that churches renew their covenants in the hope that such reexaminations and reaffirmations of their basic ties might reinvigorate corporate piety and action. Third, he urged individual intro-spection to increase personal piety and commitment. Fourth, he asked that all remember New England's "Errand." Among other things, this was an inspiration to didactic history. Next, he counseled the people to avoid despair, even in the midst of wartime sufferings, and to be thankful for "deliverances." Finally, there was the call to "Tell the World," to make certain that Mas-sachusetts's role in the larger drama of reformed Christianity was not slighted at home or abroad.[14]

In initial pursuit of this strategy, Mather in a February 1676 church meeting "read several of the Laws respecting Reformation, particularly those Laws which respect excess in apparel, & Towndwellers being at Taverns & solemnly exhorted the church to attend to the things there mentioned." These were evils he thought particularly prevalent in Boston and among his pa-rishioners. On the problem of catechisms, he asked members to "bring to me the Names & ages of the Children, that I might send for them & enquire into their spiritual estates, etc." Obviously he was not too busy to attend to crucial matters of pastoral care.[15]

In March 1676 on a Day of Humiliation near the Old-Style New Year, Mather worried about the continuing impact of war: "The sword not yet put up, grievous sinning and murmurings amongst the people." Meditating on unjustifiable massacres of Indians, he lamented "unreasoning rage against the enemy." Remembrance of the "errand" might be a partial cure. By August informal and formal discussions between clergy and government officials resumed, and they continued into the next spring. There was, however, little agreement, and even the ministers could not achieve consensus, particularly

14. The sins are colorfully described in 6–11, and the reform proposals are 11–26.
15. Increase Mather Diary, 4 February 1676.

on policies toward England and local Baptist and Quaker dissent. Also, as the war wound down in the fall of 1676 both Mather and one of his rivals, William Hubbard, rushed histories of the conflict into print to ensure that the proper providential and jeremiad lessons were at the forefront of interpretations of this awesome experience.[16]

On the vital matter of covenant renewal, he used the opportunity to preach to his father's old church at Dorchester on the last Sabbath of 1676 Old Style (21 March 1677) to urge this approach to a reinvigorated future. Mather sensed that for his generation the churches founded by their fathers had become customary, their ways a tradition to be followed as a matter of course rather than as an intense personal commitment. In short, he feared that the godly were becoming "merely civil." The solution was a formal ceremonial re-creation of church bonds, which would require conscious, overt acts of commitment. Then those traditions would more directly belong to the new generation, not as something inherited but as something embraced. Mather's program would be followed by churches far into the eighteenth century.[17]

In contrast, Solomon Stoddard of Northampton, the foremost advocate of the Half-Way Covenant, also sought ways to revive both personal and corporate piety, but he doubted the legitimacy and efficacy of Mather's approach. In line with his more liberal view of church membership he tended to regard the Lord's Supper as a means of conversion and regeneration for both individuals and the church. The disagreement enlivened the upcoming synod and subsequent religious debate for many years, a sign of continuing intellectual vitality and social responsibility within the American Puritan movement. Similar problems and debates were also characteristic of the Protestant and reformed Catholic churches of contemporary Europe.[18]

The days of Humiliation and Thanksgiving, whether called by the government or individual churches, were another ritual Mather saw as integral

16. Increase Mather Diary, 1 March, 10 August 1676; M. Halsey Thomas, ed., *Diary of Samuel Sewall, 1674–1709* (New York, 1973), 1:29–30; Increase Mather, *A Brief History of the Warr with the Indians of New England* (Boston, 1676); William Hubbard, *A Narrative of the Troubles with the Indians in New England* (Boston, 1677).

17. M. Hall, *Last American Puritan*, 148–49; D. Hall, *Faithful Shepherd*, 243.

18. Philip F. Gura, "Solomon Stoddard's Irreverent Way," *Early American Literature* 21 (1986): 29–43; Paul R. Lucas, "'An Appeal to the Learned': The Mind of Solomon Stoddard," *WMQ* 30 (1973): 257–92; Michael Schuldiner, "Solomon Stoddard and the Process of Conversion," *Early American Literature* 17 (1982): 215–26; John Bossy, *Christianity in the West, 1400–1700* (New York, 1985), 167–71.

to reform. "And indeed," as he wrote, "dayes of Humiliation without Reformation, are no other, nor no better than a Form of godliness without the power of it." Proper observance followed by action would help fulfill his suggestions in *An Earnest Exhortation* (1676) on recalling the "Errand," avoiding despair, and giving thanks for deliverances. To this end he had Thomas Thacher's *A Fast of God's Chusing*, delivered in 1674, published in 1678 (the year of the author's death) as a guide and a memorial. Thacher had observed that "All the self-denying acts that are required in a Fast" would be "but a shallow performance" unless individuals examined their consciences by asking such questions as, "Do you oblige and ingage your hearts to return to God, and to reform what is amiss in your persons, Families, Churches, etc., according to the object of your work & where you may have influence to the utmost of your power?" Among the several and occasionally conflicting functions of these rites, the linking of personal piety to social reform was one of the more significant.[19]

Yet however strongly the churches became committed, Mather was convinced that success would remain elusive without the active support of the government. Spurred by the disastrous Boston fire of 27 November 1676, which destroyed Mather's church and most of the buildings in the town center, the conversations between magistrates and ministers continued through the winter of 1676–77 and eventuated in the House of Deputies inviting Mather to deliver the election sermon in May 1677. In a ringing call to reform, *The Danger of Apostasy* began like most jeremiads by noting a declension from the founders' vision. "What Land under Heaven," he intoned, "has been more noted for professors and Religion than New England? If Apostasy prevails amongst such a people, it is like to be a sad Apostasy indeed." He addressed both blame and advice to the "People," the ministers, and particularly the magistrates.[20]

He scolded the clerics over the Half-Way Covenant and the unnamed Stoddard's "designing to bring all persons to the Lord's Supper, who have an Historical Faith [i.e., by tradition and custom], and are not scandalous in life, although they never had Experience of a work of Regeneration in their Souls." The "merely civil" remained unfit for full membership. Rather, he urged, "Let us make Converting Work our main design" by strong preaching and good

---

19. Thomas Thacher, *A Fast of Gods Chusing* (Boston, 1678), A2–A3, 22; Richard P. Gildrie, "The Ceremonial Puritan: Days of Humiliation and Thanksgiving," *NEHGR* 136 (1982): 3–16; Horton Davies, *The Worship of American Puritans, 1629–1730* (New York, 1990), 58–67.

20. M. Hall, *Last American Puritan*, 129–31; Increase Mather, *A Discourse Concerning the Danger of Apostasy* (Boston, 1685), 93.

moral example. Mather's intransigence on this point still hindered clerical unity.[21]

Having denounced "Covetousness" and "formality in Religion" among the populace, he made a strong plea to them to encourage enforcement of Sabbath laws—which was also a way of pressuring magistrates. The implication was not lost on Mather's critics in the government. He went on to urge a defense of congregational polity as a particular obligation of godly laymen. Church discipline he related directly to the problem of "manners" and, using a historical example, laid the issue not at the ministers' but at the people's feet. "Some learned men have well observed, that the Neglect of Discipline in the Churches of Asia brought in Corruption of Manners and Corruption of Manners was (through the just revenging hand of God) attended with Corruption of Doctrine, and these together provoked the Lord to lay those Churches most desolate." Could that be New England's destiny? Then, after urging the folk to "Look unto Your Families" and to pray regularly, he concluded with another veiled threat to the magistrates by urging the electorate to "Be Faithful in Improving of your Civil Liberties," meaning, in part, the "wise use" of the vote to support those interested in reform and continued resistance to England.[22]

The burden of his address to the government was on the question, "Where do you read of any great and general Reformation brought to pass, except the civil magistrate forward it?" In elaborating, he had recourse to the standard moral theology underlying Anglo-American reform thought. "I know you cannot change mens hearts, yet you may doe much (if God help you) towards effecting an outward Reformation, which will preserve outward blessings and prevent outward Judgments and desolations." In other words, "civility" was the government's obligation, while "godliness" was a problem for the churches. However, the most important role of civility to Mather, besides fending off "Judgments," was to provide the milieu in which godliness might flourish. To this end the government ought to support education, for "If ignorance over-spread the Land, Apostacie will do so too." Naturally, the magistrates were also to see to the support of "Learned Ministry" and "Publick Preachers." In Mather's mind at this point, civility did not include "Liberty of Conscience" because "the Toleration of all Religions and Perswasions is the way to have no true Religion at all left." He also suggested that the government sponsor "a collection of special Providences" so that "the great things that God did for our Fathers . . . be faithfully recorded and transmitted

21. Mather, *Danger of Apostacy*, 116–21.
22. Ibid., 62–63, 84, 88, 122–31.

to Posterity." Ignored by the state, this idea became a major project among the clerics and played an important role in forming New England's culture as well as in furthering the Reformation of Manners. In prodding the magistrates he explicitly raised one of their most painful and divisive fears, the loss of the Charter, and tied this nightmare to the cause of reform and the problem of the "profane." "If the Lord should be provoked to pluck up the Hedge of civil government, what a fearful flood of Iniquity would soon break in! How would madded and inraged Prophaneness know no Bounds! Yea, this Land would become as Sodom."[23]

The sermon so angered Governor Leverett and members of the Court of Assistants that they refused to have it printed, a most unusual occurrence. But Mather had a sadly ironic revenge: it was finally published in 1685, when the loss of the Charter had become a virtual certainty. Meanwhile, the election sermon had mixed results. The supporters were rallied by another strong statement of the program, but in the process the divisions among the clergy and between them and the magistrates were, if anything, exacerbated.

As if in response to Mather's prodding, the General Court passed a new Sabbath law in that session. Parliament had enacted one in 1675. Perhaps to some Massachusetts legislators such an act seemed a rare opportunity to do something that might please both the English government and the most vociferous local pastors. The main difference between the new law and its 1658 predecessor was its enforcement procedures. Towns were to choose "tithingmen," ideally one for every ten families, to watch over Sabbath observance, paying particular attention to "tipling" in taverns during services. The legislators, however, could not forbear annoying the clergy by ordering that the Sabbath regulations be read aloud by the ministers during services in March and September. John Higginson of Salem, who habitually had to cope with an unruly community, was one pastor who objected strenuously to Mather that such a procedure exposed "us to the reproach & contempt of ill-minded persons." He also worried about the precedent, should the Puritans ever lose control of the government. "It seems to be an injunction & imposition of such things as cannot be clearly made out to be the minister's duty, & it may be made use of by, we know not who, that may come after, to impose worse things." Even more absurdly, the new code ordered towns to maintain "cages" for violators, an injunction generally ignored.[24]

23. Ibid., 93–112.

24. G. E. Aylmer, "Collective Mentalities in Mid-Seventeenth-Century England. I. The Puritan Outlook," *Transactions of the Royal Historical Society,* 5th ser. 36 (1986): 15; "Mather Correspondence," 80, 81, 242; *Mass. Recs.* IV, pt. 1, 347; V, 133.

Significantly, the demand that pastors read the laws to their churches was not repealed until October 1679, after the synod began its deliberations. For two years it remained an ironic statement of the magistrates' prevailing attitude toward their clerical goaders. It is hardly surprising that in these years even a minister on his deathbed grumbled about the "need to reforme" and observed, "Methinks the Magistracy is more decayed than the Ministry."[25]

In January 1678, amid this almost openly rancorous impasse, the idea of a synod was broached by one of Mather's English correspondents, Thomas Jollie, a Lancashire Puritan pastor, "for your awakening to duty in the reforming of your manifest evils and for preventing of threatning ruin." As Parliament's 1675 Sabbath law indicates, English reformers, Anglican and Dissenter, were again active, and there was renewed interest in New England's opportunities and troubles. Jollie's suggestion promised a means of establishing a more satisfactory relationship among the churches and with the government. From Mather's point of view, however, the problem remained the magistrates' adamancy. For the time being, debates on covenant renewal and calls for Days of Humiliation were the only means readily available to the reformers.[26]

The stalemate broke in March 1679 at the death of Governor Leverett. He was replaced by Simon Bradstreet, member of the founding generation, widower of the famed poet, and a man of vast prestige among reformers. In May 1679 Bradstreet was confirmed in office by the voters. The election sermon by James Allen of Boston's First Church reiterated the reformist position to the electorate. "A praying, zealous, reformed and reforming Magistracy, Ministry, and People . . . that promote and keep up the separation between the precious and the vile, these are your gap-men who prevent Gods going away, and ruine coming." Triumph may have been at hand, but Allen worried about the populace's response to the reformers: "but doe you not think them the troublers of Israel? Are you not weary of them, and fain would be rid of them?" In times of relative calm, indifference is the agitator's perennial problem. But there hung over the late seventeenth-century world a continual disquiet that guaranteed reformers a hearing, if not agreement.[27]

The disquiet was reflected in the 1678 publication of a new, posthumous edition of Anne Bradstreet's *Tenth Muse* "at the desire of some friends that

25. "Mather Correspondence," 279, 279n.
26. Ibid., 289–90, 320, 322–23; Bremer, "Increase Mather's Friends," 83–84; Cressy, *Coming Over,* 51; Plum, *Restoration Puritanism,* 59; Michael R. Watts, *The Dissenters: From the Reformation to the French Revolution* (Oxford, 1978), 423.
27. James Allen, *New Englands Choicest Blessing* (Boston, 1679), 5.

knew her well" containing additional poems "which she never meant should come to public view." One of these was the thirty-three stanza masterpiece, "Contemplations," which is a subtle jeremiad distinguishing between what Mather called the "vanity" of the profane and civil and the deeper spiritual tensions and commitments of the godly. Stanza 32 is climactic:

> So he that saileth in this world of pleasure,
> Feeding on sweets, that never bit of th' sowre,
> That's full of friends, of honour and of treasure,
> Fond fool, he takes this earth ev'n for heav'ns bower.
> But sad affliction comes and makes him see
> Here's neither honour, wealth, nor safety;
> Only above is found all with security.[28]

As she died in 1672, the poems were not written to assist Mather in his campaign for a synod and continued reform, but the decision "of some friends" to publish them in 1678 may well have been. Whatever its immediate political implications, the new edition was in any case an exquisitely moving statement of the religious and social vision of the godly at a crucial time.

Certainly no time was lost in the spring of 1679. Within days of the May election Mather prepared a petition to the General Court, signed by eighteen clergy of the Boston vicinity, calling for a synod to reaffirm the Cambridge Platform. Believing that the churches, and by implication the society at large, was "much endangered both by Ignorance & error," the petitioners hoped that the meeting might encourage ministers and laymen to "have a more right & full understanding one of another." Thus reconciled, "we may bee the better prepared to hold fast our profession, & to stand fast together in an hour of Temptation." In that way the churches and people of Massachusetts "may clear ourselves of the suspicion & scandal of defection." The General Court responded with a formal call for a synod of clergy and lay leaders to meet in Boston during September 1679 to consider the double problem of identifying "provoking evils" and then rectifying them.[29]

The delegates duly assembled at the Boston Townhouse on 10 September and quickly discovered that several churches had sent ministers but no

---

28. Charles E. Hambrick-Stowe, ed., *Early New England Meditative Poetry: Anne Brad-street and Edward Taylor* (New York, 1988), 24, 109. I am grateful to Laurel Thatcher Ulrich for suggesting "Contemplations" in this context.

29. M. Hall, *Last American Puritan,* 147; Williston Walker, ed., *The Creeds and Platforms of Congregationalism* (1893; Boston, 1960), 413–15.

laymen. Given the goal of improving clerical-lay cooperation and presenting a united program of reform credible to the society at large, this was a serious problem. The members decided to begin deliberations and write to the churches urging that laymen be sent. The next day they also "determined noe Vote should passe till they had answer from ye Churches." The reform leadership must not be a clerical monopoly. During the first three days, while awaiting word on the absentees, the delegates read over the Cambridge Platform, discussed "provoking evils," and created a committee of five ministers (including Increase Mather) and three laymen to consider "remedies." Of great political importance was the fact that Governor Bradstreet "came into ye Synod" for an afternoon, thereby demonstrating his support. An adjournment, including a Day of Humiliation, was voted until the sixteenth to allow the late delegates to arrive.[30]

On the appointed day they reassembled for prayers and sermons. Serious debate began the next morning when the new members appeared. After the Cambridge Platform was reread and confirmed by unanimous vote, the committee's report, largely written by Mather, "was read over & [there was] some debate upon it." The controversial matter of "remedies," particularly the Mather-Stoddard dispute over covenant renewal and broad communion, was put off. Nonetheless, an angry debate erupted on the afternoon of the eighteenth over one of the "provoking evils," the "sins of oppression." Ralph Wheelocke, a substantial farmer and deputy to the General Court from the relatively egalitarian farming village of Medfield, "declared that there was a cry of injustice" in that ministers and magistrates were not taxed as heavily as others. An outraged Solomon Stoddard accused Wheelocke of lying while the deputy governor, Thomas Danforth, exclaimed that "he deserved to be Laid by the heels." A most tender nerve had been struck, not only by what Wheelocke asserted but also by who he was. Nearing eighty, he had been an original settler of Dedham and the "Father of Medfield," which made him a representative of the revered founding generation. Nor could he be faulted for lack of piety or weak service to the community. The session broke up in confusion. Massachusetts's egalitarian impulse in the respectable figure of Ralph Wheelocke had run headlong into its equally prevalent hierarchical presumptions personified by the minister Stoddard and the magistrate Danforth. The episode was an apt illustration of Stephen Foster's observation, "The Puritan social ethic, then, was hierarchical, though New England

---

30. The minister of Boston's Old South, Peter Thacher, kept notes, which are in Walker, ed., *Creeds and Platforms*, 417–19.

society was not necessarily so."[31] It seems, at the risk of confusion, that one could also reverse the terms, suggesting that Wheelocke's Puritanism embraced popular egalitarian values in a larger society always tending toward elaborating social distinctions.

Having encountered so graphically one aspect of the social tensions besetting them, the delegates assembled on the last day of the fall session to debate remedies "at the end of each Paragraph" of Mather's proposals. As expected, "there was much debate about persons being admitted to full communion." An attempt was made to simplify the dispute by allowing Stoddard to present an argument and Mather to respond in turn, but the delegates, late on a Friday, soon tired of the matter. So Stoddard's final points "were deferred & at present It was eased." Apparently convinced by his arguments, however, the synod voted to accept Stoddard's wording. Massachusetts churches now had the synod's sanction for admitting members by a statement of faith rather than requiring examination and conversion narratives. Of course, the Stoddard-Mather argument went on beyond the synod, but a major turning point had been reached in more closely aligning the colony's views on the sacraments and their social implications with those of other established churches in Western Christendom. Stoddard and the synod had given "nonseparatism" more reality. The rest of Mather's report passed virtually unchanged.[32]

The final issue, a general statement of faith, was deferred until the opening of the May 1680 session of the General Court. A committee including Mather and Samuel Willard, who was noted for his theological sophistication and who favored both covenant renewal and broader admission practices, suggested the expedient of adopting the Savoy Declaration of Faith issued by English independents in 1658. This too was an important reaffirmation of transatlantic unity among reformers. It is not surprising that Jollie wrote to Mather congratulating him on the success of the synod and informing him that "Wee have here in our circumstances been endeavouring something to the same purpose."[33]

During fall 1679 Mather, with his son Cotton as secretary, prepared the report on the first session of the synod that was published by the General

31. R. E. Wall, Jr., "The Membership of the Massachusetts General Court, 1634–1686" (Ph.D. diss., Yale University, 1965), 30–35; Stephen Foster, *Their Solitary Way: The Puritan Social Ethic in the First Century of New England* (New Haven, 1970), xii.

32. M. Hall, *Last American Puritan,* 151; Francois Lebrun, "The Two Reformations: Communal Devotion and Personal Piety," in Robert Chartier, ed., *A History of Private Life,* vol. 3, *Passions of the Renaissance,* trans. Arthur Goldhammer (Cambridge, Mass., 1989), 80.

33. "Mather Correspondence," 326–27; M. Hall, *Last American Puritan,* 149, 153–54.

Court as *The Necessity for Reformation* (1679). This repeated, occasionally verbatim, the strictures of the 1675 Provoking Evils Law. The synod and the General Court thus were offering not only a depiction of their society amid the shocks and uncertainties of the 1670s but also a logically developed compendium of problems that had bothered reformers at least since Erasmus. A solemn assembly of clergy and pious laymen, backed by the government, was announcing that Puritan Massachusetts would reassert its leadership role in the international, indeed cosmic, drama of the Reformation of Manners. More than a "purgation by incantation," *The Necessity of Reformation* was a battle plan describing the enemy and outlining a strategy that was in fact pursued.[34]

The first and foremost problem was a "visible decay of Godliness" among church members. Following the classic notion of dispositions underlying deportment, Mather stressed personal piety. If "Worship, especially in Secret, is much neglected," then "men cease to know and fear, and love and trust" God, "but take up their contentment and satisfaction in something else." That "something else" became an "Idol" that blighted the spirit and warped conduct. Such "Apostacy" among the putatively godly endangered the whole society by both bad example and poor governance. Hence personal piety was at the core of the Reformation of Manners, and the covenant renewal idea was aimed directly at this need.[35]

Ungodly dispositions and the resultant dangers were understood in classic Christian terms to be rooted in the "Pride that doth abound in New England." This seminal sin was most immediately revealed in "refusing to subject to Order," rushing into "contention" ("This Malady hath been very general in the Country"), and violating the sumptuary codes. It was not simply that "Servants and poorer sorts of People . . . goe above their estates and degrees" but that others, "not of the meaner sort," indulge in "strange Apparel." A quarrelsome, often egalitarian, individualism typical of traditional English popular culture was being noted here.

In the colony's religious life the symptoms were neglect of "Church Fellowship" and "Discipline," especially for the "Rising Generation." While the orthodox churches decayed, "humane invention and Will-Worship have been set up even in Jerusalem," referring to Quakers and Baptists. Naturally this institutional weakness resulted in "irreverence" expressed "By Oaths and

34. The nifty, if misleading, phrase is from Miller, *New England Mind,* 33–34.
35. *The Necessity of Reformation* (Boston, 1679), 2. Quotes in the next several paragraphs are from 2–15. See also Harry S. Stout, *The New England Soul: Preaching and Religious Culture in Colonial New England* (Oxford, 1986), 97–98.

Imprecations in ordinary Discourse," in "profaneness" at worship as folk "sit at prayertime, and some . . . give way to their own sloth and sleepiness," and even in "Sabbath-breaking." Prevalent Sabbath violations included not attending services ("especially in the most populous places"), "walking abroad and Travelling" for recreation, attending to "particular servile callings and Employments," and indulging "unsuitable discourses . . . upon the Lord's Day." These criticisms were heard as insistently in France and England.[36]

As with religious institutions, so with "Family Government." There were "Houses . . . full of Ignorance and Profaneness." Further, "many Householders who profess Religion, doe not cause all that are within their gates to become subject unto good order as ought to be." Servants and children were "not kept in subjection" because "Masters and Parents especially" were "being sinfully indulgent towards them." The argument here concluded, "In this respect, Christians in this Land have become too like unto the Indians." Not for the first nor the last time, native Americans—who were understood to be models of "incivility" or "barbarity"—were used as a rhetorical mirror to reflect an undesirable element of European popular culture, in this case an emerging sense of the independence and individualism of children.[37]

After a listing of those faults at least partially attributable to poor family and church discipline—"Sinful Heats and Hatreds," "evil surmisings," talebearing, and litigiousness—there followed a section on the tavern. That ubiquitous and necessary institution, when abused, served as a subversive alternative to church and family. Other signs of the lack of proper discipline were the "too common" temptations to sexual laxity and display. Similarly, "there is much want of Truth" reflected in "Promise-breaking," "false Reports," "Slanders," and "Reproaches."

Finally, there was a long criticism of common economic conduct, arising out of the certainty that "Covetousness is Idolatry." Here again, perhaps surprisingly, was evoked the image of the pagan Indian. "There have been in many professors an insatiable desire after Land and worldly Accommodations, yea, so as to forsake Churches and Ordinances, and to live like Heathen, only so they might have Elbow-Room enough in the World." Leaving the formerly pious frontiersman who, according to Mather, was coming to resemble his enemy, possessive individualism was also denounced in the

36. Gerald R. Cragg, *Puritanism in the Period of the Great Persecution* (Cambridge, 1958), 129; B. B. James and J. Franklin Jameson, eds., *The Journal of Jaspar Danckaerts* (New York, 1913), 29.

37. Michael Zuckerman, "Identity in British America: Unease in Eden," in Nicholas Canny and Anthony Pagden, eds., *Colonial Identity in the Atlantic World, 1500–1800* (Princeton, 1987), 115–58, esp. 154–55.

form of "excessive rates" and "unreasonable demands" by "Traders," "Day-Labourers," and "Mechanics." A final symptom of "the prevailing power of a Worldly Spirit" was a lack of generosity "as to the publick concernments." Reflected in the "languishing state" of "Schools of Learning and other publick concerns" and in the "unreasonable complaints and murmurings because of publick charges" was "a private self-seeking Spirit," surely "one of those evils that renders the last times perilous." Mather's and the synod's economic ethics were fully congruent with the civic humanism of the era.[38]

In a not so veiled criticism of Restoration mores generally as well as those of some Massachusetts merchants and magistrates, the synod's first "remedy" was that leaders should be moral exemplars, for "People are apt to follow the examples of those above them." Most of the proposals, however, were more institutional. The magistrates were to pass and enforce laws designed to "promote the interests of Reformation," which included special care "respecting Schools of Learning." Despite the preoccupation with finances, frontier defense, and English pressures, the General Court responded. Immediately after the synod's first session a committee of the court was formed to review the colony's laws to see "whether they were sufficiently warranted by the word of God, and other lawes not so well worded as may be effectuall to the end intended, or honorable to this Court." Also, the duties and powers of the tithingmen, who were intended by the legislators to be the primary enforcers of moral reform, were more fully defined. They were to watch the taverns and unlicensed alehouses "to inspect the manners of all disorderly persons." If "private admonitions" failed, violators were to be indicted. The goal was to suppress "the course or practice of any person or persons whatsoever tending to debauchery, irreligion, prophaness, & atheisme among us, wherein by omission of family government, nurture, & religious duties, & instruction of children & servants, or idleness, profligat, uncivill, or rude practice of any sort." The new law also included an oath of office. In 1681 the General Court passed a comprehensive tavern law, establishing definite licensing procedures and setting quotas for each town. Nor did the legislature neglect education. Towns delinquent in contributions to Harvard were pressured, and the famous law requiring each place of more than five hundred families to support two grammar schools and two writing schools was passed in October 1683.[39]

38. J.G.A. Pocock, "The Varieties of Whiggism from the Exclusion to Reform: A History of Ideology and Discourse," in his *Virtue, Commerce, and History: Essays in Political Thought and History, Chiefly in the Eighteenth Century* (Cambridge, 1985), 215–310.

39. *Mass. Recs.* V, 240–41, 244, 305, 414–15.

Despite the legislation success was slight, given the few years left under the Old Charter, the intractability of ancient "profane" customs, and the general weakness of enforcement machinery in the seventeenth-century world. Yet the effort was sincere and had some impact even if sporadic and partial. Indeed, one of the last orders given by the General Court near its dissolution was a call to local grand juries, tithingmen, selectmen, and constables "to doe their utmost to be faithful" in suppressing "Sabaoth breaking" and tavern abuses. Commending the proposals of the "late Synod," the court also urged "renewing our covenant with God" and using "all possible wayes and means for the upholding of church discipline."[40]

The covenant renewal program and improved church discipline increased the visibility, élan, and even numbers of the "godly." Solomon Stoddard himself used the ceremony soon after his return to Northampton and then preached a half-year series on Joshua's restoration of the Mosaic covenant. Characteristically, he followed that cycle with one on conversions based on the Twenty-third Psalm. Increase Mather's church reworked its 1650 covenant to make the document more comprehensive and specific, particularly in matters of discipline and the "rising generation." The resultant *Confession of 1680* became a model republished several times up to 1812. Although covenant renewals had precedents reaching back in Massachusetts to the 1630s, these ceremonies became a characteristic means of revitalizing corporate piety and reinvigorating moral and religious reform from the synod to the Great Awakening. With renewed ceremony came what Jon Butler has termed "a major resacralization of the landscape after 1680" as new and larger meetinghouses were erected throughout much of New England.[41]

Coming at the end of the 1670s, a decade that saw both a notable increase in social and moral tensions and a flowering of American Puritan thought and action,[42] the synod became an important benchmark laying out themes of cultural and moral criticism and inspiring reform efforts for a century. For example, in 1696 during an election sermon Cotton Mather explicitly alluded to the standard by wishing "we could say that we are mended some since the Admonitions of that faithful Synod." The synod itself became a jeremiad theme. In 1710 John Danforth lamented of New Englanders that

---

40. Ibid., 469–70.

41. Stout, *New England Soul,* 100; D. Hall, *Faithful Shepherd,* 244; Walker, ed., *Creeds and Platforms,* 409; Charles E. Hambrick-Stowe, *The Practice of Piety: Puritan Devotional Discipline in Seventeenth-Century New England* (Chapel Hill, 1982), 131; Jon Butler, *Awash in a Sea of Faith: Christianizing the American People* (Cambridge, Mass., 1990). 109–10.

42. M. Hall, *Last American Puritan,* xiv; Kenneth Silverman, *The Life and Times of Cotton Mather* (New York, 1984), 56.

although "their Sins, and ways of sinning have been set in Order before their Eyes & Particularly Testified against by the Prophets of the Lord, and by a Synod . . . they Reform them not." As late as 1774, as another revolutionary crisis engulfed New England, the terminology and agenda of the Reforming Synod were deemed not only relevant but also essential. For instance, that year on a fast day in Worcester, Thaddeus Maccarty preached two sermons published in Boston as *Reformation of Manners, of Absolute Necessity in order to Conciliate the Divine Favour in Times of Publick Evil and Distress.* Over the entire provincial era, the jeremiad form and themes shaped not only sermons of all sorts, but also histories, captivity narratives, poems, accounts of "special providences," and criminal biographies. The goal was to recast the attitudes and manners of persons of all classes at least in the direction of "civility."[43]

On this theme in 1684 William Hubbard published as an addendum to his *Well-Ordered Conversation* a meditation on public morality by a recently deceased magistrate and major general of the militia, Daniel Dennison. Consistent with the synod's assumptions, Hubbard felt the need to add the voice of a godly layman to his own clerical study of contemporary manners and morals. The judge began with an analysis of the vices of excessive individualism: "Pride and Self-concernedness," "Ambition and Envy," and "Censoriousness." In the process he lamented the chronic antiauthoritarianism of the colony. "Where have you a people less regardant of the judgment & determinations of their Leaders in Church and State?" Observing too that "Covetousness is the root of all evil" but that "Honour is as desirable to many men as Riches, and possibly here more attainable," he went on to denounce "ambition," which "must raise commotions, that thereby it might have an opportunity of advancement, and employes envy to depress others that they fancy may stand in their way, and will oblige any parties that may be subservient to their Design." Dennison was explicitly linking competitive individualism and antiauthoritarianism to social disorder in a manner reminiscent of Thomas Hobbes a generation earlier.

Increase Mather and others in the Bay Colony were familiar with Hobbes's work, but in this analysis the philosopher and the magistrate were merely stating a learned truism of their age. Rejecting Hobbes's despairing totalitarianism, Dennison instead embraced a biblical respect for the "Va-

---

43. Cotton Mather, *Things for a Distress'd People to Think Upon* (Boston, 1696), 10–11; John Danforth, *The Blackness of Sins against Light* (Boston, 1710), 29; David D. Hall, *Worlds of Wonder, Days of Judgment: Popular Religious Belief in Early New England* (New York, 1989), esp. 183.

rieties of Gifts" among men and a social contract "on Fundamentals and Superstructures of Faith and Order" allowing disagreement "in details." But most important were the "virtues" essential to sustain fairly open, contractual institutions in church and state, which included "fear of God," "humility," and "charity." The "Virtue most necessary to fit for Society," however, was "meekness," his term for civility, which he saw as "making us gentle, tractable, persuadable, willing to bear the yoke in a Society; without it men are like wild beasts." Indeed, he insisted, "The meek spirits are the Glue and Soader [solder] that unite Societies"[44]

The godly layman Dennison, much more than the clerics Hubbard and Mather, was willing to see civility as an essential end in itself and less inclined to denounce its possible self-seeking motivations. The conduct itself was the standard by which civility was to be urged and evaluated. It was civility and not necessarily piety "that unite[s] Societies." In this view, Dennison pointed to a tension already present in the clerical view of the conflicts among the godly, the civil, and the profane. Even more, he forecast a possible resolution that emerged more frequently in public debate in New England after the Glorious Revolution.[45]

To reach a resolution that was contractual and not authoritarian, one that engaged virtually the entire society and culture, required the taming of excessive individualism whether civil or profane. The most obvious target and opponent of the Reformation of Manners, as renewed by the 1679 synod, was the profane conversation. Thus, to comprehend the successes, limits, and compromises of the reformers after 1679, it is essential to understand the ethos of the profane as well as the godly.

44. Daniel Dennison, *Irenicon: Or a Salve for New England's Sores,* appended to William Hubbard, *The Benefit of a Well-Ordered Conversation* (Boston, 1684), 192–214; Increase Mather Diary, 25 May 1666; Keith Thomas, "The Social Origins of Hobbes' Political Thought," in K. C. Brown, ed., *Hobbes Studies* (Cambridge, Mass., 1965), 185–236.

45. Bercovitch, *American Jeremiad,* 119; Bruce Tucker, "The Reinterpretation of Puritan History in Provincial New England," *NEQ* 54 (1981): 481–98, esp. 488.

TWO

The Ways of the Profane

In the March 1681 session, two years after the Reforming Synod, the Essex County Quarterly Court sentenced Elizabeth Perkins, the youthful wife of an Ipswich farmer, to be "severely whipped on the naked body, and to stand or sit in some open place in the public meetinghouse at Ipswich" during Sunday services "with a paper pinned on her head on which is written in Capital letters, 'FOR REPROACHING MINISTERS, PARENTS AND RELATIONS.'" Being from an affluent family, she avoided the whipping by paying a substantial three-pound fine, but she could not avert the public humiliation.[1]

Goodwife Perkins was an accomplished gossip and slanderer whose favorite but not sole target was her mother-in-law, of whom she once remarked that the older woman "had one foot in hell already and the other would be there quickly." Her husband Luke also had a tart tongue, saying of their revered seventy-year-old pastor, Thomas Cobbett, that he "was more fit to be in a hogsty than in a pulpit, and that he had been a vile man in his former days." Being purveyors of such abuse, the couple became victims as well. A young woman professed shock at a town braggart's version of his alleged adulteries with Perkins. "What he said to her surpassed all bounds of civility or modesty concerning his relations with Luke Perkins' wife." The couple was even involved in rumors of witchcraft as both accused and accusers.[2]

Much of the animus as well as the opportunity sprang from her in-laws' position in the community. Her father-in-law, John Perkins, was a large landholder, owner of one of Ipswich's two licensed ordinaries, and longtime quartermaster of the Essex Regiment of the militia. An elderly man by the

1. *Essex Recs.* VIII, 89–91.
2. John Demos, *Entertaining Satan: Witchcraft and the Culture of Early New England* (New York, 1982), 324, 403; James E. Kences, "Some Unexplored Relationships of Essex County Witchcraft to the Indian Wars of 1675 and 1689," *EIHC* 120 (1984): 185.

late 1670s, he turned the daily running of the inn over to one son, Abraham, and the farm to Luke. Luke apparently found the arrangement constraining, for by 1686—to the scandal and delight of the whole town—Abraham, as agent for their father, was suing Luke for appropriating land and income from the farm beyond the terms of the agreement. Meanwhile Elizabeth, who seemingly spent much of her time helping and loitering about the ordinary, probably resented the at least tacit rebukes of her prominent mother-in-law as much as she shared her husband's seething rebelliousness.[3]

Also, the ordinary was earning an unsavory reputation. With a population of about 1,200 in 1680, Ipswich was an important shire and market town. Perkins's inn became a place where visitors could meet local women. In 1679 the old man found himself prosecuted "for disorders in his house at night, caused by strange men walking and talking" after closing with "two maids . . . of Ipswich." A boarder at the inn during spring 1682, James Creeke, was prosecuted for "heinous, lascivious and adulterous carriages" with Elizabeth Perkins herself, "some of which acts were done on the Sabbath day when others were at the public exercises." Creeke's defense was "that he accounted his kissing her to be good manners and as other men did," a revealing commentary on her reputation.[4] One young woman thought her "making a great deal more of him than she ever saw her make of her own husband." Others "marvelled that she should so carry herself with such a one as he, who was a poor fellow." Elizabeth, oddly, was not charged.

In 1683 a local militia sergeant was charged with "frequenting the company" of a servant "at unseasonable times" at Perkins's. While the tavern was crowded with folk during a court session he was busily "clapping her on the head and back . . . and hugging her," and she remarked to another servant that "she thought the devil was in him to follow her up and down the house." Eventually that evening he got her into the "brewhouse and had blown out the candle" only to be interrupted by Elizabeth Perkins, who was looking for the missing woman. There followed several more incidents. Finally, some weeks later, after a training day, the couple enjoyed a mock wedding in the tavern teeming with militia, consisting of a round of toasts followed by their withdrawal "into the leanto, etc."[5]

3. *Essex Recs.* IX, 584–88.

4. For an excellent description of propriety in those circumstances, see Laurel Thatcher Ulrich, *Good Wives: Image and Reality in the Lives of Women in Northern New England, 1650–1750* (New York, 1980, 1982), 94–97.

5. *Essex Recs.* VII, 271–72; VIII, 285–86; IX, 29.

Amid this rollicking ambience Elizabeth Perkins worked, flirted, ran her tongue, and, on at least one occasion, indulged in serious thievery. The victim was a Boston trader staying at the ordinary in order to peddle fancy cloth. In September 1683 she stole three pounds in cash and goods from his room, including satin ribbons, stockings, a silk hood, a lace handkerchief, a lace cap, a silk neckcloth, and a pair of "fall" [hairpieces]. Imprisoned briefly, she was released on a hefty twenty-pound fine. Goodwife Perkins and her family were required to return the goods, plus triple damages and all costs of the court and witnesses.[6]

Impulsive, hedonistic, spitefully impatient of restraint by family or church, willing to cheat and steal, Elizabeth Perkins and her husband seemed driven, as Increase Mather would have said, by "the lust of the flesh, the lust of the eye, and pride of life." They were "vain persons" who led "profane lives." To the Puritan moralists "profane" did not mean "secular," but rather denoted a contempt, irreverence, or flagrant disregard for things sacred. The idea implied deliberate and open defiance of official standards of conduct, not as random misdeeds but as a pattern. The moral reformers of the era thought of this pattern, as we have seen, as a "course or frame of life," which they often termed a "conversation."

The "profane conversation" was not, strictly speaking, a social-class phenomenon in orthodox New England. The servants, mariners, and laboring poor were more inclined to it than others, but, as the example of the Perkins family indicates, there was no necessary connection. Indeed, there are strong indications that adolescents may have used elements of it as a form of rebellion. It is better to think of the "profane life" as one moral tradition among several, a "conversation" available to people by which they could orient their ideas and conduct. In New England some were bred to it, others fell into it by "vain company," and still others deliberately chose it. But very few were forced into this mode of life by grinding poverty or lack of alternative styles. After all, providing alternatives to it was a major goal of American Puritanism from the start.

Because the "profane life" was a tradition and not a fate, it resembled the ways of the godly in that the degree of commitment to that manner of life varied from person to person and from time to time in the life of the same individual. Cotton Mather may have believed that "'tis a Rare Thing to see an Old Sinner Converted unto God and Serious Piety," but nonetheless there were conversions both ways. More commonly, the godly indulged in a "vain

6. *Essex Recs.* IX, 142–44.

practice" while the profane had their moments of social responsibility and orthodox piety. The Reformation of Manners was not, in New England at least, a class struggle. It was a more profound contest within and among people to shape systems of manners and morals that expressed and defended differing notions of human dignity.[7]

The "profane conversation" was not identical with traditional English popular culture but was a vital element within it during the early modern era. The Georgian "mob," which one historian described as that "society's id—the sump of forbidden thoughts and proscribed actions, the locus of the raging will to survive," does not seem markedly different from the "giddy multitude" of the sixteenth and seventeenth centuries.[8] English settlers in America both carried these ideas and practices with them to the New World and remained in contact with their practitioners in the home island.

Recent scholarship on the early Chesapeake amply demonstrates that the "profane life" emerged and flourished in at least parts of English America. As the royal governor of Virginia during Bacon's Rebellion (1676), Sir William Berkeley, lamented, "How miserable that man is that Governes a People when six parts of seaven at least are Poore, Endebted, Discontented, and Armed." Disorderly, violent, fiercely exploitive, and competitive in their approach to both economic life and diversions, the people of early Virginia adapted the moral codes of the profane strain of traditional popular culture to a new, harsh social environment. The usual sources of discipline—government, church, and even family ties—were too weak to inhibit seriously the bent of that tradition at least until the 1680s. The results of that failure shaped Virginia society and politics far into the eighteenth century. The character of the Virginia gentry and yeomanry, as well as the definitions of liberty prevalent

7. David D. Hall, *World of Wonder, Days of Judgment: Popular Religious Belief in Early New England* (New York, 1989), esp. 14–18; Roger Thompson, *Sex in Middlesex: Popular Mores in a Massachusetts County, 1649–1699* (Amherst, 1986); Cotton Mather, *Advice from the Watchtower: In a Testimony against Evil Customs* (Boston, 1713), 14.

8. Keith Thomas, *Religion and the Decline of Magic* (New York, 1971), 17, 163; Richard S. Dunn, "Servants and Slaves: The Recruitment and Employment of Labor," in Jack P. Greene and J. R. Pole, eds., *Colonial British America: Essays in the New History of the Early Modern Era* (Baltimore, 1984), 161; Christopher Hill, "Pottage for Freeborn Englishmen: Attitudes toward Wage Labour," in his *Change and Continuity in Seventeenth-Century England* (Cambridge, Mass., 1975), 219–38, esp. 221–22; David Nokes, *Raillery and Rage: A Study of Eighteenth-Century Satire* (New York, 1987), 10; Robert Hughes, *The Fatal Shore: The Epic of Australia's Founding* (New York, 1987), 24, for the "id" observation; Paul Fussell, *The Great War and Modern Memory* (New York, 1975), ix, on the literary quality of life.

in revolutionary Virginia, was profoundly influenced by the drive for personal autonomy inherent in the "profane life."[9]

In early Massachusetts, of course, the forces of social control in family, church, and government were much stronger and consequently more effective in shaping conduct and cultural and moral development from the founding. But that does not mean that the "profane life" was absent or irrelevant. Puritan success at creating a relatively orderly society was not won without resistance but was rather a continuous achievement born of struggle and compromise. Before and after the Reforming Synod, American Puritan moralists were anxious about what Cotton Mather once called "the Vain Conversation received by Tradition from our Fathers."[10] Attempting to deal with it and the more elitist political and intellectual pressures from England manifestly shaped the theology and practice of the movement in America. But the "profane life" was something more than a titillating foil for an evolving New England culture. For all its obnoxious and occasionally dangerous forms of expression, it contributed to the broader sense of human dignity and personal autonomy developing through the Western world in the early modern era.

Although the profane conversation was not synonymous with criminality, many of its characteristic modes of expression were illegal. Hence, one way to understand the "profane life" is in the aggregate by looking at the statistics of crime and punishment. Major crimes such as murder, rape, and grand theft were rare in Massachusetts, as was generally the case in rural England and similar regions in northwestern Europe. In Essex County, Massachusetts, from 1651 to 1680 the most common offenses, other than crimes against the churches whose numbers were swelled by Quaker prosecutions, were contempt of authority and various types of theft, the characteristic marks of roguery. Sexual crimes, mainly fornication, were also prominent. In Middlesex County the situation was similar. Statistically, poorer folk were more likely to commit property and sexual crimes, while contempt, shading into heresy, tended to increase in incidence as one went up the social scale. Needless to say, theft was not restricted to the poor, the servants, and

9. The now classic picture of Virginia is Edmund S. Morgan, *American Slavery, American Freedom: The Ordeal of Colonial Virginia* (New York, 1975). See also T. H. Breen, "A Changing Labor Force and Race Relations in Virginia, 1660–1720," *Journal of Social History* 7 (1973): 3–25; and Bernard Bailyn, "Politics and Social Structure in Virginia," in James Morton Smith, ed., *Seventeenth-Century America: Essays in Colonial History* (Chapel Hill, 1959), 90–115.

10. Cotton Mather, *Advice from the Watchtower*, 27–28. Mather used "conversation" in the same sense as William Hubbard to indicate public character.

laborers, nor were various forms of contempt unheard of among the lower orders. These statistics indicate the existence of a profane milieu. One-half of the offenders in the Middlesex study came from families with other criminal members.[11]

In other words, there was a sort of "tribalism" among the profane just as there was among the godly. As Increase Mather interpreted that condition in 1685, "As for the wicked transgressors, they are cursed not only in their persons but in their posterity." Although he granted exceptions, Mather believed that children reared among the profane "shall be punished for their Fathers' and Mothers' sins as well as for their own because they justify them by doing like them." Mather and fellow moralists also recognized nonfamily networks of the profane, often under the label "vain company-keeping." Typical of this perennial theme was Thomas Foxcroft in 1733: "For how naturally does evil & foolish Company lead to and cherish the Vices of Idleness & Extravagance . . . ?" Wrote another in 1726, "If you willingly keep Company with loose and profane Sinners, you'll become as *vile* and *wicked* as they are. There is nothing in the whole World more infectious than the evil Manners and Conversation of profane Sinners."[12] Thus criminality arising out of the "profane life" was not merely a matter of isolated, furtive deeds but often grew out of and helped constitute groups. And in this competition for adherents, the Puritan moralists believed that the profane had the advantage.

Theft was a prime example of a commonly collaborative criminal enterprise. Although stealing was so common as to seem banal, it was for the public imagination of seventeenth- and eighteenth-century England the archetypal crime, as murder was for the Victorians or espionage for the twentieth century. This fascination may have reflected the growing importance of property as an element of a person's social standing or identity. In early New England the crime was not so frequent nor apparently so intriguing, but interest was high.[13]

11. David H. Flaherty, "Crime and Social Control in Provincial Massachusetts," *Historical Journal* 24 (1981): 342; Kai T. Erikson, *Wayward Puritans: A Study in the Sociology of Deviance* (New York, 1966), 175; Eli Farber, "Puritan Criminals: The Economic, Social, and Intellectual Background to Crime in Seventeenth-Century Massachusetts," *Perspectives in American History* 11 (1977–78): 83–144, esp. 108–21, 127–34.

12. Increase Mather, *A Call to the Rising Generation* (Boston, 1685), 17; Increase Mather, *Practical Truths Tending to Promote the Power of Godliness* (Boston, 1682), 170–72; Thomas Foxcroft, *Lessons of Caution to Young Sinners* (Boston, 1733), 47; John Webb, *A Seasonable Warning against Bad Company Keeping* (Boston, 1726), 16.

13. Michael Weisser, *Crime and Punishment in Early Modern Europe* (Atlantic Highlands, N.J., 1979), 16; Pat Rogers, *The Augustan Vision* (New York, 1974), 99–100.

Generally, collaborative theft was of three types in Massachusetts. First were servants' pilfering and sharing of household goods and foods not only among themselves but also in the neighborhood. As one minister described the custom in 1712, "Servants will take Money, Victuals, Drink, Cloths, or any goods, anything belonging to their Masters or Mistresses; and will sell them, give them away, or imploy them in Junkets and Merry meetings." Being regarded as virtually a natural phenomenon, incidents of this type were rarely prosecuted in England or America. Second were festal thefts in which a group stole food and drink in order to spite the victim and treat companions to a feast at his expense. In 1685 Deputy Governor Thomas Danforth, for instance, lost two turkeys on a fast day to some Harvard students and Cambridge townsfolk who obviously wished to flout authority and an official ceremony. Finally there were the more profit-oriented thefts. Most often, such crimes seemed more opportunistic than carefully plotted; as one drunken denizen of Salem harbor urged a companion in 1679, "now is the time to get money, the privateer wants horses." However, there were organized rings, especially along the Boston, Salem, and Marblehead water-fronts, complete with elaborate, even intercolonial fencing operations. In Boston during the early 1670s, for example, there was an extensive organi-zation based in a brothel. In the midst of a flood of prosecutions for theft and "idleness" in Boston, the Suffolk County Quarterly Court clerk entered a stray warning in the record about others implicated but not prosecuted: "Take care that if they live not orderly & industriously to proceede with them according to law." In the Connecticut Valley in the mid-1680s roguery slipped into villainy as the activities of a band of brigands, estimated by terrorized citizens to number sixty, caused five towns to raise a force of ninety men to hunt the gang down. The actual number encountered was five, but the excitement they generated reached to Boston. Some of the more persistent and flagrant thieves were articulate about their commitment to the profane life. While trying to recruit a new member, a longtime Salem underworld character bragged about his gang: "What a gallant life they lived, not wanting pork, rum, molasses, corn, or mutton, which . . . they procured at their pleasure."[14] Stealing, not merely to survive but to defy official moral

14. Laurel Thatcher Ulrich, "It 'Went Away Shee Knew Not How': Food Theft and Domestic Conflict in Seventeenth-Century Essex County," in Peter Benes, ed., *Foodways in the Northeast* (Boston, 1984), 94–104; Benjamin Wadsworth, *The Well-Ordered Family, or Relative Duties* (Boston, 1712), 118–19; Roger Thompson, "Adolescent Culture in Colonial Massachusetts," *Journal of Family History* 9 (1984): 134; *Essex Recs.* VII, 245; IX, 276; Richard P. Gildrie, "'The Gallant Life': Theft on the Salem-Marblehead, Massachusetts, Waterfront in the 1680s," *EIHC* 122 (1986): 284–98; *Suffolk Recs.* 82–83, 88, 112, 114–15;

standards and to support "idleness" in a "gallant life" shared with others, was a deliberate inversion of the Puritan social ethic of hard work and personal asceticism. Thieves were not conspicuous by their absence from early New England.

"Idleness" was, in the reformers' view, a natural concomitant of thievery and reflected a similar commitment to an alternative moral vision. Richard Baxter, a notable seventeenth-century English moralist, gave voice to this consensus. "Idleness," he wrote, "is no small sin itself, and it breedeth and cherisheth many others: their time is lost by it and they are made unfit for any honest employment or course of life." Not surprisingly Massachusetts authorities attempted to prevent this "course of life" from the beginning, including a section of the Provoking Evils Law that denounced it as "a sin of Sodom." Nonetheless it remained a temptation, since the common picture of an American Eden of ease and plenty readily combined in the imagination of the era with the traditional medieval English utopian Land of Cockayne, where labor was abolished. Tradition and opportunity seemed to hallow "idleness" in English America.[15]

For some, "idleness" was not merely a "nursery of vice" but also a right. In Salem in 1678, for instance, a sailor charged with "idleness" and "disorderly carriage" objected, claiming that the local rates spent on the poor "were made to maintain him" in his preferred way of life. In 1682 the Essex court issued a "Hue & Cry" for a "Jerseyman" (a native of the Channel Islands), Thomas Russell, who had been stealing from New York to Maine, following "a very lewd Course of Life by drunkenness, Idleness" and not "providing sustenance" for his family in Marblehead. When he was home "his wicked violence" made his wife "dreade his societie." Nor was that pattern restricted to mobile sailors and recent immigrants. For example, in 1684 John Hodge of rural Suffield was prosecuted "for squandering away his time & estate in Idle Company . . . drinking, and beating his wife."[16]

Hampshire Recs. 30 March 1686; M. Halsey Thomas, ed., *Diary of Samuel Sewall, 1674–1709* (New York, 1973), 1:69.

15. Richard B. Schlatter, *The Social Ideas of Religious Leaders, 1660–1688* (1940; reprint, New York, 1971), 64; *Essex Recs.* I, 109; *Mass. Recs.* V, 62, 373; Stephen Foster, *Their Solitary Way: The Puritan Social Ethic in the First Century of New England* (New Haven, 1971), 135–36; Michael Zuckerman, "Identity in British America: Unease in Eden," in Nicholas Canny and Anthony Pagden, eds., *Identity in the Atlantic World, 1500–1800* (Princeton, 1987), 124; Hill, "Pottage for Freeborn Englishmen," 235.

16. *Essex Recs.* VII, 1; VIII, 344–45, 423–24; Hampshire Recs. 30 September 1684.

Seen in another light, "idleness," according to an eighteenth-century English wit, "is only a coarse name for an infinite capacity for living in the present." In Maine in the 1660s, where the Puritan writ did not reach, those of a "droanish disposition" flourished, according to English traveler John Josselyn. "They have a custom of taking Tobacco, sleeping at noon, sitting long at meals sometimes four times in a day, and now and then drinking a dram of the bottle extraordinarily." The temptations of the Land of Cockayne were never far off, literally or figuratively. In orthodox Massachusetts and Plymouth "wandering, vagabond persons," living much as did their English counterparts, were a problem. The authorities responded in the English mode with attempts to settle people in towns and in work.[17]

Contempt or abuse of authority was another prominent trait of the profane outlook. Its milder, less articulate forms arose out of the fact that English folk tradition tended to condone immediate emotional responses to challenges. Hence verbal and physical attacks against constables, watchmen, tithingmen, and other officers were virtual staples of local court records. In Hatfield in January 1678, for instance, the constable went to the rescue of a townsman threatened by an irate neighbor. Requiring the assistance of three other men, the constable managed to drag the angry fellow to the constable's house. There he "fell into a rage" so severe that he attacked his restrainers "with his fist severall tymes," shouting "foole, Rogue" and, as the constable testified, "saying and offering to Beate out my Brains." The constable also asserted "that I was forced to ty him fast and to have help to hold him and carry him in and keepe him, he being in a Rage and resolving to kill, damming, vowing, and swearing he would be revenged." In the tiny hamlet of Bradford in 1681 a group attempting to pay their "country rate" (colony taxes) in corn became exasperated with the constable's lengthy accounting procedure. Shouting "must we waight upon you all night?" several pushed the officer into a chair, poured a few bushels out on his doorstep, and challenged him to count them by the grain. Then someone said, "Com, we will go into the Seler and Brack out the hed of a barrill of sider and drink." To the cheers of onlookers, two women "rumaged his cupboards and knocked in his barrels of cider." Unwillingly, the Bradford constable hosted an event similar in spirit to a festal theft.[18]

17. Lance Bertelsen, *The Nonsense Club: Literature and Popular Culture, 1749–1764* (Oxford, 1986), frontispiece; John Josselyn, *An Account of Two Voyages to New England* (London, 1675; reprint, Boston, 1865), 159; *Ply. Recs.* V, 169; VI, 54, 71, 94, 113; XI, 32, 90–91, 94, 143–44, 168, 206; *Suffolk Recs.* 870–71; *Essex Recs.* IX, 452–53; Hampshire Recs. 30 March 1680, 5 June 1686.

18. *Pynchon Recs.* 288; *Essex Recs.* VIII, 213–16.

Ready indulgence of rage and exasperation against minor officialdom may be part of the human condition, although the particular forms of expression—such as impromptu involuntary drinking parties—seem specific to this culture. Most incidents, like those above, also seem to reflect only momentary pique; but there were others that apparently arose out of deep-seated, persistent contempt of official constraints. A respected "ancient man" of Haverill, a church member, was prosecuted in 1686 for behaving "in a tumultuous and seditious manner" during a town meeting. He objected too strenuously to a Quarterly Court order that two men of the town be required to support their bastard children. When the relevant statute was read, he spat out "That men were led about by the Lawes like a Company of Puppy-dogs" and followed that "with other taunting and reproachful words and expressions towards some men in particular," presumably local magistrates and other representatives of distant authority at Ipswich and Boston. Although his attitude may have reflected a residual antinomianism, his appeal to the town meeting was based on the presumed superiority of popular custom, as he understood it, and on personal autonomy. When first brought to book, he felt "not as yet convicted in my own conscience of anything criminal," but was willing, in the church way, to "seek all lawfull means for a Reconciliation." To this man, who was hardly a "rogue," the colony's law code and its agents were an alien, intrusive presence, limiting rather than embodying his and his neighbors' sense of justice.[19]

The less respectable characters could make the same profane point as clearly. One Salem rascal missed a court hearing, hardly his first, and then rode off to Marblehead with a boon companion, a Salem Village farmer. Meeting another crony at the bridge, he requested him to "tell anyone who inquired for him that he had gone to Bailey's to drink sack, etc." Later when asked at a Salem tavern about his absence from court, his response was to assault the questioner. In Scituate at about the same time a fellow was whipped for expressing the common profane view of authority. He had called the local pastor "a false prophett" and the magistrate "a false, hypocritical fellow." He noted that a pious local merchant who joined the minister in catechizing "had received stolen goods," which accounted for his prosperity, and that the merchant must have taken perverse pleasure in "going up and down from house to house, to intice young persons to come to heare their false teachers."

Richard Bryar of Ipswich, not content with denunciation, preferred parody. Being held in the garret of an Ipswich tavern in May 1682 for abetting

19. *Essex Recs.* IX, 601–4.

a jailbreak, Bryar was whipped and told by a minister that he ought to repent. "Soon after he was punished," claimed a witness, he "began with a great Singing & presently after he kneled down against a Chest & sayd he would go to prayer." After that came the sermon, in which he averred that "if he had known he should have come to the ordinary & stayd so long there, he would have brought his money & would have been as drunk as Davids Son." One of his fellow prisoners was so impressed that he "commended him that he was of such a stout heart and that he was not daunted." Bryar, appreciating his audience, asserted that "he did not value his whipping the skip of a flea, onely for a little shame and that it smarted onely a little upon one side."[20] Such bravado, expressed in this case through parody of church life and studied indifference to the lash, was a prized attribute of profane élan.

Another characteristic mode of expression among the profane was verbal and physical assault against peers, which reflected the aggressive, competitive individualism inherent in traditional popular culture. Slander and assault were seen in early modern Europe as closely related, not merely because violence often arose out of verbal challenges but also because both were attacks on the honor of persons, on their social standing in a milieu where status was fragile—particularly among common folk. Reputations for courage, physical prowess, honesty, or sexual probity were valuable economic and social assets well worth defending and attacking.[21]

In orthodox New England, even though the pressures of poverty and the oppressions of church and state were considerably less onerous, these sorts of attacks were frequent and were taken seriously by both the authorities and the populace. As the editor of the Suffolk court records, Samuel Eliot Morison, observed, "Slander was the commonest tort to appear in these cases."[22] The usual slanders were accusations of theft, perjury, drunkenness, promiscuity, and economic dishonesty, as in Europe. In a typical case from Rowley, a pair of sisters watched as a woman called a neighbor "a crooked-back slut and a thief, and gave her a box on the ear." Reputation was so vital to a Windsor resident that he journeyed to Springfield in 1655 to bring charges against one of the town's least credible characters for saying of his wife that "shee was a light woman and that he could have a leape on her when he

20. *Ply. Recs.* V, 240; *Essex Recs.* VII, 141–42; VIII, 303.

21. Weisser, *Crime,* 14–15; Thomas Brennan, *Public Drinking and Popular Culture in Eighteenth-Century Paris* (Princeton, 1988), 38; Robert St. George, "'Heated' Speech and Literacy in Seventeenth-Century New England," in David D. Hall and David Brayson Allen, eds., *Seventeenth-Century New England* (Boston, 1984), 275–322.

22. *Suffolk Recs.* lvi.

pleased." The man from Connecticut had the pleasure of witnessing the slanderer receive eight lashes and of collecting forty shillings, about fifteen days' wages for a farm laborer. Women were particularly important in slander cases as both victims and perpetrators because traditionally they were the main regulators of general reputations, a crucial role in social control.[23]

Physical assault among women was not rare. In Salem in 1683, for instance, two mariners' wives were charged with "fighting in the open street." Occasionally husbands and wives attacked as a team, as when a Rowley couple was charged with threatening a neighbor, "saying he would split him down with a spade, and his wife for saying that she would run him through with the fork she had in her hand and for hitting the oxen so that they ran away with the cart" upon which the inebriated victim was standing.[24] Most commonly, however, assault was a male crime involving matters of honor reflected in property or respectful conduct. For instance, in 1686 when a Springfield tavern-keeper told a customer that "he had had enough," the man "rose up from the Table's end . . . and said, By God I wil make you fetch me Cider." He then slammed the taverner "in the forehead" with a fist in which a coin was held, "which cut a great gash." If the victim of an assault did not respond immediately and in kind he was liable to be subjected to the further humiliation of being kicked while down, having ears pulled, and being called "cur" or "cowardly whelp," implying doglike submission to abuse by one's betters. Such violent episodes were more frequent in maritime towns where the profane life was more deeply established but, as we have seen, hardly restricted to them.[25]

These episodes of theft, idleness, contempt, slander, and assault illustrate "profaneness" as "conversation" in the sense of commentary on profane and official manners and morals. But because profaneness was also a "frame or course of life," it is instructive to follow the careers of some of the "rogues" in order to discern the underlying patterns of their attitudes and conduct. In Plymouth Colony in 1675 Matthew Boomer and two companions were summoned "for their residing in the government without order, and not attending the publick worship of God." Indifferent to the rules of state and church, they also ignored the prevalent social and economic codes by "living lonely and in a heathenish way from good societie." The court ordered them

23. *Essex Recs.* VIII, 14; *Pynchon Recs.* 236–37; Ulrich, *Good Wives,* 55, 57, 96.
24. Ulrich, *Good Wives,* 184–201.
25. *Essex Recs.* VIII, 145; IX, 82, 149; *Pynchon Recs.* 315; Daniel Vickers, "Work and Life on the Fishing Periphery of Essex County, Massachusetts, 1630–1675," in Hall and Allen, eds., *Seventeenth-Century New England,* 100.

to attend church, without specifying where, and to "live otherwise orderly, or that they depart the government." Boomer, who was apparently an Indian trader, did neither. In 1686 he was prosecuted for breach of the Sabbath "by sufering his Indian servants to hunt on the Lords Day," which cost him twenty shillings.[26]

He was also tried for "lascivious carriage" or, more properly, attempted rape. John and Mary Brandon of Freetown complained of Boomer that "att sundry times he hath attempted to abuse her, attempting by force to lye with her, & for other lascivious carriages toward her." Because her husband objected, Boomer "sundry times beat him . . . & given out [before witnesses] threatning speaches against him, in soe much that, as he saith, he goeth in fear of his life of him." Boomer was fined ten shillings for "breach of peace" and four pounds for "lascivious carriage." Obviously not a poor man, Matthew Boomer over an eleven-year period violated virtually every element of the Puritan sense of "good societie." An arrogant, aggressive, indeed violent egoist living on the fringes of settlement, he was better suited to be a boon companion for his contemporary Nathaniel Bacon of Virginia than a Pilgrim.

The Massachusetts ports, of course, were an even more prolific setting for rogues than the frontier. In Boston in January 1672 Alice Thomas was convicted on a five-part indictment for running an unlicensed alehouse, "entertaining Idle persons," that also served as a brothel and a rendezvous for thieves. The court claimed that her house was frequented by "Lewd, Lascivious & notorious persons of both Sexes, giving them opportunity to commit carnal wickedness & that by common fame she is a common bawd." No less than seven thieves convicted of more than one crime used her services "in receiving buying & concealing severall goods stol'n" out of ships and warehouses. The judge ordered her to stand on the gallows "with a rope about her necke" for an hour and then to be "stript to the waste, and there tyed to a Cart's taile, and so whipt through ye streets to prison" with at least thirty-nine lashes. Afterward she was to be held at the "pleasure of this Court." In April the court in effect put her on work-release by allowing her out during daylight. Apparently rehabilitated, she was readmitted as an inhabitant of Boston in 1676 "during her good behavior."[27]

Alice Thomas was a criminal entrepreneur providing essential services for a developing profane milieu in Boston. As her motives seemed primarily economic, the authorities could persuade her to change her ways. In contrast,

26. *Ply. Recs.* V, 169; VI, 178. For similar Plymouth characters, see *Ply. Recs.* V. 8–9, 16, 27, as samples.

27. *Suffolk Recs.* 82–89, 126, 721.

Joseph Gatchell of Salem was a rogue on principle. Born in Salem in 1652, Gatchell was only the most prominent and persistent of a family of "vain persons." Gatchell, a tailor by honest trade, made his court debut in November 1678 by fathering two children from his brother Samuel's wife. Although Samuel was a sailor, the Essex magistrates—suspecting his collusion—prosecuted him "for not living with his wife, according to law, which is a common fame." Joseph and Bethiah were bound over to the Court of Assistants, but he "broke prison and escaped." The next year he was caught and imprisoned for a week, plus more time in lieu of a fine of three pounds. He petitioned for release, claiming damage "to his poor wife at home" and "his good Customers." He also objected "that any humane creature should endure to live in so pestiferous a stinke." He was released. Meanwhile Samuel and Bethiah continued to face charges of slander, adultery, and theft. Barely out a year, Joseph was charged with a drunken assault upon a constable and promptly missed his first hearing on the count.[28]

In his subsequent trial in June 1680 Gatchell, besides assault, was also charged with "reviling and reproachful speeches against the magistrates and ministers." A habitué of Salem taverns, Gatchell liked to "scoff and jeer at ministers" before appreciative audiences. Parody was part of his repertoire: "He also made a game of praying and acted very strangely in deriding the most grave and wise in the town." In explaining his absence from worship, he claimed that he would appear "when the order of the Church of England shall be sett up with the organs." For others he claimed to be "one of those sum Call singing Quakers." "If any are the true Servants of God," he asserted, "they are, for they sing ye Songs of Moses and Miriam." His specific criticisms, however, resemble those of the Ranters of mid-seventeenth-century England: "The Ministers preach Nothing but Damnation; and that which they Called ye Scriptures was not ye Word of God, but ye Sayings of Men, and that those that they Called Preachers did only say that the Scriptures was the words of God to make simple People believe so to keepe them in Ignorance."[29]

Indeed, the Ranter point of view suited Gatchell because it provided another ideological justification for the profane life, while more profoundly shocking respectable sensibilities. An English pamphlet of 1650 outlined the position: "That there is no occasion for them to read the Scriptures, nor to hear sermons, because Father, Son, and Spirit are all in them, therefore they are above all commandments whatsoever. That there is no such thing as what

28. *Essex Recs.* VII, 113, 146–47, 149–50, 194, 224, 227, 289, 378, 381, 475.
29. *Essex Recs.* VII, 407–8.

men call sin. That sin and holiness are all one to God." One version of Ranter thought held that all religious ideas were inward experiences having no objective reality. In 1684 Gatchell had his tongue bored through with a hot poker for asserting, among other things, that "there was no God, Devil, or Hell." He also claimed that the biblical or historical Jesus was an "Imperfect Savior & a foole." This idea corresponds to the famed English heretic James Naylor's assertion that "He that expecteth to be saved by Jesus Christ that died at Jerusalem shall be deceived." If there was a savior, he "dwelt within." Thus, "the disciples of God shall not enjoy Christ till they have rejected him." Obviously "there is a full end of sin for all men," and a wise man would say, "I will delight myself with the worst of men as well as with the best."[30]

Tailors in early modern England had a reputation for heresy, bred of time to read, but also for weakness and timidity. Gatchell lived up to the first but not the second part of the stereotype. He recurrently was in court for assault, "contempt of authority," Sabbath violations, public drunkenness, adultery, and theft until his career was cut short by his "blasphemous and atheistical speeches." No lone wolf, he craved companions in crime. Indeed, he was one of the principals of a large theft ring that plagued the Salem-Marblehead waterfront for years. He also enjoyed shocked audiences. He followed a profane "course of life" openly and on principle.[31]

Such roguery was not restricted to the frontier and maritime fringes of Massachusetts. The rural towns of the Connecticut Valley also had some persistent, self-conscious offenders against respectability. The Towsley family of Suffield made frequent court appearances over a twenty-year period for the full range of profane activities except contempt of church authorities. Charged with "pound breach" (stealing animals) in 1684, Mary Towsley, wife of Michael, was also convicted of "making a trade of wicked lying, slandering, cursing, wretched scolding & dangerous language" and was given ten lashes. However, her "reviling the Court" was so severe during the Suffield hearings that she earned fifteen more lashes at the Springfield sessions. The next year she took a quart pewter pot from a neighbor. The owner and his wife saw her do it and protested, but "shee said shee would have it and Caryed it away." The owner chased her into the street, where "shee denied shee had it" and called her husband. Together they then struck the poor fellow "severall Blows,

30. Ronald A. Knox, *Enthusiasm: A Chapter in the History of Religion, with Special Reference to the Seventeenth and Eighteenth Centuries* (New York, 1961), 153, 173; Christopher Hill, *The Experience of Defeat: Milton and Some Contemporaries* (New York, 1984), 45–47, 100–101, 118–19, 122, 141; *Assistants Recs.* II, 253–54; *Essex Recs.* IX, 269.

31. Gildrie, "Gallant Life," passim; *Essex Recs.* VIII, 377–78; IX, 26–28, 82, 110, 132, 148–49, 215.

He with his fist and shee with a stick." Michael was able to make five pounds bond for his wife's good behavior.[32]

The Towsleys supplemented their small farm income by stealing household goods and animals while relying on intimidation to avoid prosecution. In 1691 the combination failed to stop James King from issuing a complaint. A constable's search of the Towsley house turned up linen, fine thread, four trenchers, and yarn allegedly belonging to King, who also had "vehement suspicions" that Towsley "killed and made use of others swine." By common report the children "were theevish, pilfering, lying, etc." King and his wife also accused the Towsleys of "threatning them and offering Mischiefe to their Cattle, threatning to burne his house whereby he is in feare of Mischiefe to him and his family." The accused were not released on bond but held for trial before the Hampshire Quarterly Court, which encouraged others to come forward. The Towsleys and their eldest daughter were convicted, ordered to pay restitution, and whipped at Springfield. The daughter in effect turned state's evidence, which she tried to recant but then repeated, charging "her father before authority, as killing [swine] and Stealing, and teaching her to steale." She agreed to become the servant of a Suffield selectman "with whom she may be wel educated, the Child herself Saying, that she can do no better or reforme whyle She continues with her Parents or father." This disaster did not prevent Michael Towsley from making court appearances in 1697 for theft of a mare and in 1701 for bad debts.[33]

In his analysis of the moral styles of his time William Hubbard remarked, "It is as natural for man to breed himself trouble, as for sparks to fly upward." Lying, stealing, blustering, and intimidating, the Towsleys compounded what was "natural" by cultivating the profane tradition. The penalties for the family were serious. But for those who—often in fits of passion—passed into villainy and were caught, the consequences could be fatal. Public executions were, of course, normal throughout the Atlantic world. Involving the agents of both church and state, these grisly rituals were intended to punish the offender and to assert the vitality and righteousness of the standing moral order. A contrite confession from the malefactor was the most affecting evidence of the latter, for raw intimidation was hardly sufficient persuasion in that era of sporadic and weak law enforcement. The more talented of the American Puritan moralists, such as Increase and Cotton Mather, saw these confessions and the obligatory sermons as opportunities not merely to denounce sin and point out

32. Hampshire Recs. 30 September 1684; *Pynchon Recs.* 308–9.
33. Hampshire Recs. 19 September 1691; *Pynchon Recs.* 326–28, 353, 372.

the consequences but also to analyze these extreme examples of a profane "course of life."[34]

In 1686 Increase Mather published the confession of a murderer, James Morgan, together with an execution sermon. The confession he elicited connected all the essential elements of the profane life except theft. Of these traits, Morgan stressed drunkenness, "for when in drink, I have been guilty of Cursing and Swearing, and quarrelling and striking others." However, the "Sin which lieth most heavy upon my Conscience is," he declared, "that I have despised the Word of God, and many times refused to hear it preached." The elder Mather was, nonetheless, more interested in the profane sense of wounded honor and mutual challenge that seemed at the heart of the crime. Morgan, as Mather put it, "told me that the other gave him some ill language whereby he was provoked and that he said to him, if he came within the door, he would run the Spit into his Bowels, and he was as wicked as he said, so that he is guilty of murder." Lacking his father's intimate involvement in the case, Cotton Mather's sermon on the same event from Isaiah 45:22 ("Look to me and be saved, you peoples from all corners of the earth; for I am God, there is no other") was aimed first at the felon, urging repentance, and then to the populace in the jeremiad mode.[35]

Four years later the younger Mather produced a more insightful piece, probably because he was now the principal cleric hearing and trying to shape the confession. Hugh Stone, an Andover farmer who was often "distempered with drink," slit his wife's throat over a dispute "about selling a piece of land." The marriage had long been an unhappy one, as Stone stressed in his confession. Noting that he "had been used unto something of Religion," he observed that "upon Contention between me and my wife, I left off the wayes of the God, and you see what I am come to." A bad marriage led to escape in drink and then to murder. Mather in his sermon was on occasion crudely denunciatory: "O thou that takest no care to lead thy life civilly and honestly, . . . here is this Murderer, look upon him; and see how many are come with their eyes to behold this man, that abhors himself before God." But wondering, "I have hardly met with so unintelligible a man, as this Hugh Stone," the minister tried to gain a fuller understanding. Stone, while in

34. William Hubbard, *The Benefit of a Well-Ordered Conversation* (Boston, 1684), 70; Hughes, *Fatal Shore*, 31; Ronald A. Bosco, "Lectures at the Pillory: The Early American Execution Sermon," *American Quarterly* 30 (1978): 156–76; Richard Weisman, *Witchcraft, Magic, and Religion in Seventeenth-Century Massachusetts* (Amherst, Mass., 1984), 96–97.

35. Increase Mather, *A Sermon Occasioned by the Execution of James Morgan* (Boston, 1686), 10, 27; Cotton Mather, *A Call of the Gospel* (Boston, 1686); Worthington Chauncey Ford, ed., *Diary of Cotton Mather* (New York, 1912), 1:122.

prison, "thought himself sometimes haunted with the Ghost of his Murdered Wife," which led Mather to speculate on "whether the use of his *Reason* were not sometimes disturbed by the Horrour of his mind." Yet underlying and preceding that condition was the psychology of the profane. "His *Passions* upon any Provocation were so inordinate, as that we did not wonder to see what he was come unto." Mather also added a picture of the umbrageous pride of profane individualism: "And as on one side, I never saw a Man express less *fear* of Dying, so on the other, I never heard a Man express more *Care* about every Trifle, which he counted himself concerned in."[36]

By use of these extreme examples as well as their daily pastoral encounters, the American Puritan moralists, like their compeers throughout Catholic and Protestant Europe, detected and attempted to suppress both specific misdeeds and the matrix of attitudes and conduct that, together with Original Sin, seemed to be the root cause of "provoking evils."

The profane conversation whose extremes shaded into criminality was a way of life, a reasonably coherent moral structure found throughout the Atlantic world in the early modern era. In New England the reformers described it as "vain," "disorderly," and "contemptuous of authority." Pointing to another facet of this tradition, the Massachusetts General Court in 1682 denounced "Vagrant, Idle" folk who "doe not follow any lawful imployment for a livelyhood."[37] Although not so numerous or so chronically impoverished as their fellows in England and Europe, the Towsleys, Gatchells, Boomers, and other profane persons of New England evinced similar attitudes and conduct.

As reflected in a popular and influential literary genre of the early modern era, this particular moral vision of the profane might also be thought of as "picaresque." Picaresque ballads, stories, and novels centered, in the words of a recent critic, on "the individualistic will of a hero determined to resist the discipline of external authority."[38] Generally these works were comic biographies and autobiographies of wandering young men from humble origins who made their way by cunning or petty criminality. Having no secure position in respectable society but being unwilling or unable to live fully outside of it, the picaro (or "rogue" in English terminology) had his own moral code, sanctioned by long tradition, which was an ironic commentary on or inversion of official standards.[39]

---

36. Cotton Mather, *Speedy Repentance Urged* (Boston, 1690), 67–68, 76–77, 82; *Essex Recs.* IX, 27, 568, for Stone's drinking.
37. *Mass. Recs.* V, 373; *Ply. Recs.* XI, 32, 90–91, 168, 206.
38. Michael McKeon, *The Origins of the English Novel, 1600–1740* (Baltimore, 1987), 97.
39. Barbara Babcock, "'Liberty's a Whore': Inversion, Marginalis, and Picaresque Narra-

As with his more privileged counterpart, the rake, the rogue's exaggerated egocentrism was expressed in the pursuit of sensual pleasure, material objects, or wealth, and the delights of outwitting or outfacing others. Usually heedless of long-term consequences or gains, he sought immediate gratification. The rogue tended to regard those who lived by the respectable codes of hard work or legal privilege as dupes, if relatively powerless, or hypocritical oppressors, if powerful or influential. Thus the rogue's characteristic view of society was satiric as well as exploitive. His most typical crime was theft in its various modes. Those with a penchant for sustained or extreme violence (murder, brigandage, piracy) were on the far margins of roguery, being "villains." The villain abandoned society or created his own; the rogue would not. The rogue lived by his wits, not bloodlust, and his anger and rebellion often took a mocking rather than a desperate form. The chief targets of mockery were the legal system, religious institutions, and those who ran them, for they were the main defenders and teachers of a moral standard the rogue despised.[40]

This picaresque literature clearly reflected a social and cultural reality. It described a moral imagination that shaped people's lives in Europe and English America. New England was not exempt from this presence, a moral code that greatly alarmed the godly.

In order to shape manners and morals, the reformers, as they made clear in the Reforming Synod of 1679, intended to improve the social and educational milieus in which people formed their ideas and conduct. Hence they were interested in such things as tavern reform and improvements in "family government." It was through them that the Puritans hoped to overcome the world of impulsive, aggressive, and hedonistic individualism, which, they believed, threatened both worldly and cosmic disaster.

---

tive," in her *The Reversible World: Symbolic Inversion in Art and Society* (Ithaca, N.Y., 1978), 104–5.

40. Frank W. Chandler, *The Literature of Roguery* (1907; reprint, New York, 1958), 4–5; Harold Weber, "Rakes, Rogues, and the Empire of Misrule," *Huntingdon Library Quarterly* 47 (1984): 13–32, esp. 15–16. For a mild but nonetheless intriguing eighteenth-century American picaro tale, see Susan E. Klepp and Billy G. Smith, eds., *The Infortunate: The Voyage and Adventures of William Moraley, an Indentured Servant* (University Park, Pa., 1992).

ARENAS OF
CONFLICT

THREE

Tavern Milieus

Taverns and the conduct proper to them were crucial to the Reformation of Manners, and, accordingly, "intemperance" was addressed by the Reforming Synod of 1679.[1] The reformers' understanding of the problem, their attempts to cope with the issue, and the reactions to and effects of their efforts were central to New England Puritanism's struggle with the profane. In part the synod's report confirmed the General Court's worry in the Provoking Evils Law of 1675 that "the shamefull and scandelous sin of excessive drinking, tipling & company keeping in tavernes, etc., ordinarys, grows upon us." The 1675 law, essentially a summary of evolving tavern regulations reaching back to 1634, asked the "County Courts not to license any more publick houses than are absolutely necessary in any towne, and to take care that none be licenst but persons of approved sobriety and fidelity to law and good order." As a corollary, the legislature reiterated that "all private, unlicensed houses of entertainment be diligently searched out" and suppressed. To that end, selectmen were authorized to choose "some sober and discrete persons" to assist. This office was, in essence, an early form of the tithingmen whose role was clarified in 1679 in response to the synod.[2]

Both the law and the synod's report restated the official view that "the proper end of Taverns, etc." was "for the refreshing & entertainment of travailers & strangers only." The law "strictly enjoyned & required" towns-folk "to forbeare spending their time or estate in such common houses of

1. This chapter is an expanded, extensively rewritten version of Richard P. Gildrie, "Taverns and Popular Culture in Essex County, Massachusetts, 1678–1686," *EIHC* 124 (1988): 158–85. The author is grateful to the Essex Institute, Salem, Massachusetts, for permission to reuse this material.

2. [Increase Mather], *The Necessity of Reformation* (Boston, 1679), 5–6; *Mass. Recs.* V, 61–62. See also Mark Edward Lender and James Kirby Martin, *Drinking in America: A History* (New York, 1982), 9–21.

enterteynment, to drincke & tiple." Nor were the New England Puritans unique in this unrealistically restrictive view. In 1604 Parliament asserted that "the ancient, true, and principal use of Inns, Alehouses, and Victualling-houses was for the Receit, Relief, and Lodging of Wayfaring People." They were "not meant for Entertainment and Harbouring of lewd and idle People to spend and consume their Money and their Time in a lewd and drunken manner."[3] The populace in England and Massachusetts, however, thought otherwise. As the report noted, "it is a common practice for Town-Dwellers, yea, and Church-Members, to frequent Publick Houses, and there to mis-spend precious Time. . . ."

The tavern and its less respectable sibling, the alehouse, were ubiquitous and necessary institutions of traditional English popular culture. Indeed, they were as central a physical and symbolic setting for the sociability and ceremonies of the "profane" as churches were for the "godly." Beginning at least with the Licensing Act of 1552, English attempts to suppress the alehouse and regulate the tavern arose from a fear that the attitudes and conduct of the habitual patrons of such places not only encouraged vice and criminality but also threatened proper social order. In the mid-seventeenth century in England, "as reforming enthusiasm was channeled increasingly into a demand for a reformation of manners," one recent English historian has observed, "popular drinking customs and the alehouses which supported them were swiftly identified as obstacles to the realization of the reformers' aspirations."[4]

In England, Massachusetts, and even Virginia there were renewed efforts to control excessive drinking and tavern customs during the 1670s. In the aftermath of Bacon's Rebellion the Virginia House of Burgesses passed in 1677 a highly restrictive law, confirming a 1668 statute that limited each county to two licensed houses (except the shire in which the legislature met) and adding a requirement that every licensed place be able to "provide for travellers good dyett, lodging," and proper care of horses. The burgesses shared with their peers elsewhere in the English world a distaste for the rebelliousness, "idleness and debaucheryes" that the reformers, Puritan and

3. Quoted in Paton Yoder, "Tavern Regulation in Virginia: Rationale and Reality," *Virginia Magazine of History and Biography* 87 (1979): 274.
4. Keith Wrightson, "Alehouses, Order, and Reformation in Rural England, 1590–1660," in Eileen Yeo and Stephen Yeo, eds., *Popular Culture and Class Conflict, 1590–1914: Explorations in the History of Labour and Leisure* (Brighton, England, 1981), 11–17, quote on 17; Peter Clark, "The Alehouse and the Alternative Society," in Donald Pennington and Keith Thomas, eds., *Puritans and Revolutionaries: Essays in Seventeenth-Century History Presented to Christopher Hill* (Oxford, 1978), 47–72, esp. 61–62.

Anglican alike, believed endemic to tavern culture.[5] Such similar worries, reactions, and rhythms of reform suggest that, at least from the point of view of the authorities, the tavern culture of Massachusetts closely resembled that of other English places.

In pursuit of the Reformation of Manners after the Reforming Synod, the Massachusetts General Court passed an extensive elaboration on the tavern code in March 1681. The law reiterated the requirement of annual licensing during the spring sessions of the quarterly courts and insisted that selectmen must approve of all persons to be licensed in their towns prior to county court action. This answered complaints from Increase Mather and others that magistrates were occasionally too quick to grant licenses to persons local authorities found questionable. Also, the quarterly courts were required to hear grand jury presentments before issuing licenses. If a tavern-keeper was convicted on a first offense, the fine had to be paid before renewal. On a second offense the license was to be revoked.[6]

For the first time the General Court also set quotas resembling those of the Virginia statutes of 1668 and 1677 rather than leaving the question to the discretion of the county courts. Boston was allowed six wine taverns, ten inn-holders, and eight retailers of wine and "strong licquors out of doors." For Salem there were to be two wine taverns, four inns, and four retailers. Charlestown was limited to "three publick houses" and one retailer. Two public houses and one retailer were deemed sufficient for Ipswich, while the towns of Gloucester, Lynn, Hingham, and Newbury were each allowed two public houses. All other Massachusetts towns were restricted to "one such publick house or retayler."

The legislature assumed, as it had for decades, that the ports and market towns—havens for "strangers and travellers"—had greater need, while agricultural places regardless of population required but one. On the other hand, the insistence on the more expensive and respectable "wine taverns" and "innholders" for the ports of Boston and Salem rather than the more general "public houses" indicates a strong suspicion of waterfront drinking places and their denizens. Indeed, the terminology of the law reflected an antipathy toward cheap, easily established taverns: the terms "public house" or "ordinary," as used in late Stuart England and Virginia, were meant to contrast with "private," often ephemeral places that might require little more than a

5. Peter Clark, *The English Alehouse: A Social History, 1200–1830* (London, 1983), 1–3, 166–221; Yoder, "Tavern Regulation," 261–63; George L. Haskins, *Law and Authority in Early Massachusetts: A Study in Tradition and Design* (New York, 1960), 78.

6. *Mass. Recs.* V, 305.

bench and a few mugs to begin business. The "public house" was a licensed establishment offering lodging, meals, and alcohol, as the Virginia law stressed. The unlicensed "private house" certainly offered drink, but other services beyond that varied considerably and often in directions the authorities found distasteful.[7] In any case, the great variety of types of drinking places from the elite wine taverns to the poorest alehouses unable to provide even beer and cider suggests their importance to the whole society.

Their numbers are another indication. Peter Clark, in his study of English drinking houses, estimated one for every 89 to 104 people from 1630 to 1690. In Paris in 1750 there was approximately one tavern for every two hundred inhabitants. A recent estimate for Essex County, Massachusetts, in the 1680s puts the ratio at 219 persons per tavern, licensed and unlicensed. On average, then, the frequency of drinking places in this well-settled area of the Bay Colony was about half that of contemporary England and close to that of Paris seventy years later. In Plymouth Colony the density was much lower. In 1669 there were approximately 110 adult males for each licensed tavern. Assuming the usual multiplier, the ratio would have been about 550 people per house in the Old Colony. On the whole, these figures suggest that orthodox New England, and especially Plymouth, was, compared to seventeenth-century England, a relatively "sober" society, as was eighteenth-century Paris. At the opposite extreme, one historian has claimed that Jamestown, Virginia, and Port Royal, Jamaica, in the 1670s rollicked with a tavern for every ten inhabitants.[8]

These averages and common sense suggest that there were vast differences in demand among varying social settings. The most obvious distinction, and one embodied in the 1681 law, was between the major ports and the agricultural towns, with the smaller ports and market towns in the middle. In Essex County, for instance, Salem Town averaged eighty people per tavern in the 1680s, a greater density than the English average. The General Court authorized six licenses for the port. The Quarterly Court, responding to local demand, allowed nine in 1681, and yet there were still indictments of six

---

7. Clark, *English Alehouse,* 124, 195. For other signs of official concern for order along waterfronts, see Daniel Vickers, "Life and Work on the Fishing Periphery of Essex County, Massachusetts, 1630–1675," in David D. Hall and David G. Allan, eds., *Seventeenth-Century New England* (Charlottesville, Va., 1984), 83–117; Richard P. Gildrie, "Salem Society and Politics in the 1680s," *EIHC* 114 (1978): 185–206, esp. 191–92.

8. Clark, *English Alehouse,* 44–45; Thomas Brennan, *Public Drinking and Popular Culture in Eighteenth-Century Paris* (Princeton, 1988), 76; Gildrie, "Taverns"; *Ply. Recs.* XI, 22; George D. Langdon, Jr., *Pilgrim Colony: A History of New Plymouth* (New Haven, 1966), 55n.; Stephen S. Webb, *1676: The End of American Independence* (New York, 1984), 58.

illegal alehouses that year as well. Meanwhile Andover, the county's most populous agricultural town, was well served by one ordinary for its 850 people. There were no recorded prosecutions of unlicensed houses or illicit sales in Andover, nor in the next largest farming community, Rowley, from 1681 to 1686. Similar conditions held in Suffolk County in the 1670s before the passage of the law. Dedham, Milton, Weymouth, Medfield, Hull, Braintree, and Roxbury all had but one ordinary, while Dorchester and Hingham, each with two, were also bothered by only an occasional indictment over the decade. In Boston, however, twenty-seven houses were licensed in 1678, supplemented by nine retailers, and yet five more places were prosecuted that year.[9]

Frequent complaints about the "excessive number of drinking houses," both legal and illicit, naturally centered on the ports of Boston and Salem and, to a lesser extent, on the market towns and smaller ports such as Ipswich and Marblehead. Increase Mather and other critics understood "that in such a great Town as this [Boston], there is need of such Houses, and no sober Minister will speak against the Licensing of them." Rather, they worried that "there be not more of them then there is any need of." Of particular concern were the "private, dark Alehouses, which do more mischief, then all the Publick Houses do good, as being the very Sinks of Sin." These places, in the view of the critics, often became the haunts of those "not so well affected to Sobriety, Law & good order." Nor were the patrons of either licensed or unlicensed houses restricted to mariners or other itinerants, for "most of them are known to be frequented by town-dwellers, to ye great impoverishing of ye town [in this case Salem], ye increas of tipling, drinking & company-keeping to the dishonor of God & further provoking of his wrath."[10]

Regulating drinking places and controlling their numbers were difficult problems throughout the English world. Not only were the cheaper sorts of alehouses easily established and often ephemeral; they also had strong warrant in traditional patterns of sociability and economic custom. Among the poorer folk of Tudor-Stuart England, according to Keith Wrightson, the informal movement of alehouse business from house to house "could constitute a system of circulating aid in which economic activity, neighborly assistance, and festivity were subtly blended." On occasion these informal arrangements evolved into more permanent establishments. In Salem in 1678, for instance, John Wilkinson was charged with running an unlicensed house. He claimed

9. Gildrie, "Taverns," 162; *Suffolk Recs.* passim.

10. "The Reverend John Higginson's Letter on Taverns, June 25, 1678," *EIHC* 43 (1907): 180–81; Increase Mather, *Wo to Drunkards* (Boston, 1673), 29.

that friends "brought me sum fish" and, as "it was very could wether and ther being ayght [eight] in company, I Burned one pint of rum and that we drank together." He heartily denied that he "sould rum for fish . . . but only the rum that I gave them was to requit them for a Kinys [kindness] for, as the ould provarb hath it, one good turne desarvs another." He also likened his practice to that of his betters, "as when the porters have done any kinys for a marchant my Judges hear knows it that they used to bestow a dram or a glass or two of wine on one that hath done them any kinys." It was not his fault that some of his guests wandered off to "drink rum at another publick house that I am not willing to name" and subsequently were arrested for "being overtaken with drinke." Whatever the truth of this defense, by the next year Wilkinson had transformed an exchange of "kinys" into a notorious dive and was charged with "excessive drinking and keeping bad order in his house," including "fiddling and dancing." John King, also of Salem, professed surprise at his indictment in 1680 because he believed that "the approbation of forty or fifty of the neighborhood to sell liguor by retail" was sufficient license. For three years, backed by local custom, he "supposed he was at liberty to supply the necessities of the neighborhood."[11]

The magistrates too were often ambivalent about enforcement because the granting of licenses was a traditional form of poor relief and even of patronage. In Boston in July 1672 two women were convicted "for giving entertainment to persons drincking in their houses at unseasonable times of the night." Too poor to make bond, they were imprisoned. In October one of them was licensed to "sell Sider by the quart." In the disastrous aftermath of King Philip's War the pressures to increase the numbers of licenses so as to care for some of the widows and disabled soldiers was intense. From 1676 to 1678 the number of Boston ordinaries licensed to sell beer and cider, but not the more expensive wines and brandies, went from thirteen to eighteen. In 1675 and 1676 there were no prosecutions for unlicensed houses, but over the next two years there were ten. The minister at Salem, John Higginson, noted in 1678 that although "within this few years 2 ordinaries were judged sufficient for Salem" there were currently fourteen operating, some without licenses, while another four persons were applying to the Essex Quarterly Court. As local tax rates climbed to cope with refugees, shattered families, and soldiers "uncapable & disabled from following [their] callings," the temptation to use this traditional means of relief was strong indeed.[12]

11. Wrightson, "Alehouses," 5; *Essex Recs.* VII, 109, 251; VIII, 46.
12. *Suffolk Recs.* 24, 148; "Higginson's Letter," 180–81; *Essex Recs.* VII, 78, 80; IX, 65–66, as examples.

That there were no signs of similar pressure in more rural towns probably indicates their lesser demand for taverns and their superior capacity to absorb admittedly fewer victims of war into families and communities through church and town relief.

Thirty years later during Queen Anne's War, Boston minister Benjamin Wadsworth complained about both the magistrates' licensing practices and the traditional system of mutual aid. "It may be a Man has met with *Losses,* or his *Trade fails,* he's become low and indigent; the next thing is, he seeks a *License to Sell Drink.*" But rather than neighborly assistance Wadsworth saw moral and economic peril, fueled by poverty and entrepreneurial attitudes, outweighing the communal sense of good will.

> Licenses are so multiplyed (especially in some Places) that those who have them can get no tolerable gain by them, unless their Neighbors prove *Wicked Customers* in spending *more money* with them than they should. When men have Licenses, they're under a Temptation to Sell what Drink they can; tho' they know their Neighbors do *Wickedly* in buying *so much* as they do. And the *Poorer* those that have *Licenses* the greater are their Temptations to allow ill practices in others, for their own gain.[13]

In his view, it was not aid that was being circulated but poverty. "I fear *many* are *made* poor, by being *Wicked* customers to others that were poor before them."

Wadsworth's observation on the economics and ethics of tavern-keeping is consistent with a long-term trend toward commercialization of the liquor trades. What was missing in New England, even in the eighteenth century, was the tendency toward concentration and control by large-scale brewers and distillers typical of contemporary England. Governed only by the licensing regulations and by economic realities and popular traditions that often undermined those official controls, the tavern milieus of early New England were highly diverse. Some of these drinking establishments were even mobile. In 1671 John Chandler of Roxbury was "admonished" by the Suffolk Quarterly Court for "selling beere & Cider (upon publique fame) without a license" from a cart "upon & about ye Last Court Day of Elextion & the Last General Trayning Dayes at Boston." More infamous was the "walking Tavern," a ship, usually financed by merchants, that followed the fishing fleets, especially along

---

13. Benjamin Wadsworth, *An Essay to Do Good; by a Disswasive from Tavern-Haunting & Excessive Drinking* (Boston, 1710), 20–21.

the Maine coast. The operators were not averse to "taking ashore two or three Hogsheads of Wine and Rhum" not only for shoremen drying fish but also for local farmers. Because the trade often worked by credit, not only in liquor but also in "shooes and stockins, shirts and wastcoats," fishermen frequently and coastal farmers occasionally found "they must enter into the Merchants books for such things as they stand in need of, becoming thereby the Merchants slaves." As their debt rose, some were "constrained to mortgage their plantations, if they have any," and, upon failure to pay, the merchant was "sure to seize upon their plantations and stock of Cattle, turning them out of house and home, poor Creatures, to look out for a new habitation in some remote place where they begin the world again."[14]

The drinking trades were so easy to enter, often becoming a periodic supplement to other sources of income, and so difficult to regulate that the possibilities of corruption were obvious. Most notoriously during the Dominion of New England, "Excise men would pretend Sickness on the Road, and get a Cup of Drink of Hospitable People, but privately drop a piece of Money and afterwards make Oath that they bought Drink at these Houses, for which Innocent Persons were fined most unreasonably." The excisemen, of course, got an informer's share. The difficulty of even defining a drinking business amid the welter of transactions involving liquor further testifies to the importance of taverns and alcohol in the daily lives of English people on both sides of the Atlantic.[15]

Despite the problems of enforcement, licenses were valuable, particularly in those places restricted by law after 1681 to one ordinary. Commonly the privilege was held by a prominent local leader, often a militia officer or a selectman, whose right and performance went unchallenged for years if not decades. Some of these ordinaries became famous. The Anchor Tavern of Lynn, for instance, was owned and operated for some forty years by Thomas Marshall, a Cromwellian veteran and a local commissioner for the Essex court. Halfway between Boston and Salem, the tavern became an important watering hole for the colony's elite.[16]

At other times the selections were not so obvious. In Amesbury in the 1680s the selectmen supported Sarah Rowell, a woman deserted by her hus-

14. Clark, *English Alehouse*, 182–84; Clark, "Alehouse," 51–52; *Suffolk Recs.* 22; John Josselyn, *An Account of Two Voyages to New England* (London, 1675; reprint, Boston, 1865), 161–62.

15. William H. Whitmore, ed., *The Andros Tracts* (Boston, 1868–74), 1:116; Clark, "Alehouse," 49; Lender and Martin, *Drinking in America*, 2–4.

16. *Essex Recs.* IX, 147, 469; Edward Field, *The Colonial Tavern: A Glimpse of New England Town Life in the Seventeenth and Eighteenth Centuries* (Providence, 1897), 49–56.

band; but a local man, Samuel Colby, opened an unlicensed, competing tavern. When Rowell complained to the county court that Colby's sales "had been greatly to her damage," Colby responded that she was "a lone woman and very unfit for that employment." He claimed that her poverty prevented her from fulfilling the obligations of an ordinary: her place was "destiteud of lodgings and of all other conveniences for ye entertainment of straingers." The court "saw no cause" to question the selectmen's choice, "judging [Colby's complaint] to be irrational and illegal." In this case charitable custom was more potent than utility or free enterprise.[17]

Sometimes the competition was protracted both in and out of court. In September 1682 Walter Fairfield's license for Wenham was not renewed, although he was allowed "to draw by retail" to deplete his stock. The selectmen made that recommendation because Fairfield and his wife sold liquor to Indians and "unseasonably entertained town people and some others on Sabbath." They wished to issue the license to Ezekiel Woodward, who had "become disabled" fighting a fire. The result was a series of suits and countersuits over "irregular selling" and allowing "illegal pleasures" in their houses, of which both were guilty according to the tithingmen. The arguments were heard in every session of the court until Fairfield finally lost in June 1683.[18]

The tensions between the charitable and commercial impulses, exacerbated by the perceived need to limit licenses for moral reasons, were occasionally and plainly severe. Indeed, those pressures may help explain why there were so few prosecutions for illegal selling in the countryside. Laxity in formal enforcement, avoiding the county courts and relying on local compromises and adjustments, may have constituted a partial solution for this problem, as it was for other difficulties.[19] It may be significant, for instance, that it was not the Amesbury tithingmen or selectmen who charged Samuel Colby but Sarah Rowell who objected to the competition. But this is conjecture based largely on negative evidence. The pressures, even in the countryside, were visible enough; the solutions were less obvious.

Those places able to grant more than one license naturally enjoyed more flexibility in resolving the conflicts among charitable, commercial, and moral imperatives. The nuances of what was permitted to whom both reflected and institutionalized a highly complex tavern milieu, particularly in the ports.

17. *Essex Recs.* IX, 528, 593, 600.
18. *Essex Recs.* VIII, 383; IX, 17–18, 78, 82.
19. See David T. Konig, *Law and Society in Puritan Massachusetts: Essex County, 1629–1692* (Chapel Hill, 1979), for development of this argument on local conflict resolution.

The most elaborate, of course, was Boston's. In 1673 twenty-three tavern licenses were granted, excluding "off-licenses." Thirteen of them were the standard ones, found throughout the colony, for "public houses of entertainment," meaning lodging, meals, and alcohol. However, in Boston these places were limited to beer and cider sales. Only four other, more expensive establishments could legally sell wine and brandy. Then there were five "cook's shops" offering no lodging but licensed for "wine, beer, and victuals." In effect, these were restaurants. However, one of them, run by a widow, Elizabeth Connigrave, was restricted to "one penny quart beer." The next year she (perhaps understandably) was accused of "exceeding her license." One other woman, Mrs. Jane Barnard, ran a public house but could serve only coffee and "bottle cider," a rather genteel restriction. All four of the more elaborate inns were owned by men, two of them with militia titles. Of the thirteen standard licenses, three were held by widows, while two of the five cook's shops were run by women.

Salem, with fewer licenses, observed the same general distinctions. There were also some signs of specialization in the smaller ports and market towns. In Ipswich, for instance, John Sparkes's tavern near the meetinghouse, the preferred site of Essex Quarterly Court proceedings in the town, was apparently a model of elegance and decorum compared to the tavern run by the Perkins family. Similarly in Haverhill, where the county court allowed two licenses, the tavern run by Daniel Ela saw frequent violations while Sargeant John Johnson's place seems to have been a quiet, local ordinary.[20]

Despite the official caveat that taverns serve only travelers and strangers, the clientele of these places—both licit and illicit—was at least as broad and diverse as their ownership. Just as women owned and served in New England taverns, so too did they patronize them. In England, in contrast to southern Europe, the alehouse was not a male enclave. As a surprised Swiss visitor in England noted in 1599, "What is particularly curious is that the women as well as the men, in fact more often than they, will frequent the taverns or alehouses for enjoyment." Indeed, some taverns, particularly in the larger towns, were gathering places for neighborhood wives. When the irate wife of William Dicer of Salem was charged with "railing at Mrs. Hollingsworth," a licensed tavern-keeper, as "a black-mouthed witch and a thief," the witnesses were three married women in their twenties and a young sailor.[21]

20. *Suffolk Recs.* 259–63; *Essex Recs.* VII, 180, 377–78; VIII, 272–73; IX, 447, 451, 593.
21. Linda Woodbridge, *Women and the English Renaissance: Literature and the Nature of Womankind, 1540–1620* (Urbana, Ill., 1984), 243; Nicole Castan, "The Public and the Private," in *Private Life*, 3:413; *Essex Recs.* VIII, 238, 251; *Plymouth Recs.* XI, 195.

Common complaints that "Children and Servants" frequented "such Houses" are confirmed in court records wherein witnesses to tavern abuses occasionally include eleven- and twelve-year-old girls. "Heads of Families," admonished one cleric, "should watch over their Young Ones, not suffer them to *haunt* Taverns and drink to Excess. They should not teach their Children, their Boys and Girls to drink Rum (as I have heard some very Foolishly & Sinfully do)." Men of all professions, including an occasional minister, and of all classes entered into the life of the tavern in early New England.[22]

Ubiquitous, diverse in form, and broad in appeal, the tavern's influence—as a social setting in which basic values were expressed and inculcated relatively free of magisterial or clerical control—was pervasive. In effect, public drinking places were seen by reformers throughout the early modern world as competing with churches, families, and courts in the formation of popular attitudes and conduct. As Increase Mather complained to his congregation in 1682, "Thou canst find time it may be to sit in some Tavern and there to discourse the Lord knoweth about what. If that time, which is spent in vain, unprofitable discourse, were spent in Communion with God, it would be happy for thee. Canst thou find time for vain discourse, and yet not find time for prayer?" Obviously many, including pious laymen, understood that different, even conflicting codes of conduct were appropriate in different settings and saw the tavern as a temporary and generally harmless release from the pressures of labor and godliness. They sought that respite in traditional ways among the profane. "Alas!" lamented the elder Mather, "that as to the company which men keep, there is little difference to be observed between some Professors and the profane. . . . Are there not some *Church Members*, that if a man would speak with them, he must look for them in some Tavern or in some Publick House, and there he shall find them amongst vain persons, mispending their precious time?" On occasion the otherwise respectable misread and abused the opportunity. For instance, John Davis, a Lynn farmer, entered a Marblehead tavern in 1680, and there, "being deprived of the right use of his reason by excessive drinking, he affronted two sober and chaste women." Apparently he did not realize that even in the raucous, infamous taverns of Marblehead one could encounter "sober and chaste women." Chagrined, he "promised . . . that he would be more watchful of his tongue in the future."[23]

---

22. Wadsworth, *Essay to Do Good,* 20–22.

23. Brennan, *Public Drinking,* 7; Increase Mather, *Practical Truths Tending to Promote the Power of Godliness* (Boston, 1682), 71, 184; *Essex Recs.* VII, 400.

Yet the sense of competition between meetinghouse and drinking house was not restricted to the reformers. While most expressed their attitude by largely ignoring the critics' more extreme complaints, the more militant of the profane vehemently, sometimes even violently, defended the taverns and their mores from official attempts to regulate or suppress them. The Marblehead selectmen, seconded by several employers of fishermen, complained to the Essex court in 1678 about "much Disorders In the towne . . . By Reson of ye manifould ordinaries . . . whether nither Constable, grandjuryman nor Tithingman can com Nere them to prevent them." In Boston and Salem, constables and tithingmen attempting to enter taverns to quell brawls or enforce Sabbath curfews were subject to verbal and physical assault. Encountering such resistance, officers could not rely on help from bystanders, even from the "soberest," as the tavern milieu was deemed sacrosanct by many of its denizens. Also, some patrons assumed that their real enemy was Puritan authority, often embodied in the local pastor, rather than the intruding constables. Seeking "a pot of beer and a cake" in an unlicensed Salem alehouse on a Sunday morning in 1678, a man explained that "he scorned to go to hear old Higginson [the Salem minister] for he was an oppressor of the poor." On occasion a constable would provoke "a rage" by attempting to collect ministerial rates in taverns and find himself abused as "a pitiful cur," suggesting cringing obedience to unjust authority.[24] Hence, the critics' antipathy to "vain persons" who "haunted" taverns was often reciprocated, particularly in port towns, which strongly implies the existence of a self-conscious "alehouse culture."

Opportunity to indulge traditional forms of sociability and recreation deemed disreputable by the guardians of official standards was, of course, a major element of the tavern's allure. Despite laws to the contrary, "fiddling and dancing" were so common that local courts seem largely to have ignored violations unless they occurred "at unseasonable times of night" and thereby disturbed complaining neighbors. Gambling with dice and cards, and even with shuffleboards and tenpins, was virtually universal in Bay Colony taverns just as in contemporary England. There was also an atmosphere of greater sexual and verbal freedom. Taverns were places for "nightwalking" and "lascivious carriage," as well as for "jests," "banter," and "mockery."[25]

24. *Essex Recs.* VII, 1, 13–14, 70–71, 110, 151–52, 246–47; *Suffolk Recs.* 26.
25. For samples, see *Suffolk Recs.* 237, 676, 941–42, 1061; *Essex Recs.* VIII, 12–13; IX, 564–65; Josselyn, *Account of Two Voyages,* 149; *Mass. Recs.* II, 180, 195; III, 201–2; IV, pt. 2, 449; *Pynchon Recs.* 257–58; Wadsworth, *Essay to Do Good,* 12, 20; Cotton Mather, *Advice from the Watchtower: In a Testimony against Evil Customs* (Boston, 1713), 32–33.

The prevalence of these activities points to the contrapuntal rather than homogeneous nature of New England culture. Underlying these officially proscribed customs was the hedonism endemic to traditional popular culture, which reformers such as Benjamin Wadsworth found particularly pernicious. "Those that were *Sweating* while you were *Drinking;* diligently *working* while you were *Idling* and *Playing;* those were *Frugal, Diligent,* and *Prudent,* while you acted like *Prodigals;* must now Support you and yours, else you would perish. And what a shame is it, that should be thus burdensome." Further, the "waste" and "idleness" of tavern sociability had about it a competitive edge. Gambling was an obvious example. More fundamentally the tavern was an arena for verbal and physical challenges, a court of popular opinion and rivalries. "The good Companionship of rude Sinners, is (as one expresseth it) no better than *Horse-play,*" observed Increase Mather in 1699. "They will strike one another. When they are in their drink, and in their mad frolicks, they will tell one anothers Secret sins, and so expose their Neighbours to reproach & shame. And this is their sport." "They will," he claimed, "glory and boast of their being drunk, or wanton, or of their lying and cheating. Nay, some are so wicked, as to brag of their committing abominations which they did not commit."[26]

The impulse to competitive self-assertion sometimes transcended the festal intimidations and braggadocio of "horseplay" and led to violence. In tiny rural Wenham on a town meeting day in January 1681, Fairfield's tavern was crowded. It was a time and place for the visible display of the community's hierarchies of prestige. Deep in his cups, Thomas Abby, a young farmer proud of his physical prowess, was challenged by the tavern-keeper's daughter "that she would give him a quart of wine if he could whip" a rival, John Hutton. Abby immediately "laid hold" of Hutton, who asked him "to forbear because there would be taking of parts" among the patrons, perhaps provoking a brawl. Instead Hutton offered "to do it at some other time." But "some other time" would not meet Abby's need for a large audience on a significant day, together with the symbolic trophy of wine. Abby swore "he would do it if Betty Fairfield would be as good as her word" and "fell upon" Hutton. At that point a cousin of Abby's, Nathaniel Waldron, "pulling him off that the house might not be abused," separated the combatants by pushing Abby into an adjoining room, "followed by the company." The outraged and thwarted Abby cried, "Let me alone & be hanged, what doe you medele with me for?" and "flew at Waldron . . . and down they fell on

26. Wadsworth, *Essay to Do Good,* 7; Increase Mather, *The Folly of Sinning* (Boston, 1699), 61–62, 73.

the floor together." As bystanders finally pinned the flailing Abby he expressed his wounded pride by challenging the deferential assumptions of respectable society, "saying that if the best man in the land or if Mr. Gerrish [Salem merchant and Essex marshal] offered to pull [him] off from another he was fighting, he would strike him" as well.[27] The basis of the challenge was individualistic, an insistence on personal autonomy rather than any group solidarity.

As were drinking places throughout the early modern Western world, New England taverns (particularly in ports and market towns) were convenient arenas for slander and assault, because in those settings persons expressed not only their friendships but also their rivalries.[28] In order to express and control these complex relationships, there evolved a set of tavern rituals based partially on the symbolic similarity of drinking in company to religious communion. In its preparations for receiving the cup, for instance, the Book of Common Prayer included a prayer that all present might "live in unity and godly love." Virtually unheard of in England before the 1560s, these secular drinking ceremonies, according to Peter Clark, "seem to have reached their zenith" in the Restoration era. While denouncing them as episodes of "idle company-keeping," Increase Mather in 1687 noted the conciliatory motives of participants: "There are those who excuse themselves by pleading, they are loth to be Uncivil, or that any should take occasion to think them morose or ill-humored."[29]

Mather's understanding of tavern mores as "idle company-keeping" pointed to the necessity for the profane to establish coherent, readily understood rules of conduct within their major institution. Because the profane conversation was, by definition, a form of communication and hence of social interaction, hedonistic individualism as an assertion of personal merit and autonomy ironically could be fully expressed only in "company-keeping." Being an individualist by oneself is pointless. But, as we have seen, competitiveness—at times even violence—was a preferred means of establishing one's worth. Hence there had to be rules, not merely to limit physical danger, but also to help the participants in the tavern milieu to understand the competitions and relationships as they developed. In effect, the customs and rituals of the tavern were ways to create an alternative community

---

27. *Essex Recs.* IX, 13–15.

28. Brennan, *Public Drinking*, 25–26, 38, 62–63, 72–73; Gildrie, "Taverns," 163–65.

29. Clark, *English Alehouse*, 163n., 212; Increase Mather, *A Testimony against Several Prophane and Superstitious Customs now Practiced by Some in New England* (London, 1687), 28.

among competitive hedonistic individualists much the way a marketplace develops opportunities for expressing and controlling possessive individualism.[30]

One of the more widely followed and certainly most roundly condemned of these ceremonies was what the Reforming Synod termed "that heathenish and Idolatrous practice of Health-drinking." Essentially a series of toasts, "health-drinking" required the naming of an admired person or event and "a draining of the cup." Elaborations usually included "putting off the Hat, yea, of kneeling, (a gesture of adoration)." In 1686 John Dunton, an English bookseller and Grub Street denizen, "went to take a glass" with a Salem merchant at a local tavern in order to "make acknowledgments for his former favours." He "drank a kind remembrance in wine" to the merchant, a ship captain, "and the rest of our Ship's Crew" who "had saved my life at sea." The merchant answered by toasting Dunton's wife "with much honour and respect; and I believe we drank her health five times in an hour's sitting."[31]

This convivial episode was an example of the traditional urge, as the contemporary saying went, "to drink it out" whenever favors or debts required recognition. Yet there was often an element of coercion in "drinking by numbers and measure, as is usual amongst Health-drinkers." As reformers argued, "The Incivility is on their part, who urge the health, and not in those who out of Conscience refuse it." Indeed, the extent of compulsion marked a distinction occasionally made between drinking "for a Remembrance and a Health." As Increase Mather explained in justifying the former custom, "In a Remembrance (as it is called,) a man is not obliged to drink up the whole Cup. Nor is the Person to whom he drinks obliged to pledge him, except as he seeth cause." This "Liberty to Pledge where, and in what, and how he pleases" was "contrary to the Laws of an Health." The ritualistic intimidation of "health-drinking" was also, in the view of critics throughout the Atlantic world, an unwarranted assertion of power relationships both in and beyond the immediate tavern setting. "A Remembrance is usually of Friends and Equals, when as an Health is commonly to Superiors. So that these two differ the whole Heaven over." Thus, there were political as well as social implications in "health-drinking"—as illustrated in the common Noncon-

30. For a similar argument on the importance of ritual applied to the genteel taverns of eighteenth-century Philadelphia, see Peter Thompson, "'The Friendly Glass': Drink and Gentility in Colonial Philadelphia," *Pennsylvania Magazine of History and Biography* 113 (1989): 549–73.

31. *Necessity of Reformation*, 5; I. Mather, *Wo to Drunkards*, 31; John Dunton, *Life and Errors* (London, 1705), 126–27.

formist saying, "I would pray for the King's Health but drink for my owne." Of course the possibility of parody was always present in, for example, ornate expressions of respect to persons or institutions held in contempt. So too other elements of competition and self-assertion were preserved in contests over elaborate wording of toasts or numbers of glasses downed. In 1710 Samuel Danforth in a summary denunciation pronounced, "Wo to those who use their Wit and Fancy to applaud and commend hard and long and frequent Drinkings, as being Generosity and Sociableness" when to his mind those were the very virtues undermined by such tavern ceremonies. "Consider," he pleaded, "it cannot be love and friendship, to lead and betray our Friends into Temptation."[32]

Nor were those practices, which Cotton Mather called "but a Continuation of the Old Paganism," restricted to those of putatively evil lives. "To Drink Healths," he noted in 1713, "growes a very common Usage; even among such Professors of our Holy Religion as ought least of all to Learn the Wayes and Workes of the Heathen, or keep the vain Conversation received by Tradition from their Fathers." His own uncle, the Reverend Seaborn Cotton, had confessed in 1665 to the elder Mather that he "drank health onely, not with Punctilios of it, . . . not kneeling nor compelling to drink up the cup." "Health-drinking" was a prime example of the vitality, universality, and creativity of traditional popular culture as displayed in New England's taverns.[33]

Just as the function of "health-drinking" was the ordering of personal and social relations through ritual exchanges, the effect of "excessive drink" was liberation from propriety. In the physiological theories of the era inebriated persons were understood to be not only free from conventional constraints but also in extreme cases bereft of conscience and reason. As one cleric explained in 1710, "Men are hereby let loose to all those Sins to which they are either by Nature or Custom inclined." Or as another argued in 1727, "A Man is greatly expos'd to Sin and Vanity, when he is too much rais'd with Drink. He then loses his Fear, and is shamefully off his Guard. *Noah's*

32. I. Mather, *Testimony*, 25, 28; John Flavell, *The Reasonableness of Personal Reformation* (London, 1691; reprint, Boston, 1725), 77; Gunter Lottes, "Popular Culture and the Early Modern State in Sixteenth-Century Germany," in Steven L. Kaplan, ed., *Understanding Popular Culture: Europe from the Middle Ages to the Nineteenth Century* (Berlin, 1984), 168–69; Michael G. Hall, ed., "The Autobiography of Increase Mather," AAS *Proceedings* 71 (1961): 284; Samuel Danforth, *The Woful Effects of Drunkeness* (Boston, 1710), 40–41; Thompson, "'Friendly Glass,'" 553–56, 564–67.

33. Cotton Mather, *Advice from the Watchtower*, 34; Michael G. Hall, *The Last American Puritan: The Life of Increase Mather, 1639–1723* (Middletown, Conn., 1988), 74.

Drunkenness should be a Christian's Warning." In short, where there are explanations and precedents there are also excuses. Indeed, in the popular tradition this license had almost cosmic warrant, for, as the common proverb had it, "A Drunken Man gets no Harm."[34]

Interpreted in terms of the prevalent faculty psychology, the virtual cult of "excessive drink" in popular culture seemed to the moralists a most direct affront to human dignity itself, which in their view depended heavily on self-discipline. The psychological basis of sins was that "the Inferior faculties are not kept in due subordination to the superior; but the Will and Passions get a head above the Reason and Understanding." Inebriation was a particularly vivid and dangerous example. "Drunkenness is justly termed a brutish Sin, and a voluntary Madness; Sense & Reason being laid asleep, thereby nothing remains in exercise but that part of man wherein he resembles a Beast, which produces beastly action and behaviour."[35]

The consequent lack of restraint opened for the reformers an animalistic, nightmare vision.

> Drunkenness has various effects on men; some in their Drunkenness act like *Fawning, Flattering, Slavering Fools,* they seem mighty *Loving* and *Good Humour'd.* Others in their Drunken fits, are much for *Discoursing* and *Disputing* about *Religious* things, and it may be will *Weep* and seem much *affected* with them. . . . Some in their Drunken fits, are like *raving mad dogs,* are ready to quarrel and fight with any they meet with. . . . When men are drunk, how often do they *Quarrel, Fight, Wound, Bruise, Maim* one another; and hurt Sober Persons that come in their way?[36]

"Excessive drinking" was thus an opening to the "World Turned Upside Down" because "Drunkenness hath a natural Tendency to bring Confusion and Disorder into all Societies that are infected with it." In such societies adults "are Intemperate, Disorderly, and bruitish; there the Children and Servants are brought up in Ignorance and Impudence; in Idleness, Lewdness, and Profaneness."[37]

34. Clark, *English Alehouse,* 108–15; Wrightson, "Alehouses," 5–6, 12; Danforth, *Woful Effects,* 22; John Barnard, *The Nature and Danger of Sinful Mirth* (Boston, 1727), 128; Cotton Mather, *A Sailour's Companion and Counsellor* (Boston, 1709), 13.
35. Danforth, *Woful Effects,* 18–19; Linder and Martin, *Drinking in America,* 14–17.
36. Wadsworth, *Essay to Do Good,* 10–11.
37. Danforth, *Woful Effects,* 25.

Although the moralists' worries were exaggerated, there were sufficient prosecutions of persons (to quote a Plymouth case) "for theire abusive frequenting the ordinaryes . . . , spending their time theire, and expending theire estates, soe as they are become very poor" to lend them plausibility. The besotted Essex County wife who in September 1684 had to be lifted out of a muddy lane "when the hogs were teasing her clothes" seems a prime example of the sort of self-debasement, or "voluntary Madness," that concerned the reformers. Also worrisome were cases where the liberating effects of "excessive drink" led to abuse of persons, property, and authority. In Hatfield in 1678 four men broke into a tavern cellar whose owner apparently annoyed them by his absence. While "playing at cards," they drank his stock. Finally, answering the call of nature, they "layd their Tailes" over a "Beame and Loome" and spread excrement over the tavern's "implements" as a parting gesture. Late in 1670 "on the evening before Sabbath Day," John Sprague, one of Plymouth's more colorful profane characters, was engaged in "drinking, gameing, and uncivill revelling" with several companions at a tavern when he decided to protest the Saturday sundown curfew by "bringing in . . . a mare into the parlour" of the establishment.[38]

More serious brawls, assaults on tavern-keepers and constables, and other "abuses" were common concomitants of "excessive drink" in New England and throughout the English world. Whatever its physiological or psychological causes, the cultural meaning of "excessive drink" was to fuel, and partially to justify, flamboyant expressions of the profane conversation the moralists wished to curtail. Many of the profane were as aware as their critics of that quasi-ideological function of inebriation.

Along with "health-drinking" and "excessive drink," the Sunday tavern customs provide good illustrations of the complex interplay between the profane and godly elements of early New England thought and conduct. By law taverns were to be closed, except for the convenience of "sojourners," from sundown Saturday until dusk Sunday. Not surprisingly, given the traditional rivalry between church and alehouse in rural England, violations were frequent. Saturday night curfew was particularly resented and at times forcibly resisted, especially in the port towns. Also, persons were occasionally "found in a Tavern in the time of publique worship with Liquor standing before them."[39]

38. *Plymouth Recs.* V, 53; VI, 7; *Suffolk Recs.* 721; *Essex Recs.* IX, 336; *Pynchon Recs.* 289–90.

39. Clark, *English Alehouse,* 157; Wrightson, "Alehouses," 17; *Suffolk Recs.* 1018; *Essex Recs.* VII, 246–47; VIII, 227.

A more common, indeed virtually ubiquitous, practice in the country-side was for "Families . . . that live remote from the Publick Meeting-House" to go to "Near Drinking Houses that may receive them, and refresh them in the Intervals of Divine Worship" between the morning and afternoon services. This necessary convenience for some naturally attracted others more concerned with "Sensual Pleasure and Temporal Profit." In Haverhill in 1680 Daniel Ela, an unsavory local character, defended himself against indictment for keeping an illegal alehouse by claiming that "necessity caused him to do it partly for dwelling next to the meeting house upon Sabbath days especially sacrament days and other public days his house was so thronged with sometimes twenty, thirty or forty or more persons, some so young and some so weak that they were not able to go to the ordinary." He admitted that he had no license but asserted that he "was encouraged to sell liquor by some of the inhabitants, not the meanest, and some of the selectmen." Throughout the colony clerics believed that this custom, however necessary and popular, was "an occasion for Discourses and Actions, not very suitable to the Religion of the Sabbath." Sociability, secular conversation, even jocular commentary on the sermon regularly punctuated the pious works of the Lord's Day. And the practice was stoutly defended. Regardless of whether the drinking houses were kept "by men of Probity or persons of another Character," complained one pastor in 1704, "Have them they *must,* and have them they *will:* and if a Godly Magistracy, at any time (tho' for the most scandalous and detestable Enormities) put any of them down; Good God! What a cry is raised up!"[40]

The taverns of early New England, like their counterparts throughout the English world, were essential to daily life and multifarious in form and atmosphere. They were frequented by the whole spectrum of the populace, female as well as male, merchant as well as servant. The patrons shared a desire for recreation lubricated by drink and a commitment to a set of mores about personal autonomy, competition, and occasionally rowdy sociability not readily satisfied elsewhere. At times the taverns were also havens for those "not so well affected to sobriety, law, and good order." Critics in England, New England, and the Chesapeake interpreted these mores as "idleness," "vain company-keeping," "debauchery," and "disorder." They were, Cotton

---

40. John Danforth, *The Vile Prophanations of Prosperity by the Degenerate* (Boston, 1704), 20; *Essex Recs.* VII, 104, 377–78; VIII, 272–73; Cotton Mather, *Advice from the Watchtower,* 32. See also Roger Thompson, "Adolescent Culture in Colonial Massachusetts," *Journal of Family History* 9 (1984): 132; and Yoder, "Tavern Regulation," 266.

Mather thought, "foolish customs," part of the "Vain Conversation received by Tradition from our Fathers."

As such they were the universal targets of those wishing to further the Reformation of Manners whose goal was to tame, but not eliminate, the drinking house. This effort was, by the early eighteenth century, a partial success. As a result of moral suasion and such experiments in regulation and enforcement as the Massachusetts tavern law of 1681, the taverns of England and America seem, on the whole, to have become more "polite." Contributing factors were economic improvement and increasing political stability throughout much of the empire after 1690.[41]

For instance, in Essex County, Massachusetts, after 1690, as the waterfronts became better integrated economically and socially into the whole society, the level of alehouse violence and episodes of overt contempt for authority diminished. Indeed, prosecution rates for such serious crimes as theft and assault declined throughout the Bay Colony during the early eighteenth century. From 1700 to 1740 indictments in the Essex County Court of General Sessions for illegal liquor sales and public drunkenness averaged about 3.4 per year, compared to an annual average of 9.5 in the Essex Quarterly Court from 1678 to 1686. Such a statistical comparison is probably more dramatic than accurate, given the changes in court structure and shifts in prosecutorial priorities. Yet it suggests a notable decline, if not in the crimes themselves, then certainly in concern about them. However, tavern life was not wholly transformed. As a recent student of Essex County's crime statistics concluded, "There was a close relationship, then, between illegal liquor sales, excessive drinking, and public disorder in eighteenth century Essex County," just as there had been in the earlier period. Naturally the moralists' complaints too echoed through the new century.[42]

The tavern was, and remained, a place where people went to release the bonds of propriety, if only temporarily. In that role it played a vital part not only in daily recreation and sociability but also in the development of an

41. Clark, *English Alehouse,* 166–249; Wrightson, "Alehouses," 11; Yoder, "Tavern Regulation," 260–65.

42. Daniel Vickers, "Work and Life on the Fishing Periphery of Essex County, Massachusetts, 1630–1675," in David D. Hall and David G. Allen, eds., *Seventeenth-Century New England* (Boston, 1984), 113–16; Paul Donald Marsella, "Criminal Cases at the Essex County, Massachusetts, Court of General Sessions, 1700–1795" (Ph.D. diss., University of New Hampshire, 1982), esp. 115, 127; Gildrie, "Taverns," 164; David H. Flaherty, "Crime and Social Control in Provincial Massachusetts," *Historical Journal* 24 (1981): 339–60; Yoder, "Tavern Regulation," 275; Clark, *English Alehouse,* 239–42.

Anglo-American ethos that prized individual autonomy and fostered a healthy skepticism about the pretensions of authority. New England's taverns provided a milieu in which these elements of traditional English popular culture thrived, while the Reformation of Manners helped refine their expression into forms more appropriate to the formation of an independent, responsible citizenry.

FOUR

Family Government and the Rising Generation

Creating and sustaining what they deemed proper family life were perennial goals among early modern moral reformers. Indeed, in their view the success of the Reformation of Manners, with all its implications for an improved social and political order, hinged on the family. As one Massachusetts cleric explained in 1693, "The Foundation of a whole Peoples or Kingdoms REFORMATION or DEFECTION, RELIGION or REBELLION is laid in Families. Families are the Constituent Parts of Nations and Kingdoms; hence as Families are Well or Ill Disciplined, so will the whole be Well Disposed, or Ill Inclined." There were, in short, both godly and profane patterns of family life. Not surprisingly, the issue—together with a related concern for the "rising generation"—was central to the Massachusetts Reforming Synod of 1679. As Increase Mather succinctly put it in his campaign to have the General Court call the synod, "Families are the Nurseries for Church and Commonwealth, ruine Families and ruine all. Order them well & the Publick State will fare the better."[1]

The reformers' version of proper "family government" was not so much an imposition on an unwilling populace as it was a clarification and reinforcement of one of the conflicting tendencies in traditional popular culture. Whatever their degree of concern about the "Publick State," many of the common folk of early modern Europe and America found practical value in the reformers' approach to family life. The late medieval ideal was that marriage, permanent and monogamous, established cohesive and stable fam-

---

1. Deodat Lawson, *The Duty & Property of a Religious Householder* (Boston, 1693), 51; Increase Mather, *A Discourse Concerning the Danger of Apostacy* [1677 election sermon] (Boston, 1685), 127.

ilies. Children who honored and obeyed their parents were raised to be dutiful and productive members of society. The form was patriarchal, but the fathers' effective power was supplemented and thus limited by the wife's essential control of household matters and by the children's right to establish new families whose claims superseded those of the older unit.[2] With some elaboration and modification, this model, long supported by the medieval church and popular aspiration, was the reformers' ideal as well.

In practice, the relative autonomy and internal coherence of families implied by the ideal were difficult to attain. In early modern villages, families were often tightly interdependent, economically and socially, and thus each was subject to outside scrutiny and pressure. An ethic of social harmony stressing forbearance, respect for elders and superiors, hard work, and mutual aid among families and individuals was enforced by popular opinion amid countercurrents of competition for scarce resources of honor and wealth. As the formal procedures of church and state became more influential in daily life, the possible sources of outside pressure on families increased. Internally, there were contradictions between the personal impulses of family members and the collective sense of identity and fate that animated family life.[3]

The reformers' efforts at reinvigorated family government offered at least a partial solution. Proper order and conduct within the household encouraged good behavior outside, which in turn redounded to the person's and the family's credit. A good reputation was a valuable asset economically, socially, and politically. It was also a defense against unwanted interference from neighbors and the authorities. Good family government, encouraged by reformers in the church and the state, became a bulwark for the gradually emerging ideal of privacy, centered in the home. As a recent French historian has explained, "Privacy manifested itself primarily as discipline, but it could also be nourishing and life sustaining. Without it, people with a bare minimum of resources could not have risen to the daily challenge of surviving with dignity."[4]

2. David Herlihy, *Medieval Households* (Cambridge, Mass., 1985), esp. 132–35.

3. G. R. Quaife, *Wanton Wenches and Wayward Wives: Peasants and Illicit Sex in Early Seventeenth-Century England* (New Brunswick, N.J., 1979), 16; Carole Shammas, "The Domestic Environment in Early Modern England and America," *Journal of Social History* 14 (1980): 1–24.

4. Yves Castan, "Politics and Private Life," in Robert Chartier, ed., *A History of Private Life,* vol. 3, *Passions of the Renaissance,* trans. Arthur Goldhammer (Cambridge, Mass., 1989), 50, 61–62; David H. Flaherty, *Privacy in Colonial New England* (Charlottesville, Va., 1972), 45–84.

Nor were the reformers blind to this benefit. In 1712 Benjamin Wadsworth of Boston, in a long discourse on family life, observed that although husbands and wives "should by no means allow or approve what is sinful in one another, yet they should not needlessly expose each others failings, indiscreet words or actions, but rather cover them with a mantle of love; they should be tender of each others credit or reputation." He was certain that "strife and discord" within families was "bad," but that it was "very bad indeed if this strife comes to be blaz'd and nois'd among the Neighbourhood!"[5] Wadsworth was expressing a genteel ideal that nonetheless had relevance to the aspirations of many common folk. Family discipline, on which reputation and honor depended, ultimately relied on self-discipline; a concern for shame further encouraged the development of guilt, one of the essential regulators of relatively autonomous, responsible individuals.

In Europe and America the reformers' considerations of family government usually developed under four headings, one of which was ceremonial and instructional while the others were relational and ethical. These were "family prayers," husbands and wives, parents and children, and masters and servants. First and foremost was "family prayers," an emphasis that may seem odd to moderns. The point was not some sentimental and quaint piety but what the Puritans called "practical godliness," a form of godliness that could be taught and was reflected in conduct. As Cotton Mather asked rhetorically in 1707, "In a family where Good Orders are kept and Prayer is every Morning and Evening Seriously carried on, are not the Children and Servants likely to be more Orderly, more Dutiful, more Virtuous, than in a family where God is not sought unto? And are not Religious Families likely to be the best Support and Safety for the Common-wealth?" The object of household devotions, thought English moralist Richard Baxter, was for family members "to help each other in the knowledge and obedience of God," which ideally led to both solidarity and decent conduct. As Increase Mather put it, characteristically reversing the priority, "They that are contending and quarrelling with one another, are very unfit to go to prayer together: Therefore, Husband and Wife should live in love that so they may not be indisposed to pray together in their Family."

It was essential to instruct children and servants in piety and good conduct "by example as well as precept" through family ritual. Nor was this view of family devotions restricted to English Protestants. During the 1690s the French church issued a directive to its clergy that "you must do all that you

5. Benjamin Wadsworth, *The Well-Ordered Family, or Relative Duties* (Boston, 1712), 35.

can to exhort each family to gather in the morning and evening for common prayer, with a member of the family reciting each prayer out loud."[6] Household ritual, supplemented by direct instruction in religion, was to reflect and encourage proper conduct in and out of the home.

The most fundamental relation to be sustained in part by family prayer was between husband and wife. The ideal was both patriarchal and companionate, a difficult combination. Love was the virtue, according to European and English moralists, that would ameliorate the worst tendencies in patriarchalism. Without love, marriage was "only bargain and compact, a tyranny perhaps on the man's part, a slavery on the woman's," proclaimed a 1677 English pamphlet popular among both Anglicans and Nonconformists. Although sexual pleasure for both partners was a major theme, the essence of love was to be found in "perfect friendship," a union of two souls resembling divine love in which passion was subordinate to reason. Indeed, in the "perfect friendship" of marriage each soul was to illumine the other, thus overcoming the conflicts between reason and passion in a higher, more embracing definition of love.[7]

Although this stress on mutuality in marriage nearly to the point of equality resembles recent prescriptions, it was in the view of one historian "utopian, a volatile ideal rather than a sustained reality" in the seventeenth and eighteenth centuries.[8] Even among the Puritans themselves there was a tendency to rely more on patriarchalism than on "perfect friendship" as a guarantor of discipline in family government. The pressures of patriarchalism, perhaps aggravated as much as ameliorated by the ideal of rational love, were intense for both husband and wife.

The responsibilities of the "family head"—husband, father, master of servants—were onerous. These patriarchs were accountable not only to their families but also to their peers, to the authorities of church and state, and ultimately to God. As Increase Mather warned of families prone to "Trans-

6. Cotton Mather, *Family Religion* (Boston, 1705, 1707), 8; Edmund Leites, "The Duty to Desire: Love, Friendship, and Sexuality in Some Puritan Theories of Marriage," *Journal of Social History* 15 (1982): 389–90; Increase Mather, *Practical Truths Tending to Promote the Power of Godliness* (Boston, 1682), 59; Francois Lebrun, "The Two Reformations: Communal Devotion and Personal Piety," in Chartier, ed., *Private Life*, 97.

7. Edmund Leites, *The Puritan Conscience and Modern Sexuality* (New Haven, 1986), esp. 3, 12, 15; Richard B. Schlatter, *The Social Ideas of Religious Leaders, 1660–1688* (1940; reprint, New York, 1971), 1–30, esp. 14; Laurel Thatcher Ulrich, *Good Wives: Image and Reality in the Lives of Women in Northern New England, 1650–1750* (New York, 1980, 1982), 106–25.

8. John R. Gillis, *For Better, for Worse: British Marriages, 1600 to the Present* (Oxford, 1985), 14.

gressions that provoke the glorious eyes of the Holy Majesty of Heaven, . . .
Let the Masters of such Families look to themselves. For the Sabbath Breaking
& other prophaness that are indulged in their Families will be charged upon
them, who ought to rule their Houses better."[9]

With the moral, economic, and even political burdens of New England's
version of patriarchalism came a preferred bearing, a style of conduct within
the household derived in part from the classical *gravitas* of the Roman
paterfamilias. In 1727 a noted Massachusetts minister recommended that
"Those who are Heads of Families should carry themselves very *gravely* and
soberly in their Houses: Not that I commend to you Moroseness and Sower
Carriage in your Families; but Heads of Families should avoid all those
Levities which may give those under their Charge occasion to suspect their
conscientiousness, and which may tend to render their *Persons* and *Authority*
contemptible." If such dignity be maintained by the fathers, then "their
Commands will have the more weight with them, their *Charges* will be more
impressive, their *Reproofs* the more heeded, their *Corrections* more likely to
answer the end."[10]

The widespread appeal of patriarchalism with its heavy demands on fathers
rested as much on its putative advantages in the competition for economic
security and honor as on its religious warrant. In 1715 an anonymous Boston
satirist chided this common aspiration by announcing his defection. "To be
a Husband, Father, a Master, to be deckt with many pendulous and gaudy
Additions; to Soar with the Wings of Honour, to abound in Coin and Cattle,
to possess sumptuous Buildings, and large Territories, I will not be Ambitious;
for I see what Inconveniences attend the Flow of Temporals." Having evoked
the ancient Judeo-Christian suspicion of material success with the Puritan
jargon "Temporals," he went on to reverse the logic of patriarchalism for more
worldly reasons: "This Abundance, and these Titles, I cannot call them (as
some) Privileges from, but rather Sluces and immediate Inlets to, Trouble and
Danger."[11]

The essayist's argument that "Trouble and Danger" for adult males can
best be avoided not by taking responsibility but by evading it was an appeal
to the profane tendencies which most prized personal autonomy. To illustrate
by extreme example, informal separations and desertions (usually initiated by

9. I. Mather, *Practical Truths*, 68–69.
10. John Barnard, *The Nature and Danger of Sinful Mirth* (Boston, 1727), 120–21. For the
general importance of classical ethical ideals in Puritan thought, see Theodore Dwight Bozeman, *To Live Ancient Lives: The Primitivist Dimension in Puritanism* (Chapel Hill, 1988).
11. Anonymous, *Select Essays* (Boston, 1715), 24.

husbands) was an admission of a failed marriage in terms of both the relations between the spouses and the struggle for economic stability and communal respect. However intense the sense of failure may have been among some who took this course, within the picaresque hedonistic ethic there was honor to be gained by abandoning wife and family for a more independent existence. In 1678, for instance, the Massachusetts Court of Assistants heard the divorce petition of Hope Ambrose, who asserted that her husband "hath absented himself from hir upwards of fower yeares & left hir not only without due provission for the maintenance of hirself & children but as Appeares" by the testimony of witnesses from Jamaica "hath broake his marriage Covenant & keepes another woman at Jamaica as his whore & hath had carnall fellowship with hir severall times & with others as he hath boasted."[12]

Although there was no consensus, the general Protestant position allowing divorce for desertion was an attempt to protect women and society in general from such conduct. But that does not mean that attaining a divorce was common or easy even in New England, where the Church of England's adherence to the Catholic doctrine of marital indissolubility was ignored. From 1620 to 1699 in all of New England, including heterodox Rhode Island, there were fewer than 110 petitions for separation or divorce, two-thirds of them by women and commonly for desertion. Although these petitions were usually granted, the decided preference—enforced by both informal pressure and legal proceedings—was to force the errant spouse back to the original marriage. Again, patriarchal order, together with economic and social need, overcame the ideal requirement of "perfect friendship." An additional advantage to this practice of returning wandering spouses was that, in cases where the offender had abandoned a wife or husband in England or elsewhere, the custom sanctioned the expulsion of profane or picaresque characters who were annoying on other grounds besides family desertion.[13]

In pursuing the ideal of family government the role of the proper wife was, if possible, even more difficult. As wife, mother, and mistress of servants, her responsibility was both to direct and to serve the household. Her authority, delegated by her husband and codified by customs enshrined in a plethora of household handbooks and religious tracts, centered on feeding, clothing,

---

12. Keith Wrightson, *English Society, 1580–1680* (New Brunswick, N.J., 1982), 100; *Assistants Recs.* I, 27.

13. Schlatter, *Social Ideas of Religious Leaders,* 124–25; Roderick Phillips, *Putting Asunder: A History of Divorce in Western Society* (New York, 1988), 65, 77, 115, 243, 250, 284–85; *Suffolk Recs.* 942, 943, 1158; *Plymouth Recs.* V, 10, 33, 50; D. Kelley Weisberg, "'Under Greet Temptations Heer': Woman and Divorce in Puritan Massachusetts," *Feminist Studies* 2 (1975): 183–94.

and instructing people within her home and tending to them in birth, illness, and death. In the competition for honor and economic well-being, her role was crucial because she was expected not only to be effective in these household functions but also to demonstrate the virtues of frugality, modesty, devotion to her family and religion, and a becoming generosity among her neighbors. In her relations with her husband she was to be loving and obedient while at the same time sharing in his responsibilities and powers, a most delicate matter. As Laurel Thatcher Ulrich has summarized, "A married woman in early New England was simultaneously a housewife, a deputy husband, a consort, a mother, a mistress, a neighbor, and a Christian." This complex definition was shared among Catholic and Protestant reformed circles throughout the North Atlantic world.[14]

Women's daily lives were not restricted to their houses and gardens. "Good Neighborliness" meant that goods and services circulated among women, usually by barter but often by money, thus sustaining a female economy crucial to the success of households but virtually invisible in historical sources. Women also trafficked in creating and destroying reputations, that other vital area of competition. Given their significant role in social and moral control in and out of the household, the prominence of women in the religious lives of Reformation and Counter-Reformation churches constituted a vital element of the Reformation of Manners. There are indications that in the Middle Ages women were generally less exposed to institutions and customs inculcating self-discipline than were men. The reformed churches, on the other hand, deliberately encouraged female piety at all levels of the social order. Except among the more radical sects, women never emerged as overt leaders; men remained the instructional and institutional heads of religious bodies. Nonetheless, women had vast influence and responsibility in religious life as elsewhere. Their commitment to and effectiveness in cultivating "practical godliness" was of vital concern to the reformers.[15]

The burdens of approximating this ideal sometimes provoked dissent among women just as the responsibilities of patriarchy annoyed some men. Occasionally in Massachusetts a wife found herself in court, indicted "for her

14. Ulrich, *Good Wives*, 3–86, quote on 9; Suzanne W. Hull, *Chaste, Silent, and Obedient: English Books for Women, 1475–1640* (San Marino, Calif., 1982), 132–35; John Demos, "Towards a History of Mid-Life: Preliminary Notes and Reflections," in his *Past, Present, and Personal: The Family and Life Course in American History* (New York, 1986), 127.

15. Ulrich, *Good Wives*, 51–67; Leites, *Puritan Conscience*, 120; Charles E. Hambrick-Stowe, *The Practice of Piety: Puritan Devotional Discipline in Seventeenth-Century New England* (Chapel Hill, 1982), 47–48; Amanda Porterfield, *Female Piety in Puritan New England: The Emergence of Religious Humanism* (New York, 1992), 14–39.

ungodly speeches" against a minister, "as also for reviling her Husband & her murtherous Intent against him." The popular literature of the era was replete with scolds, nagging shrews, unfaithful wives, and women who wasted their families' resources by idleness and extravagance. Although exaggerated by male fears of female "revolt," the popularity of such satire and abuse, particularly in the seventeenth century, indicates that there was some basis in experience for the imagery. In 1640 an English pamphlet, *The Women's Sharpe Revenge,* by "Mary Tattle-well and Joane Hit-him-home," objected to female education designed "to make us men's mere vassals, even unto all posterity" and asked, "What poor woman is ever taught that she should have a higher Design than to get her a Husband?" Individualist aspiration, sanctioned by a part of popular tradition, had a female as well as a male voice in both England and New England.[16]

From husbands and wives the reformers' prescriptions usually turned to parents and children. The Erasmian focus of the early modern Reformation of Manners was on the formation of self-discipline in the young, an emphasis that remained into the eighteenth century. It was the parents' duty to "Commend, Cherish, [and] Encourage" their children so "that they shun *Idleness* and *Wickedness,* and are afraid of Sinning against God." Good attitudes were best reflected early in courteous "carriages," which of course strengthened the family's reputation as well as prepared the young to accept adult individual responsibility for their conduct. "Yea, teach them to be civil and respectful to all persons whatsoever, according to their Rank and Station: Don't suffer them to be rude, saucy, provoking in their words or actions unto any; for this would be a shame to your Children, and to you too," admonished Boston's Benjamin Wadsworth.[17]

Again, reflecting the humanist approach to moral training, the goal was to discipline, not destroy, self-respect and individual expression. To that end the rules of courtesy were to be loosely defined. As Wadsworth explained, "But though you should teach your Children to be Mannerly, I dont mean that you should spend all or great part of their time, in nicely, curiously, critically observing those various, changeable, ceremonious punctilio's of carriage,

16. Hampshire Recs. 24 Sept. 1678; David E. Underdown, "The Taming of the Scold: The Enforcement of Patriarchal Authority in Early Modern England," in Anthony Fletcher and John Stevenson, eds., *Order and Disorder in Early Modern England* (London, 1985), 116–17, 135–36; Hull, *Chaste, Silent, and Obedient,* 135–36; Antonia Fraser, *The Weaker Vessel* (New York, 1984), 226; Ulrich, *Good Wives,* 93–105.

17. Susan Brigden, "Youth and the English Reformation," *Past and Present* 95 (1982): 37–67; Cotton Mather, *The Best Ornaments of Youth* (Boston, 1707), 23–24; Wadsworth, *Well-Ordered Family,* 53.

which some very foolishly affect." This would be in his view "time very sinfully spent," not merely because it was profligate of time and effort but also because it taught the child to be a slave of fashion without considering the underlying purposes of proper conduct. "A Child may avoid such fooleries and fopperies, and yet be very civil, courteous, mannerly in his words and gestures."[18] The practice of courtesy by children was fundamental to the sense of manners that, the reformers believed, prevented adult society from descending into barbarism and anarchy.

The reformers' reflections on servants, the fourth relational category of their thoughts on family government, were similar to those on children, for the bulk of household servants, particularly in New England, were simply older children born in another household. As Benjamin Colman argued in 1721, "There are Servants in the Family and you must be very good and pious toward them. . . . An ingenious servant is like a Child in a family and should be in a manner treated as one." Enjoined Wadsworth, "Servants should in their words and actions, put respect and honour on their Masters; they must not give saucy, impudent, contradicting Answers to them." But because servants were older they were more able and likely to rebel against family government in terms of the libertarian and egalitarian strains in traditional popular culture. "Possibly some Servants are very high, proud, stout, they'll scarce bear to be commanded or restrained: they are for much liberty." This sense of personal autonomy took forms that in the view of reformers such as Wadsworth undermined the household's discipline and its social and economic performance. "They must have liberty for their tongues to speak almost what and when they please; liberty to give and receive visits of their own accord; liberty to keep what company they please; liberty to be out late on nights; to go & come almost when they will without telling why or wherefore." Another sign "may be the work they are set about, they reckon 'tis beneath or below them, they wont stoop to do it, but will rather disobey Masters or Mistresses."[19]

As heirs to Romantics, Marxists, and Freudians, we are too apt to see only the repressive elements of reformed family government and thereby to underestimate its role in empowering families and individuals among the common folk of the era. The goal was that self-assertion be tempered by self-discipline so as to maintain dignity and honor amid the uncertainties of early modern life. It is important to remember that this ideal had strong popular

18. Wadsworth, *Well-Ordered Family*, 53.
19. Benjamin Colman, *Early Piety as it Respects Man* (Boston, 1721), 18; Wadsworth, *Well-Ordered Family*, 112, 117.

appeal. But equally important were the individualistic and egalitarian aspirations that family government sought to control and channel. However difficult to balance, these conflicting values interdependently have shaped the moral basis of the modern Western world. A sense of self-control evinced as "godly meekness" was, according to Joseph Sewall of Boston in 1721, "pleasing to God, lovely in the eyes of Men, and of great benefit to Societies." The health of a social order "doth very much depend upon this, that the several members put off Wrath, Anger, Malice"—a common theme in the Reformation of Manners. Sewall particularly stressed that "the tranquillity and Good Order of Families do very much depend on this, that Young Men and Women take care to govern their Passion. Where an angry Spirit prevails, there will be strife, and then confusion and every evil work."[20] Such was the rationale for improved family government.

The patriarchal but affectionate form favored by the reformers and so many of the common folk of Europe and America was not, of course, the only type of family found in early New England. Had that godly pattern fully prevailed, the clerics would hardly have complained so frequently "that the Decay of Religion, of Practical Godliness, among us, is not more owing to any one thing, than to the neglect of Family Instruction and Government." "Without Family care," they characteristically warned, "the labors of Magistrates and Ministers for Reformation and Propagating Religion is likely to be in great measure unsuccessful."[21]

During the 1680s the family of Cornelius Merry of Hampshire County, Massachusetts, was a prime example of the sort of "neglect of Family Instruction and Government" that concerned reformers throughout the Atlantic world. A servant guilty of "several misdemeanors" in Northampton during the early 1660s, Merry served in King Philip's War and by 1680 had married, fathered children, and established a household in that town. But that year the selectmen determined that, as "Cornelius Merrys Children being many & little Care taken for their Education, it appearing that the father of them is very vicious & Rather Learns them irreligion than any good Literature," it would be best to put them out as apprentices without the parents' permission. After this humiliation Merry and his wife moved to Northfield, where after some time she tried to rebuild her life and reputation by preparing for church membership.[22]

20. Joseph Sewall, *Early Piety* (Boston, 1721), 11.
21. J. A. Sharpe, "Plebian Marriage in Stuart England," Royal Historical Society *Transactions*, 5th ser., 36 (1986): 78–90; Wadsworth, *Well-Ordered Family*, 84.
22. *Pynchon Recs.* 261; Hampshire Recs. 30 March 1680.

Enraged by his wife's new course, Merry was indicted in 1686 for "abusing his wife by flinging her downe" and for publicly calling her "a whore & a jade & no more fit for a Ch. member than any Indian." Cursing his wife, "wishing the devil had her," he threatened those neighbors who were trying to assist her, "saying he would Cutt out there guts." His opinion of the local church was no higher: "a Company of Beggars." Also charged with running an illegal alehouse "selling liquor to Indians," Merry came to court drunk. There he demonstrated the extreme oscillations of passionate temperament typical of the profane conversation; "Sometimes Seeming as though he repented . . . yet at other times in open Corte reviling Authoritie, deriding the laws of this government, saying they have little worth."[23]

For these transgressions the magistrates decided to require a heavy bond for good behavior and to send him home to his wife "under the oversight of the Constable of Northfield" and a neighbor. Merry defied the court by boasting "he would not fear as many Constables as you would make." Needless to say, he broke bond by again abusing his wife before the day was out. He was back in court within hours for "vicious crimes & notorious high handed boldness & impudence." For this he was "well whipt on the naked body with 15 stripes Severely layd on." His bond was also forfeited, and he was sent "to House of Correction" at Springfield "for the pleasure of this Corte." Five years later the impenitent Merry, with several cronies including his namesake son, were prosecuted for episodes of drunkenness and Sabbath breaking. Cornelius Merry succeeded in living the profane life and in passing the tradition on to his eldest son. What happened to his wife, never even named in the record, is unknown.[24]

The Merry family was unusual but hardly unique even in orthodox Massachusetts. In 1682 Daniel Ela, a Haverhill farmer who ran an illegal alehouse, threw his wife Elizabeth out of their house, claiming "she was nothing to him but a devil in woman's apparel." He justified this informal divorce as a matter of patriarchal honor: "his wife was his servant and his slave and he would have her whipped but that it would be a disgrace to him, for he would never have a quiet hour until he died" if she stayed. After all, "hee was a gentellman borne, she was butt a poore widdow," and he would no longer tolerate being seen as a "pimping knave." Elizabeth Ela had offended by complaining to her husband and to others of his delaying payment to and withholding the customary perquisite of "a pot of cider" from hired farm laborers during harvest, as well as of "injustices to herself." Despite English and colonial laws

23. Hampshire Recs. 30 March 1686.
24. Hampshire Recs. 30 March 1686, 31 March 1691.

to the contrary Daniel Ela had warrant in popular tradition. As an English pamphlet advised in 1582, "let not thy wife have rule over thee," and "if she walke not in thine obedience, cut hir off then from thy flesh."[25]

These attitudes, aggravated if not caused by the frequency of economic disaster among the poor of the early modern era, encouraged a tradition of informal, impermanent, and sometimes even egalitarian relations between spouses. Given the expense and trouble of complying with English ecclesiastical requirements, it is not surprising that among much of the populace marriage was sanctioned, if at all, by informal public recognition. Persons who acted married were married. As the saying went, "To eat, drink and sleep together; these things seem to make a marriage." Marriages informally created—their existence ratified by popular rituals of exchange of food, pledges, or gifts—could also be informally dissolved. The more hysterical critics claimed that "vagabonds" generally "have not particular wives, neither do they range themselves in families, but consort together as beasts," presumably because they lacked stable communities to sanctify the unions. Yet however impermanent and independent of social sanction these relations may have seemed, they were not necessarily loveless or without a sense of mutual responsibility. As another adage observed, "there 'longs more to marriage than four bare legs in a bed."[26]

There were people who operated on these assumptions in early New England. What the colonial courts interpreted as bigamy or adultery were sometimes in the eyes of the offenders the results of informal marriages and divorces. Few were as extreme as the deputy governor of Rhode Island, John Green, who argued in the 1690s that "it was no more sin in the Light of God for one man to lye with another mans wife than for a Bull to leap a Cow upon the common"—virtually an argument for free love. Yet serial marriage may well have had popular warrant. Given the difficulties of public record-keeping and distribution, it may well have been common in late medieval and early modern Europe. Opportunity often became custom and custom a matter of right unless directly challenged. In 1685 Elizabeth Gilligan of Marblehead was

25. *Essex Recs.* VIII, 272–73; Hull, *Chaste, Silent, and Obedient,* 95. For other examples, see *Essex Recs.* IX, 114–15, 203–5, 221–22; M. Halsey Thomas, ed., *Diary of Samuel Sewall, 1674–1719* (New York, 1973), 1:337. For an account of the English tradition of popular divorce, see Samuel P. Menefee, *Wives for Sale: An Ethnographic Study of British Popular Divorce* (New York, 1981); Lyle Kochler, *A Search for Power: The "Weaker Sex" in Seventeenth-Century New England* (Urbana, Ill., 1980), 66–67n.

26. Gillis, *For Better, for Worse,* 13; Phillips, *Putting Asunder,* 30–31; Sharpe, "Plebeian Marriage," 89.

indicted "for absenting herself from her husband and keeping company with John Hunniwell of Marblehead, both night and day in the fields and woods, likewise at Marblehead and at Piscatagua in their journey to the eastward when they appear to have lived as man and wife." Hunniwell, also charged with profane swearing, abusing a constable, and "other great crimes," readily admitted leaving a wife and six children in England. The new relationship apparently had the blessing of Elizabeth's husband, Alexander Gilligan, who besides "giving his consent" for the two to travel to Maine as husband and wife also habitually slept at the foot of the bed that Hunniwell and Elizabeth shared in Marblehead. The Essex court, after having the errant wife and lover whipped, sent her back to her husband.[27]

This story, while odd, had its counterparts, especially among the maritime population of Boston, Marblehead, and Salem. Even in rural Plymouth County in 1670 one wife was so shocked by her husband's lack of consent to an informal divorce or adulterous affair, depending on one's point of view, that she attacked him verbally and physically in public. By Roderick Phillips's count 308 men and women were convicted of adultery or "adulterous carriage" (meaning attempted or unproven seduction by a married person) in seventeenth-century New England. But there were only forty divorces asked for and granted on these grounds. Apparently such conduct, even when flagrant enough to eventuate in court proceedings, was not considered by the wronged spouses or the courts as an insurmountable barrier to continued family life. Massachusetts as early as 1638 allowed whipping or banishment as penalties for adultery. In 1660 the General Court added the death penalty, but only for those who had been banished but refused to leave the colony.[28] If adulterous persons could not be reclaimed into family life, then they at least theoretically could not remain as examples of a particularly heinous element of the profane life.

Besides families that could not or would not live up to the popular or reformed patriarchal ideals, there were two other anomalies that complicated family government. The first were women who were independent by virtue of their personalities or their social status, such as widows. The second were "youths," those of both sexes who had passed puberty but were as yet unmarried. The latter, as "the rising generation," were of more concern

---

27. Richard Johnson, *Adjustment to Empire: The New England Colonies, 1675–1715* (New Brunswick, N.J., 1981), 300; *Essex Recs.* IX, 535–38.

28. *Assistants Recs.* I, 10; *Suffolk Recs.* 232, 1158; *Essex Recs.* VII, 419; VIII, 101, 238; IX, 83, 151; *Plymouth Recs.* V, 31–32; Phillips, *Putting Asunder,* 350; Kochler, *Search for Power,* 146–52.

(especially the males) to New Englanders pursuing the Reformation of Manners, for they were the shapers of the society's future.

In popular European and English tradition independent women were objects of much fear, some respect, and a great deal of ribald humor. The authors of Tudor-Stuart almanacs generally agreed not only that women were inherently inferior to men but also that wives in particular were prone to rebellion. Domestic brawls, predictions that wives would increasingly "lord it over their husbands," tales of "civil wars between drunken husbands and scolding wives, mothers-in-law and their daughters," and stories of female promiscuity and extravagance were common fare in chapbooks and ballads. So strong was this tendency, according to Margaret Spufford, that the chapbook version of marriage "was to equate it with cuckoldry."[29]

In popular estimation the root of the problem was that women were more passionate and less rational than men. As the late seventeenth-century French epigrammatist Jean de La Bruyère claimed, "Most women hardly have principles; they are led by their passions, and form their morals and manners after those whom they love." For this reason "women run to extremes; they are either better or worse than men." In 1596 an English pamphlet considering "the Nature, conditions, and manners of Women" wondered "why that sex when they are angrie, are more fierce then Men, conceive anger sooner, chide more unmeasurablie, and are sooner overcome with any affection then Men." This fundamental lack of self-discipline, according to the author, explained "in what sense this saying the Wise Man is to be taken: The iniquities of a man is better then the good deedes of a Woman."[30]

These criticisms of female conduct and psychology exactly paralleled the reformers' assessment of the profane conversation generally. Passion, willfulness, and rampant hedonism undermined the sobriety, rationality, and discipline essential to an orderly, decent, "civil" society. Some recent historians have held that the image of the "shrewish wife," together with other stereotypes of fiercely independent women, "was a patriarchal bad dream rather than a social reality," an idea "whose basic function was the maintenance of existing norms through inverting them." Others, in contrast, believe that the picture was more rooted in daily experience and long-term cultural

29. Bernard Capp, *English Almanacs, 1500–1800: Astrology and the Popular Press* (Ithaca, N.Y., 1979), 112, 123–24; Hull, *Chaste, Silent, and Obedient,* 111; Margaret Spufford, *Small Books and Pleasant Histories: Popular Fiction and Its Readership in Seventeenth-Century England* (Athens, Ga., 1981), 140.

30. Jean de La Bruyère, *Characters,* trans. Henri Van Laun (London, 1963), 45–46; Hull, *Chaste, Silent, and Obedient,* 205–6; Fraser, *Weaker Vessel,* 102; Leites, *Puritan Conscience,* 118.

trends. In fact, Natalie Davis has argued that the "image of the disorderly woman" was "multivalent" enough to encourage and sanction wider latitude in conduct in and out of marriage, including various forms of dissent. Peter Burke, while noting that evidence is slim and ambivalent, contended that "women's culture was more conservative." Burke attributed this female conservatism to the relative insulation of women from the cultural ferment of books, taverns, and ecclesiastical and political institutions. While his explanation may be overdrawn, his general observation seems confirmed, at least for seventeenth-century England, by Susan Amussen and David Underdown in more recent essays.[31] At minimum it seems that women participated as fully as men in those individualistic, antiauthoritarian, bawdy elements of the popular tradition which reformers found dangerous or obnoxious, and that those tendencies when pursued by women greatly alarmed the defenders of patriarchy.

In early New England the worries were less intense, but the stereotypes were present both in rhetoric and in reality. Disorderly women, married or unmarried, made frequent appearances in court records, travelers' accounts, execution sermons, and even local criminal histories. The most famous of the latter is Cotton Mather's *Pillar of Salt* (1699), a best-seller containing a section on Sarah Smith of Deerfield, a petty thief who cuckolded two husbands and was finally executed for infanticide. Mather was greatly impressed with her "Hardness of Heart" and "astonishing Stupidity of Soul." In the 1660s English traveler John Josselyn remarked smugly of New England, "There are many strange women too, (in Solomon's sense), more the pitty, when a woman hath lost her Chastity, she hath no more to lose." Prosecutions of single women in the late seventeenth century for "lascivious carriage," sometimes including "being seen in bed with a man," were fairly frequent. Indeed, Lyle Kochler has claimed that "Adultery was one of the most common offenses in Puritan New England, yet most cases probably never came under the surveillance of the authorities." Women constituted 43.5 percent of a total of 308 convictions in orthodox New England during the seventeenth century. Other indictable signs of suspicious female independence included "excess in her apparel & living from under [family] Government." The younger Mather

31. Sharpe, "Plebeian Marriage," 88; Natalie Z. Davis, "Women on Top: Symbolic Sexual Inversion and Political Disorder in Early Modern Europe," in Barbara A. Babcock, ed., *The Reversible World: Symbolic Inversion in Art and Society* (Ithaca, N.Y., 1978), 147–90; Peter Burke, *Popular Culture in Early Modern Europe* (New York, 1978), 49–50; Margaret Spufford, *Small Books*, 34–36, 62; Susan Amussen, "Gender, Family, and Social Order," in Fletcher and Stevenson, eds., *Order and Disorder*, 196–217; Underdown, "Taming of the Scold," 116–36.

was told in the 1710s "of several Houses in this Town, where there were young Women of a very debauched Character, and extremely impudent."[32]

Yet not all the images of women violating patriarchal expectations were negative. The English traveler and bookseller John Dunton, who was conventional enough to believe that "the principal and most distinct scenes in which a Woman can act a part are, either as a Virgin, a Wife, or a Widow," praised a single woman thirty years of age whom he claimed to have met in Boston in 1685. "It is true, an old (or superannuated) Maid in Boston is thought such a curse, as nothing can exceed it (and looked on as a dismal spectacle); yet she, by her good-nature, gravity, and strict virtue, convinces all (so much as the fleeing Beaus) that it is not her necessity, but her choice, that keeps her a Virgin." That "choice" to be independent, albeit protected by exemplary conduct, was apparently respected.[33]

Of Dunton's three "distinct scenes" of virgin, wife, and widow, perhaps the latter was the most troublesome within the paradigm of patriarchal family government. Widows controlling property, likely to marry or not, complicated the male-dominated inheritance patterns. Female heads of household without property were a drain on the economic resources of families and communities. Generally viewed in the popular culture as sexually experienced, wise in the ways of the world, and self-assertive, the status of widow was definitely "multivalent" in terms of the dominant social ethic. There was respect for her experienced independence. As one seventeenth-century English ballad advised,

> He that doth woo a maiden
> Must use sometime to flatter,
> And he that would woo a widow,
> Must seriously speake good Matter.

On the other hand there was the strongly held stereotype of the "lusty widow" whose sexual appetites, having been aroused and developed in marriage but then thwarted by widowhood, were deemed insatiable. Again, as

---

32. Cotton Mather, *Pillars of Salt: An History of Some Criminals Executed in this Land for Capital Crimes, with some of their Dying Speeches* (Boston, 1699), 103–4; John Josselyn, *An Account of Two Voyages to New England* (London, 1675; reprint, Boston, 1865), 139; *Suffolk Recs.* 23, 185, 677, 751, 940, 1061; Worthington Chauncey Ford, ed., *Diary of Cotton Mather* (New York, 1912), 2:229; Kochler, *Search for Power*, 148–49.

33. John Dunton, *Life and Errors* (London, 1705), 1:102–3.

the ballad literature had it, "He that woos a maid, must fain, lie, and flatter / But he that woos a widow, must down his breeches and at her."[34]

John Dunton portrayed the model Boston widow in "Madam Brick," who "lived a life of sincere piety; and yet was so far from sourness either in her countenance or conversation, that nothing was ever more sweet or agreeable."[35] Maintaining a respectable family life, she joined the church and saw to the education of her children. In his depiction of Madame Brick's feelings for her lost husband, Dunton found a symbol of the self-control and dignity that, the reformers believed, separated the manners of the godly from those of the profane.

> Her grief for his death was such as became her, great but moderate; not like a hasty shower, but a still rain: she knew nothing of those tragical furies wherewith some women seem transported towards their dead Husbands: those frantic embraces and caresses of a carcass betray a little too much the sensuality of their love.

The widow who succeeded in this life of pious discipline became an emblem of the Christian life generally. In 1744 Ebenezer Parkman, a pastor in Westborough, Massachusetts, went to visit an ailing, aged woman. In his diary he enthused, "She gave me an Excellent Testimony of the Grace of God in her and the Evidences of a regular and thorow work from her early Age; of which may God have the Glory! And may we all pattern after her in all!" Significantly, her piety and conduct became a point of family pride. "Her children also testify that this had been the Substance of her Conversation among them all along thro' her life."[36]

In 1718 Cotton Mather, who served a maritime congregation often ravaged by storm and war at sea, noted that "the Widows of the Flock are numerous; they make about a fifth part of our Community." Besides working to ensure their economic well-being, he published a "Sermonfull of Councils and Comforts" urging the same discipline and dignified conduct crucial to the ideal of widowhood. Yet later that same year his church faced the scandal of a young widow, raised in a wealthy and pious family, charged

34. Carol F. Karlsen, *The Devil in the Shape of a Woman: Witchcraft in Colonial New England* (New York, 1987), 81–84, 168–69, 204–17; Quaife, *Wanton Wenches,* 143; Sharpe, "Plebeian Marriage," 74; Fraser, *Weaker Vessel,* 4; Hull, *Chaste, Silent, and Obedient,* 56; Ulrich, *Good Wives,* 97.

35. Dunton, *Life and Errors,* 1:107.

36. Francis G. Walett, ed., *The Diary of Ebenezer Parkman, 1703–1782* (Worcester, Mass., 1974), 104.

with "lewd Carriage towards diverse Men at Sundry Times" and "having had an unlawful offspring in the Time of Widowhood, which long remained a secret." To Mather's astonishment she, once discovered, "foolishly insisted on her total Ignorance of anything done unto her to give her any Impregnation." Her family, and particularly her father, "who is an old and great Professor of Religion," in their grief and defensiveness evinced "a strange Malice and Revenge" toward Mather and the woman's accusers, using "violent Wayes to sow Discord among the Neighbours, and the Peace of the Church is threatened." However, by unanimous vote the widow was excommunicated until she made a sincere repentance.[37]

Her and her family's strong but futile effort to preserve their reputation may illustrate the common seventeenth-century adage, "Hypocrisy is the tribute vice pays to virtue." Less pejoratively, the episode demonstrated the power of the ideal to limit self-expression. The young woman's punishment and public disgrace, which also cast suspicion on the putative respectability of her family, was meant to enforce patriarchal standards.

Yet there were women who found in the ambivalence of popular attitudes toward widowhood a freedom to challenge rather than embody the pious ideal. In 1739 Ebenezer Parkman remarked on "the Snares of a Young Widow" of New Haven who, when the target of her affections fled town, "boldly and resolutely and against the Fears and entreatys of her parents, Sisters, and her own Child mounted her Horse and rode after" him. She got her man, despite "the endearments and great Fortune of his own Wife, supposed to be in Boston."[38]

Still others, remaining unmarried, lived up to the image of the "lusty widow," apparently both abetted and punished by "common fame." For instance, Newbury's Sarah Stickney, a thirty-five-year-old widow with four children in 1679, made several court appearances from that year to 1683 in cases involving fornication, slander, "lascivious carriage," and child support. The opening case involved fornication with a young sailor of the town, Samuel Lowell. The local tavern-keeper testified "that the widow Stickney being at his house just after her husband had died, and Samuel Lowell and some other seamen being there also, he saw her very jocund and merry, sitting in their laps, etc." She then took to inviting Lowell to her home "often and asked him," according to his testimony, "to bring others, and left the back door open that he might come in." Her brother, believing that she

37. Ford, ed., *Diary of Cotton Mather,* 2:516–17, 531, 538; Cotton Mather, *Marah Spoken To: An Essay to do Good unto the Widow* (Boston, 1718).
38. Walett, ed., *Diary of Ebenezer Parkman,* 68.

"was troubled with Samuel Lowell's coming to her house at unseasonable times," offered to "lodge there." And so on a Sunday afternoon he caught Lowell, who asked him "to say nothing about it, as they had been friends formerly, and he would give him a pint of wine." A near neighbor, aware of the comings and goings, wondered aloud if the brother "would be Samuel Lowell's pimpe." Sarah admitted that Lowell and another sailor, Thomas Stevens, were frequent visitors and even that on "another night when he came, someone from Rowley was in the house with her," causing some embarrassment. Yet to another younger male she denied "all the rumors" but confessed she would not have "complained of Lowell had it not been for her brother."[39]

By late 1681 Stickney had another child, and understandably there was much speculation and confusion over who was the father. Dominant opinion favored Samuel Lowell, a source of merriment among some of the town. One day three young men in their twenties drove a cart by her house. While one mimicked the sailor another shouted, "Here is Samuel Lowell, what have you to say to him?" She replied, "A you Roge, yonder is yor Child under the tree, goe take it up and see it." Nonetheless, with even the man who "plowed for Sarah Stickney" among the popular suspects, she was able to claim that a married farmer, John Atkinson, was the "father of her last child, which fact she had concealed upon his promise to maintain the child which he now refuses to do." Despite the fact that a sometime female confidant of Stickney implied strongly that she settled on Atkinson because Lowell "had no money," the court charged the farmer for child support at eight pounds to date plus 2s. 6d. a week in future to be given to the widow. Whatever the actual economic constraints on Stickney, the court apparently did not take the possible financial motive seriously because in their view the widow had substantial property and had also remarked, when trying to entice Lowell "to marry her and carry her to Providence," that she "had money enough."[40]

The next year, however, John Atkinson and his wife, Sarah, successfully petitioned "to be wholly cleared from any further allowance toward the child's maintenance." Sarah Atkinson was especially articulate about "the imperious dealings of Sarah Stickney, who having gotten an advantage because of the unjust course of law uses it with a great deal of rigor, threatning & scoffing." Although the widow Stickney had been somewhat tender, if

39. *Essex Recs.* VII, 316–18.
40. Ibid., VIII, 260–63, 286. For a tragic parallel case of a woman, Elizabeth Emerson of Haverhill, impregnated by a married man but executed for infanticide, see Ulrich, *Good Wives*, 190–201.

imprudent, about her reputation in 1679, by 1682 she was largely uncon-
cerned about either informal or formal sanctions. Once, having been heavily
fined, she remarked "that the court did not regard the sin so long as they
could get the money," an interesting commentary on her outlook.[41] She was
a strong character who seemed to cultivate a wanton image that had both
sexual and financial compensations. She also apparently grew to enjoy the
battles over reputation, particularly the sufferings of the Atkinsons. For her
the stereotype of the bawdy widow proved part burden (witness the hoped-
for escape to Providence) and part liberation.

In her combativeness Sarah Stickney may have been a patriarchal nightmare. Yet however "disorderly," neither she nor her sisters constituted a
significant threat to the moral order of orthodox New England. Whereas in
early modern England the defenders of patriarchy seemed more concerned
with the rebelliousness of women, the New England advocates of family
government worried more about youths, both as "children" and as "servants." Both the 1662 synod in Massachusetts and the subsequent debates
on how best to incorporate into the churches the young whose grandparents
were full members but whose parents were not were strong indications of
that concern.[42]

Although Increase Mather opposed the Half-Way Covenant measures as
dilutions of the "power of godliness" in the churches, he had a keen and
broad appreciation of the problem. As the leading American theorist of the
Reformation of Manners in the late seventeenth century he saw the issue of
"youth" as central to the whole moral and social order. His approach had
wide appeal. According to Michael G. Hall, Mather's latest and finest bi-
ographer, "The Rising Generation became Mather's most popular theme,"
leading to the publication of five sermons on the problem from 1675 to
1679. No doubt the popular response to his formulation contributed significantly to support for the Reforming Synod of 1679.[43]

For New Englanders the problem of the rising generation was acute for
demographic as well as cultural reasons. In a region experiencing both
chronic labor shortages and a high birthrate, young people were not only
conspicuous by their proportion in the population but also essential to the
work force. Hence, their availability for and commitment to disciplined

---

41. *Essex Recs.* IX, 17.
42. Capp, *English Almanacs,* 126; Robert G. Pope, *The Half-Way Covenant: Church Membership in Puritan New England* (Princeton, 1969).
43. Michael G. Hall, *The Last American Puritan: The Life of Increase Mather, 1639–1723*
(Middletown, Conn., 1988), 146.

work under the direction of elders were vital. Thus an economic condition deepened the moral challenge of child-rearing. As Mather intoned in 1679, "You that are servants, young men and maids, have you not been guilty of stubborn, disobedient carriages towards your Masters? . . . And you that are children, have not you disobeyed your parents?" Being neither shortsighted nor morally obtuse, Mather called for something more than mere docility. Because the members of the rising generation were fated to replace their elders, their discipline must become self-discipline. Also, to be effective that self-control must transcend economic ambition to embrace wider moral and religious commitments. For Mather the lack of discipline was evinced in three areas: economic aspirations that were narrowly "worldly," perfunctory religious observance, and "a great Rudeness" or "degeneracy from the good manners of the Christian world," by which, of course, he meant more than proper etiquette. Lack of reform or lack of discipline, Mather characteristically warned, had not just practical but also cosmic consequences; "if when Fathers have been of a holy, exemplary Conversation, their children shall be unholy and prophane, they are forsakers of God, concerning whom he hath threatened to cast them off forever."[44]

Rhetorically Mather tied the reform of the rising generation not merely to the physical survival and prosperity of his society but also to its ultimate meaning in and beyond history. Thus not only the youths of his era but those of each succeeding generation for at least a century were exhorted and worried over in precisely the same terms. The rising generation was a perennial and central theme of the entire jeremiad tradition. Typical was this summary of the argument from the 1720s: "Nothing is more Threatening to the Welfare of a People, than to have their *Young Ones* generally *Ignorant, Irreligious, Disorderly.* When it is so, it looks as tho' Iniquity would soon abound, to the pulling down [of] heavy Judgments."[45]

To account for the vehemence and persistence of this concern, as well as for the frequency of youthful offenders in Massachusetts courts, recent historians—particularly Ross W. Beales and Roger Thompson—have convincingly identified "a separate youth culture" that embraced those persons of both sexes between puberty and marriage (or conversion among the godly)

44. Jim Potter, "Demographic Development and Family Structure," in Jack P. Greene and J. R. Pole, eds., *Colonial British America: Essays in the New History of the Early Modern Era* (Baltimore, 1984), 145–49; Increase Mather, *A Call from Heaven to the Present & Succeeding Generations* (Boston, 1679, 1685), 39–40, 59, 62, 108, 151.

45. Benjamin Wadsworth, *Nature of Early Piety* (Boston, 1721), 29. See also Solomon Stoddard, *Danger of Speedy Degeneracy* (Boston, 1705), 9–10, for another forceful statement.

and "represented an alternative to the norms and values of the adult world."[46] More broadly, it seems that young persons, including those from godly families, traditionally enjoyed greater freedom to indulge in the profane activities of the wider popular culture before they settled into the responsibilities of forming proper family governments. Indeed, the very similarities alarmed the reformers. Increase Mather made this connection in 1679, claiming that "the generality of Youth in this Land walk in wayes of loosness, profaneness, pride, drinking, gaming, or in careless neglect of God, and of their own souls." He worried about "many a young man, born of godly parents," who "hath fallen into acquaintance and familiarity with *vain persons,* whose councils he hath followed, to the everlasting destruction both of his body and soul." Two generations later in 1733 Thomas Foxcroft of Boston's First Church followed the same themes by building a sermon upon a list of "Sins of Youth" that he thought likely to become habitual into adulthood and in turn to be taught to the next generation. These included the usual failings such as "Idleness and Evil Fellowship," "Intemperance," "Lasciviousness," "sullen Discontent," and "Covetousness."[47]

As in their thinking about independent women, the reformers pointed to adolescence as a condition of life with a peculiar vulnerability to the root sin of pride revealed in excessive forms of individualism. "Pride is a lust of the mind," wrote Joseph Sewall in 1721, "and is a Sin which easily besets Young Persons." He elaborated, "Young People are apt to be conceited, and to magnify themselves; to be desirous of vain glory, and ambitious of more honour and respect than they deserve." Extremes of such self-assertion appeared to the reformers as a form of "madness," the opposite of self-control. In 1712 Cotton Mather warned, "The Young Fool runs on in his Uncontroleable Folly. He foolishly, and with a most Licentious Extravagancy & Exorbitancy values himself upon those Liberties, which are indeed the worst of Slaveries. Because Madness is in his Heart, he is madly set upon the Pleasures of Sin which are but for a Season." For the reformers, then, the

46. Ross W. Beales, "In Search of the Historical Child," *American Quarterly* 27 (1975): 379–98; Roger Thompson, "Adolescent Culture in Colonial Massachusetts," *Journal of Family History* 9 (1984): 127–44, quote on 139–40. The fullest treatment is Roger Thompson, *Sex in Middlesex: Popular Mores in a Massachusetts County, 1649–1699* (Amherst, Mass., 1986). See also Demos, *Past, Present, and Personal,* 13, 94–95.

47. Increase Mather, *A Call to the Rising Generation* (Boston, 1679), 104; I. Mather, *Practical Truths,* 178–79; Thomas Foxcroft, *Lessons of Caution to Young Sinners* (Boston, 1733), 40–49.

"youth culture" raised the same dilemmas of autonomy and discipline that fueled the more general Reformation of Manners.[48]

Yet despite this concern that the tendency to "Walk in forbidden Paths" might become habitual, the critics of youth also recognized that for many, if not most, of the young such self-indulgence was temporary and was rooted in both adolescent psychology and popular tradition. As Samuel Moody, whom Increase Mather called one of his "Academical Children," observed in 1707, "Youngsters do see, that, for the most part, those who are Young like themselves do take their swing in Youthful Vanities." Addressing the young of his congregation who took "their swing" as a matter of harmless right, Thomas Prince complained, "You seem to think as if you are not under any Obligations to be religious in your Youthful Age." He was speaking, of course, not only of formal religious observance but of moral self-control. In 1732 the pastor of Malden could assume that the adult members of his congregation had experienced the "Giddiness and Inconstancy" that the youth culture shared with the profane. "We should remember the rash Anger & Sinfull Passions of our Youth. The Envy, Hatred, and Malice, the Fierceness & Rage, the Clamour and evil Speaking, the calling of Ill Names, threatning & Cursing, Quarreling and Fighting, that we were formerly guilty of."[49] Such memory could assist in avoiding adult temptation.

The reformers, however, were not inclined to wait for the young to outgrow their indiscretions. Proper family government was an obvious and necessary remedy. In Increase Mather's early formulation, "If the Fathers follow superstitions or profane practices, it is most likely that the children will do so too. Therefore you that are parents in the fear of God look to it that you do not scandalize your children by an evil example." In this context it was "a great mercy to be born and brought up under godly parents." Although the clerics were keenly aware of exceptions, this assessment of family influence was a crucial moral aspect of the famed Puritan "tribalism," a notion hardly peculiar to early New England.[50]

Another possibility frequently pursued was a prudential appeal to reputation, an appeal to what his father called "merely civil." In 1707 the younger Mather contrasted the stereotypes of "licentious" and "godly"

48. Sewall, *Early Piety,* 7; Cotton Mather, *Repeated Warnings: Another Essay to warn Young People* (Boston, 1712), 2–3.

49. C. Mather, *Repeated Warnings,* 20–21; Samuel Moody, *The Vain Youth Summoned,* 2d ed. (Boston, 1707), 25; Thomas Prince, *Great and Solemn Obligations* (Boston, 1721), 13; Joseph Emerson, *Offering of Memorials* (Boston, 1732), 8.

50. I. Mather, *Call to the Rising Generation,* 14, 28–29.

youth. For the male, "Which is best of the two? To be thus described among the Neighbours; That Young Man is a Foolish, Profane, Extravagant Fellow: Or, to be thus described, That Young Man is a Sober, Discreet, Vertuous Person, He will never do a Base or an Ill thing, you may depend upon him." For the female the choice was "That Young Woman is a Vain, Giddy, Trifling Fool: She knows nothing but the Mysteries of the Dress and the Dance; and she is given so to Lying and Mischief, 'tis a dangerous thing to talk with her: Or, . . . That Young Woman is Vertuous, Modest, Prudent, and in everything well-accomplished." Mather left no doubt which courses were more likely to lead to honor and success. The appeal to social and economic calculation, however, had its own cosmic perils for those youth who, in the words of John Barnard in 1728, "content themselves in a State of Unregeneracy; tho' it may be, they are exemplary for Morality."[51]

The ideal was an "early piety" that would both prevent the converted youngster from full participation in the youth culture and be a sign of his or her eternal salvation. Here as elsewhere the goal was to tame, not obliterate, this aspect of popular mores. "It is not criminal for you to be cheerful and merry in Conversation. Young People may use the Divertisements and Pleasures of Life, such as are proper to their Age, so as they do but keep within the Bounds of Innocence and Moderation." As always in the Reformation of Manners, self-discipline, not overt social control, was the sign of success. As Joseph Sewall addressed the young in 1721, "Now if we would have a sound mind in a spiritual sense, we must seek to get our minds enlightened with Saving knowledge of the truths of God's Word, and make use of the Excellent Rules there laid down, for the right government of our Lives."[52]

To carry out this campaign to improve family government and the character of the rising generation, the clerics were not content merely to preach and to leave the more egregious offenders to the magistrates. Educational programs and pastoral care, including visitations of homes and "careful catechizing" of children and whole families, were major clerical activities. Through such ritual devices as covenant renewals and fast days they sought to mobilize church members in the effort. They also inspired voluntary associations of young people and others to carry on reform from the 1690s through the colonial era. In this effort the American

---

51. C. Mather, *Best Ornaments*, 14; John Barnard, *Piety Described, and Early Religion Recommended* (Boston, 1728), 80–81.
52. William Cooper, *Objections to Early Piety Answered* (Boston, 1721), 8; Sewall, *Early Piety*, 3.

Puritans were participants in humanist tendencies stretching back at least as far as fifteenth-century Florence to see the young both as possible "ritual saviors," with "early piety" being a general sign of success for a social order, and "as the special objects of intense religious and educational concern."[53]

53. George Selement, *Keepers of the Vineyard: The Puritan Ministry and Collective Culture in Colonial New England* (Landon, Md., 1984); Donald Weinstein, "Critical Issues in the Study of Civil Religion in Renaissance Florence," in Charles Trinkaus and Heiko A. Oberman, eds., *The Pursuit of Holiness in Late Medieval and Renaissance Religion* (Leiden, 1974), 265–70, quote on 266.

FIVE

Rituals, Godly and Profane

For Increase Mather, his allies, and his successors in the Reformation of Manners, family prayer was both a cause and a result of proper family government. Although American Puritans rejected what they termed "vain ceremonials," they nonetheless evinced a keen appreciation of the role of ritual in the formation, transmission, and preservation of a social ethic. As heirs to and critics of the rich liturgical heritage of late medieval Christendom, their sensitivity to the impact of ritual in religious, private, and civic life led them to recast rather than reject ceremonial modes of expressing and inculcating cosmic and moral commitments. Consequently, orthodox New England developed a distinctive pattern of rituals around the Sabbath, days of Humiliation and Thanksgiving, militia training days, election and court days, and Harvard's Commencement. Although rooted in English experience, each was significantly adapted to express the new society's sense of social and natural order under the governance of God.[1]

The process of reshaping old ceremonies and establishing new ones also included attempts to suppress those deemed "disorderly" or "superstitious." Cotton Mather thought such practices to be relics of "the Vain Conversation received by Tradition from our Fathers." Thus, as the populace variously embraced, contested, and accommodated the reforms, another arena was created in which the complex interplay between the godly and the profane was acted out. As David Hall has suggested, "Ritual represents and acts out a myth of collective identity. It is a process that reaffirms the social bond. Yet it may also become expressive of contradictions and alternatives." In 1700 Increase Mather affirmed the relationship between ceremony and moral

1. For an excellent guide to the rituals of American Puritans and their theological bearings, see Horton Davies, *The Worship of the American Puritans, 1629–1730* (New York, 1990).

discipline for the Reformation of Manners in New England. "That the Churches which are called *Reformed,* have attained unto an *Imperfect Reformation,* is a Truth not to be denied: The defect has not been so much in *Doctrine* as in *Worship* and *Discipline."²*

One measure of the strength of traditional English popular culture in early New England as a challenge to reform was the persistence of profane customs that the reformers sought to eliminate on religious and moral grounds. Christmas was a prime example. As early as 1659 the Massachusetts General Court complained of "some still observing such festivals as were superstitiously kept in other countries," including Christmas. The legislature levied a fine on those celebrating "by forbearing of labor, feasting, or any other way." That ban, as with so much similar legislation, was not effectively enforced.³

In 1677 Boston "Gallants" who pledged that they would "keep Christmas . . . were as good as their word" and celebrated with impunity. In Salem in 1685 an aged couple sued a man who bought their property in return for support. One of the charges was that he had not included them in a Christmas feast. None of the magistrates seems to have found that odd. Nor were these traditional Christmases always models of decorum. In 1679 a group of four young male carolers burst into a house in rural Essex County on Christmas Eve, sang two carols, and demanded liquor. When refused and forcibly evicted, they went to another house, where the results were a brawl and extensive vandalism. They were prosecuted not for observing Christmas but for assault and damage to property.⁴

In 1681 the ban, obviously unenforceable in New England and obnoxious to English officialdom, was formally repealed. By 1685 Samuel Sewall could take grudging comfort in the thought that only "some somehow observe the day; but are vexed I believe that the Body of the People profane it, and blessed by God no Authority yet to compel them to keep it." It was not law or "repression" that prevented Christmas festivities from becoming more general but rather custom reinforced by sermons. And, of course, some always felt free to defy Puritan opinion. After 1690 the celebration of the Nativity became increasingly common even among the "godly." By 1711 Cotton Mather was complaining of a "Christmas frolick, a revelling Feast, and Ball" held by

2. Cotton Mather, *Advice from the Watchtower: In a Testimony against Evil Customs* (Boston, 1713), 13–14; David D. Hall, "Religion and Society: Problems and Reconsiderations," in Jack P. Greene and J. R. Pole, eds., *Colonial British America: Essays in the New History of the Early Modern Era* (Baltimore, 1984), 336; Increase Mather, *The Order of the Gospel Professed and Practiced by the Churches of Christ in New England* (Boston, 1700), A2.
3. *Mass. Recs.* IV, pt. 1, 366.
4. "Mather Correspondence," 238; *Essex Recs.* VII, 331–32; IX, 479, 483.

"young People of both Sexes" from his congregation. To prevent "such Follies" in the future he preached a sermon (to Sewall's delight) denouncing Christmas observance "by Mad Mirth, by long Eating, by hard Drinking, by lewd Gaming, by rude Revelling."[5] Christmas, a vital part of the English popular heritage, could not be suppressed, particularly in the anglicizing atmosphere of the late seventeenth and early eighteenth centuries. All that could be hoped for was to dampen its more rowdy manifestations.

Observance of Saint Valentine's Day by the posting of obscene libels and of Shrove Tuesday by sharing pancake feasts presumably dedicated "to the Queen of Heaven" or by wearing costumes was less common but not unheard of before Massachusetts became a royal colony. Indeed, as early as 1645 Plymouth magistrates were bothered by "some abuses" from persons "disguising, wearing visors [masks] and strange apparel to lascivious ends and purposes." A strong indication of continuing concern was a law against masking that was repeated with minor changes in wording in 1658, 1672, and 1685. The practice was not restricted to Shrove Tuesday. In purpose the law resembled a statute of Henry VIII "against disguised persons and wearing of visors" and apparently was as ineffective.[6]

While authorities tried to suppress or at least discountenance some traditional religious customs, others were embraced and developed further. The days of Humiliation and Thanksgiving, for example, were public rituals of prayer, sermons, fasts, and feasts, based on European Calvinist reforms of common medieval practice and intended to acknowledge God's specific acts of blessing or judgment. Some of the calls were for individual churches. Others, written by clergy and political leaders and passed by the colonial legislature, were for the whole society. By celebrating providential events publicly the Puritans hoped to gain God's favor, to increase piety, and to unify the populace in pursuit of moral and social reform. These rites were popular, enjoying widespread interest and participation.

But they also rather rapidly incorporated elements of the traditional agricultural ritual cycle of harvest feasts and spring fasts, which tended to

5. M. Halsey Thomas, ed., *The Diary of Samuel Sewall, 1674–1729* (New York, 1973), 1:90, 2:701n.; Worthington C. Ford, ed., *The Diary of Cotton Mather* (New York, 1912), 2:145–46; Increase Mather, *A Testimony against Several Prophane and Superstitious Customes now Practiced by Some in New England* (London, 1687), 44; C. Mather, *Advice from the Watchtower,* 35.

6. Roger Thompson, *Sex in Middlesex: Popular Mores in a Massachusetts County, 1649–1699* (Amherst, Mass., 1986), 86, 93, 181; I. Mather, *Testimony,* 46; *Plymouth Recs.* XI, 48, 96–97, 173–74; C. J. Ribton-Turner, *A History of Vagabonds and Vagrancy and Beggars and Beggary* (London, 1887; reprint, Montclair, N.J., 1972), 70.

transcend and confuse the idea of acknowledging special providences. If one bountiful harvest was a particular sign of God's grace, then should not every harvest be acknowledged by a Day of Thanksgiving? The tendency to include traditional meanings also implied increased tolerance for traditional conduct; "thereby," as Solomon Stoddard complained in 1705, "Young People have opportunity to meet together, and spend some part of the day rudely." Youthful misconduct on such occasions (particularly feasts) was, of course, an early modern tradition. Also, in times of political division—particularly in the 1680s—there was a temptation to use the ceremonies as propaganda. Yet despite these confusions and even occasional abuses by persons in authority the days of Humiliation and Thanksgiving retained both their popularity and their central meaning in the Reformation of Manners throughout the colonial era. In 1774, as the revolutionary crisis mounted, Worcester cleric Thaddeus Maccarty preached a fast-day sermon entitled *Reformation of Manners of Absolute Necessity* in which he reiterated the essential theme of these rites.

> May it not justly be expected by God himself that a genuine repentance and reformation will follow this day's solemnity? Shall it be said that any after this go on in prophaness, intemperance, unchastity, in fraud and oppression, in bitterness, wrath, malice, anger, dishonesty, unrighteousness, sabbath breaking, neglecting the public worship of God? Shall it be said after this, that there are any more prayerless families . . . ?

Right into the American Revolution the themes of social order, moral reform, and piety remained tightly linked in an important public ritual.[7]

Of all the ceremonies of early New England none was more central to the society's sense of identity and purpose than the Sabbath. Nor were there any in which the interplay between popular and Puritan ideas and conduct was more important in the common experience of the populace. In England and America a reconstitution of the Lord's Day was a defining characteristic of the reform movement. As with so much else in Puritanism, Sabbatarianism's

---

7. Davies, *Worship of the American Puritans,* 58–67; Charles E. Hambrick-Stowe, *The Practice of Piety: Puritan Devotional Discipline in Seventeenth-Century New England* (Chapel Hill, 1982), 100–103; David D. Hall, *Worlds of Wonder, Days of Judgment: Popular Religious Belief in Early New England* (New York, 1989), 170–73; Richard P. Gildrie, "The Ceremonial Puritan: Days of Humiliation and Thanksgiving," *NEHGR* 136 (1982): 3–16; Solomon Stoddard, *Dangers of a Speedy Degeneracy* (Boston, 1705), 18–19; Thaddeus Maccarty, *Reformation of Manners of Absolute Necessity* (Boston, 1774), 36.

roots were medieval. After the Fourth Lateran Council of 1215, the church embarked on a concerted campaign to improve the morals of the clergy and laity. An important element of this reform was a more orderly Sunday observance, extended back ideally to Saturday evening, and suppression of wrestling, ale-drinking, dancing, and gambling in the churchyards on Sunday afternoons. The effort was but a partial and temporary success.[8]

The later Puritan attempt was more thorough in that it tried to reshape the religious and ideological framework of the Sabbath. By denouncing and then abandoning the annual liturgical cycle and shrines of the Church of England, the Puritans denied that there were particularly sacred places and times. All time and space were equally significant to God. By so doing the Puritans were attempting to recast an entire worldview and with it a system of meanings that for centuries had irregularly and ambiguously separated and merged the sacred and the profane, Christian and pagan, penitential and celebratory. All of this existed within the rhythms of the agricultural seasons. Maypoles, Christmas, clerical vestments, Lent, processionals, Shrove Tuesday, Sunday sports, "set prayers," and saints' days were all supposed to be sacrificed and replaced by a simplified, clarified, weekly ritual moment, the reformed Sabbath. The irony was that in trying to acknowledge the sanctity of all time and space in one celebration the Puritans were creating a uniquely holy ritual event.[9]

Nonetheless, the implications of such thorough iconoclasm were staggering and certainly not lost on contemporaries. Both secular and religious patterns of life were reoriented toward a single celebration freed from the agricultural rhythms wherein not just one element of the Christian drama but the entire cycle of creation, fall, and redemption was rehearsed. This concentration and simplification of religious experience into "the Sabbath as the devotional point of reference was," in the words of Charles Hambrick-Stowe, "a major Puritan innovation within Christianity." The Puritans themselves, of course, saw the reform not as innovation but as restoration of biblical practice, which to them gave the reform even deeper significance. They came to see "keeping the Sabbath holy" as the leading ritualistic sign of the spiritual health of individuals and communities. As Increase Mather

8. Margaret Spufford, "Puritanism and Social Control?" in Anthony Fletcher and John Stevenson, eds., *Order and Disorder in Early Modern England* (London, 1985), 50–53.

9. James P. Walsh, "Holy Time and Sacred Space in Puritan New England," *American Quarterly* 32 (1980): 79–95; Hambrick-Stowe, *Practice of Piety*, 48–51, 96–97. For the standard history of Sabbath laws, see Winston U. Solberg, *Redeem the Time: The Puritan Sabbath in Early America* (Cambridge, Mass., 1977).

put it, "Most commonly men's Religion is according to what their Sabbaths are."[10]

In essence, there were two basic principles to the reformed Sabbath: first, "resting from all servile and common business pertaining to our natural life," and second, "consecrating that rest wholly to the service of God, and the use of holy means which belong to our spiritual life." There was to be no secular labor or play, for the "work of the Lord's Day" was the recreation of the soul, not the body. The Sabbath itself began at sundown on Saturday in preparation for the round of family devotions and church services in both morning and afternoon on Sunday. Each service lasted about three hours and contained a combination of prayers, scriptural readings, sermons, and psalm-singing. There were but two sacraments: the Lord's Supper and Baptism. The former was celebrated monthly or bimonthly, usually at the end of the morning service, while the latter was held in the afternoon as needed. Also in the afternoon there were occasional collections for the poor and the admission of new members. In essence, Sunday daylight was spent in the meetinghouses except for a noon recess. It is not surprising that during the Protectorate one observer in London commented caustically, "The Religion of England is preaching and sitting still on Sundays."[11] New England's custom would have seemed identical to that jaundiced eye.

Attendance was also mandatory in the orthodox colonies, at least officially. Thus, the Puritan Sabbath with its intense version of the cosmic and human drama of sin and redemption was a central common experience of the populace throughout the colonial era. Preaching styles varied by cleric and period, as did the fashions in psalm-singing, prayers, and the sacraments. Yet the rudiments remained constant and pervasive, a major force in organizing both the mental and practical lives of thousands of New Englanders for nearly two centuries.[12]

10. Hambrick-Stowe, *Practice of Piety*, 96; Theodore Dwight Bozeman, *To Live Ancient Lives: The Primitivist Dimension in Puritanism* (Chapel Hill, 1988), 73; Increase Mather, *Practical Truths tending to Promote Holiness* (Boston, 1704), 73. See also Davies, *Worship of the American Puritans*, 52–58.

11. Hambrick-Stowe, *Practice of Piety*, 57, 97, 103–4; Thomas Lechford, *Plain-Dealing, or, News from New England* (London, 1642; reprint, Boston, 1867), 16–18; John Evelyn, quoted in Gerald R. Cragg, *Puritanism in the Period of the Great Persecution, 1660–1688* (Cambridge, 1957), 129.

12. Harry S. Stout, *The New England Soul: Preaching and Religious Culture in Colonial New England* (New York, 1986), is masterly on this point. For the implications of Lord's Supper for domestic life, see Amanda Porterfield, *Female Piety in Puritan New England: The Emergence of Religious Humanism* (New York, 1992), 127–33.

Reactions to this austere revolution were mixed. On the one hand, there were gains that helped assure the commitment of many common folk over the generations. The simplicity, clarity, comprehensiveness, and dignity of its forms, combined with the discipline and regularity of its weekly and monthly schedule, provided opportunities for intellectual rigor and emotional intensity that still shine through many of the surviving sermons and prayers. Clerical and pious lay diaries testify to the continuing impact of the Puritan Sabbath in shaping an impressive version of the Christian life.

On the other hand, there were losses derived mostly from the Puritan redefinition of the relationship of the sacred and the profane. For instance, except through the prayers and the days of Thanksgiving or Humiliation, the ritual ties between Christian experience and the agricultural cycle were severed. The church calendar based on the seasons was gone, as were the processionals to bless flocks and fields. Likewise for the maritime population, the christening of ships was discountenanced as pagan—which, however, did not stop the practice. The Church of England (following Catholic tradition) recognized the need for bodily as well as spiritual recreation on the Sabbath and thus allowed sports and merriment. Dancing, drinking, games, and military sports such as archery and wrestling were all part of the traditional Sunday "Day of Rest." Puritans generally were not opposed to physical recreation yet believed that pursuing these activities on Sunday constituted an egregious confusion of the sacred with the profane. "The word Sabbath," one English cleric explained, "signifies not common, but sacred and holy rest."[13]

Not surprisingly, many people even among the pious found this rigorous disjunction difficult to accept in theory or in practice. For some it was simply that their bodies would not be denied. Then as now, dozing during long prayers and sermons was common, a foible that much annoyed the ministers. "To Sleep in the Publick Worship of God," grumbled Cotton Mather in 1713, "is a thing too frequently and easily Practiced by very many People; and even by some noted Professors of Religion, who ought of all Men, to give a Better Example." He wished "That it might grow more fashionable" to prod one another awake. A generation earlier his father blamed this lapse on overindulgence: "When men overcharge themselves with meat and drink, and then come to hear the Word preached, no wonder they fall asleep." He urged stimulation, observing, "If sitting be an occasion of sleeping, rather stand up, then sit and sleep in sin." He was also astonished that many "account it a peccadillo, a sin not worth taking note of." Then, too, dozing in the pews offered the possibility of expressing a wry irreverence. As the senior Mather noted, "Some woful Creatures have been so wicked as to profess they have gone to hear Sermons on purpose, that so they might sleep, finding themselves at such times much disposed that way."[14] That church-going might be a cure for insomnia hardly accorded with the Puritan sense of worship.

Then too there was the impatience of children and youths to be out of the meetinghouse after the long, often tedious services. In 1682 the town of Salem admonished constables and tithingmen to keep watch "for the prevention of the profanation of the Sabbath by Boys playing in and about the meetinghouse and disorderly running down the stairs before the blessing is pronounced." Salem was responding in part to a portion of the Provoking Evils Law of 1675 aimed at preventing "persons turning their backs upon the public worship before it is finished and the blessing pronounced." Nor could persons always wait until near the end of services to indulge their sense of play. Increase Mather complained of laughter during sermons. In Springfield in 1661 a man in his twenties was prosecuted because he had "thrust and tickled" a teenager "and plucked him off his seat three times and squeezed him and made him cry out" during the sermon. It is not surprising that Jasper Danckaerts, a Dutch visitor who belonged to the strict Labadist Anabaptist sect, complained of a Boston service in 1680, "There was no more devotion than in other churches, and even less than at New York [Dutch Reformed]; no respect, no reverence; in a word, nothing but the name of Independents; and that was all."[15]

Of course, such examples of "want of reverence" reflect more the normal ills to which flesh is heir than any ritual or ideological pattern. Essentially there were three more significant types of response: absence from service, mockery, and inclusion of festal elements of the traditional Sabbath. First there was "neglect of the Sabbath," which meant absenting oneself from services in order to work, rest, or play. On occasion violators intended their acts to be interpreted not as lapses but as contempt. In April 1678, for

---

14. C. Mather, *Advice from the Watchtower*, 36; Increase Mather, *Practical Truths Tending to Promote the Power of Godliness* (Boston, 1682), 209–10, 218–19.

15. *Town Records of Salem, Massachusetts, 1629–1691* (Salem, 1868, 1913, 1934), 3:55; *Mass. Recs.* V, 60; Increase Mather, *Practical Truths . . . Godliness*, 214–15; *Pynchon Recs.* 253; Hambrick-Stowe, *Practice of Piety*, 99 for Danckaerts's quote.

instance, a professed Quaker entered a Salem tavern on a Sunday morning and ordered "a pot of beer and a cake." The tavern-keeper, despite laws to the contrary, complied and then invited the customer to join him and his wife at church. But the man refused, for "he scorned to go hear old [John] Higginson [the Salem pastor], for he was an oppressor of the poor and he bound it [his refusal] by swearing in the name of God," an act that cast some doubt on his claim to be a serious Quaker. There were those who went hunting, drove cattle, carried wood and bricks, tried to collect bad debts, "abused Indians for sport," sailed cargoes across harbors, and even pilfered from the houses of the more pious who were away at the meetinghouses. When challenged, such folk often responded with "contemptible words."[16] Thus for some, "neglect" was an overt form of resistance to authority.

"Neglect of the Sabbath" often entailed a vocal anticlericalism of the sort common throughout early modern Europe. One reason was that the ministry was supported by a specific local tax, the minister's rate. It was a visible sign of clerical privilege and status. In 1681 a woman in Lynn defamed the local miller by saying that he "was an old thief and would steal enough to maintain Joseph Whiting," Lynn's pastor. In neighboring Salem in 1685 a joiner "refused to pay, speaking reproachfully of the ministers, if ever he dealt with [them] he'd pay them, but he never dealt with them for anything." Obviously he believed that if he had to run the risks of capitalism, then so should the clergy. When the constable attempted to seize a warming pan for the tax, the joiner bodily threw him out of his house, shouting, "if they would have any rates they must fight for them." The clergy was an economic burden, particularly in the era during and after King Philip's War as the local rates for refugees, widows, orphans, reconstruction, and defense mounted.[17]

Anticlericalism was not merely an economic phenomenon. In Gloucester in 1682 a widow being prosecuted for "neglect of public worship" had also tried to prevent her married daughter from attending by observing that "to go hear your parson or priest or what you will call him is the way to hell." The next year a Marblehead man, on trial for the second time "for obstinately abstaining from the public worship of God," claimed a higher integ-

16. *Essex Recs.* VIII, 110, 147, 226; IX, 151, 455, 586; *Pynchon Recs.* 255, 280, 310; *Plymouth Recs.* V, 16, 27, 51, 61, 87, 99, 118, 152, 157, 254.

17. *Essex Recs.* VIII, 144–45; IX, 472–73; Margaret Spufford, *Small Books and Pleasant Histories: Popular Fiction and Its Readership in Seventeenth-Century England* (Athens, Ga., 1981), 219–20; Martin Scharfe, "The Distance between the Lower Classes and Official Religion: Examples from Eighteenth-Century Wurtemburg Protestantism," in Kaspar von Greyerz, ed., *Religion and Society in Early Modern Europe* (London, 1984), 157–74, esp. 165.

rity by "affirming in a railing manner that cursing was as well pleasing to God as praying, being both done by a hypocrite." Despite the variety of opinions—from Quaker mysticism to agnostic secularism—that seems to have animated articulate "neglect of the Lord's Day," the common thread running through it all was an anticlericalism rooted in an egalitarian resentment of pastoral privilege and influence.[18] Quakers, through the doctrine of the inner light, gave that attitude a more articulate theological warrant.

Nonattendance even in the face of prosecution was not the only means available for expressing egalitarian and anticlerical impulses on Sunday. The second form was mockery, a wonderful way to deflate the pretentious. Some practices, particularly of the Quaker sort, were subversive of or even overtly hostile to the central meaning of the Puritan Sabbath. Services were on occasion interrupted by persons "railing" or "speaking contemptuously" of the pastor or congregation. Sometimes disruption took the form of men or women appearing in church naked or dressed only in sackcloth and daubed with ashes, all intended to symbolize the spiritual poverty of the reformed Sabbath and its devotees.[19]

More common forms of mockery or parody were gently humorous and implied not a rejection of the Sabbath but an affectionate but ironic embrace of it. We have already noted complaints about "playing, sporting, and laughing in sermon time." In taverns on the Sabbath the mockery could become more elaborate. In 1727 one Massachusetts cleric expressed shock at the custom: "Some ridicule Prayer, Reading, and Hearing the Word of God: they'll banter the Sacraments; they'd make Mirth with all Christ's Institutions." Nor were the ceremonies of the Sabbath alone parodied. "They will especially bring the Minister of the Gospel upon the stage, and ridicule the Sons of Levi: their persons become the subject of their bold Jests; they scoff at their Messages, and flout at their offices." The clerics may have forgotten about the medieval Feast of Fools, but the common folk retained some memory of the tradition's value. Such performances were, in fact, an integral part of the traditional European Sunday, which allowed a way to assault pomposity, vent tensions, and indulge humor without denying the value of the Sabbath.[20]

---

18. *Essex Recs.* VIII, 367; IX, 83, 152; Hall, "Religion and Society," 331–32.

19. *Plymouth Recs.* V, 169; VI, 151–52; *Assistants Recs.* I, 127; Carla Gardina Pestana, "The City upon a Hill under Siege: The Puritan Perception of the Quaker Threat to Massachusetts Bay," *NEQ* 56 (1983): 331–32.

20. *Pynchon Recs.* 252, 275–76; John Barnard, *The Nature and Danger of Sinful Mirth* (Boston, 1727), 107–8.

The impulse to mockery was closely related to the third way of profaning the Sabbath, which was to reengraft the festal meanings and customs of the traditional Sunday onto the Puritan rite. On the old Sunday the churchyard was a place for sport and sociability before, during, and after services. There was a strong tendency to do the same in orthodox New England. During the 1660s Plymouth magistrates heard complaints from "sundry towns" of persons "Jesting, sleeping, or the like . . . without the doors of the meetinghouses on the Lord's Day in times of exercise." In 1668 the Plymouth government had to outlaw horse racing on Sunday, while the magistrates of Essex County, Massachusetts, held it "uncomely, offensive, and rude" to race near the "Meetinghouses on the Sabbath." Apparently during the 1670s Ipswich held an unofficial race day on Sundays in the spring, for there were court orders against "running races upon horses or jades in the streets of Ipswich, or for abetting and encouraging others, of laying wagers on any side." Despite the protests, the custom seemingly persisted at least into the 1690s. Loitering, smoking, card-playing, and even indecent exposure could occur outside the meetinghouses during services. Ministers were not slow to complain, "And is it not to be lamented, that in some parts of New England, the Sabbath is so much profaned by Frolicking and merry Diversions?—But is it not eminently sinful for persons to be in a merry frame, while they are at God's house in the time of public worship?" This critic traced the practice to a folk revival of the *Book of Sports* of early Jacobean England. Parliament in 1625, influenced by reformers, passed a law condemning "unlawful exercises and pastimes upon the Lord's Day" to little effect, just as the New England authorities later and vainly tried to suppress the same customs. Festivity could not yet be barred from the churchyards of Old and New England.[21]

For the more pious who were not outside during the services, the opportunity for Sunday sociability came at the noon break. In 1705 Solomon Stoddard noted that "Men do take a mighty Liberty with their Discourses on that day . . . : between the Exercises they will talk of anything, they will discourse of their Corn and Hay, and the prices of Commodities, or almost anything they discourse of on Working Days. They are mute about what they hear [in sermons]. . . . It were a fault in Boys, but Men and Women are guilty, yea, such as pretend high to Religion are greatly culpable in this thing."[22] Stoddard was describing a practice common in Anglican Virginia

21. *Plymouth Recs.*, XI, 214, 224–25, 236; *Essex Recs.* VII, 363–64; Esther Forbes Papers, AAS, box 4, "Introduction," 4; Barnard, *Nature and Danger*, 98–99; Ribton-Turner, *History of Vagabonds*, 147.
22. Stoddard, *Dangers of a Speedy Degeneracy*, 17–18.

or any English place. Friendships, courtships, and economic news and negotiations were all pursued on the Sabbath. Even the sincerely pious would not sacrifice this vital element of community life to the Puritan ideal of a reformed Sabbath.

The noon recess also marked the prime moment for the "Sunday Tavern." The official justification was that persons who lived too far from the meetinghouses to go and return between services could lawfully enter "near Drinking-Houses, that may receive them and refresh them in the intervals." Tavern-keepers asserted that the practice was a public service, while many lay people, even those living nearby, regarded it as a necessity and a right. While granting its inevitability and legality, many a pastor suspected "that with many, the Interest of Sensual Pleasure and Temporal Profit lay at the bottom of all." Cotton Mather rather understated the case by observing in 1713, "Sometimes this proves an occasion for discourses and actions, not very suitable to the Religion of the Sabbath." Here was the best opportunity not merely for sociability but also for commentary on and parody of religious services and ministers, fueled by a festal atmosphere of food and drink. This custom, even with its excesses, was stoutly defended by the populace.²³

In essence, the common folk insisted on the traditional alternation of penitential and festal moods, of spiritual edification and communal pleasures. Puritan pastors, committed to clarifying and separating these themes, could not avoid asking, "How can the Heart be Solemn and Serious, if there be an immediate transition from Mirth and Levity, to Prayer, singing Psalms, Reading or Hearing the Word of God?" Nor could they help suspecting, "Tis a sign our Souls have not been seriously employed in religious Duties, if, as soon as they are over, we get to Laughing and Jesting."²⁴ In this gap between the clergy's suspicions and the pious folk's insistence we have one clear sign of the distinctions between the austere, systematic Puritanism of the ministers and the more eclectic popular religious ethos of New England.

More spectacular, and to the clergy more troublesome, examples were the popular uses of Saturday and Sunday nights. The tone was set as early as 1658 when the Massachusetts General Court noted that "by too sad experience it is observed, the sun being set, both every Saturday and on the Lord's Day, young people take the liberty to walk and sport themselves in the streets or fields . . . and too frequently repair to public houses of entertainment and there

23. John Danforth, *The Vile Prophanations of Prosperity by the Degenerate* (Boston, 1704), 20; C. Mather, *Advice from the Watchtower,* 32; *Plymouth Recs.* XI, 137; *Essex Recs.* VII, 377–78; Claude M. Fuess, *Andover: Symbol of New England* (Andover, Mass., 1959), 113.
24. Barnard, *Nature and Danger,* 103.

sit drinking." To remedy the evil, taverns were supposed to be closed, except for travelers and for the licit "Sunday Tavern" of the noon recess. The regulations were but sporadically enforced, and in the port towns such efforts were likely to encounter serious, even physical, resistance. As Jasper Dankaerts remarked of Boston in 1680, "Saturday evening the constable goes round into all the taverns of the city for the purpose of stopping all noise and debauchery, which frequently causes him to stop his search, before his search causes the debauchery to stop." In Salem in the same period tithingmen attempting "to clear the houses" were occasionally forcibly ejected "with scornful speeches" and threats by both owners and patrons. For their profane denizens, water-front taverns were places where the Puritan writ did not run.[25]

Sunday dusk, marking the official end of the Sabbath, was when the more pious were most apt to enter the drinking houses to celebrate and socialize. On these nights "waggery" and even an occasional "fray" tended to erupt not only in the ports but also in the more sedate rural towns. Increase Mather, lamenting this joining of the religious with the overtly impious, observed, "I cannot speak it without some anquish of Spirit, there is more wickedness committed usually on that night than in all the week besides." It was a time for release from the rigors of the Sabbath, for boisterous humor and general rowdiness.[26]

The Puritan Sabbath, in short, reflected a complex religious and social order in which reformed and popular themes merged and contested. The sacred day provided one important setting for what Lance Bertelsen, in speaking of eighteenth-century English experience, called the "rituals of power and the counter-rituals of irreverence."[27] The line between reverence and irreverence, between assertions of power and popular affirmations of authority, was not always clear, however. Indeed, it was the very ambiguity of the symbolic language of ritual and of the intentions of those using it that provided much of the dynamism of early modern cultural and social experience.

Training Day was a civic as opposed to a religious event, which allowed opportunity, parallel to the Sabbath, to express and explore those tensions and agreements.[28] Besides a means of military preparation, this public cer-

25. *Mass. Recs.* IV, pt. 1, 347; IV, pt. 2, 562; *Plymouth Recs.* XI, 236; J. Franklin Jameson, ed., *Journal of Jasper Danckaerts, 1679–1680* (New York, 1913), 274; *Essex Recs.* VII, 110, 246–47; VIII, 232.

26. *Pynchon Recs.* 268, 279–80, 317; *Essex Recs.* VIII, 101–2, 227; Increase Mather, *A Call to Heaven* (Boston, 1679), 88.

27. Lance Bertelsen, *The Nonsense Club: Literature and Popular Culture, 1749–1764* (Oxford, 1986), 7.

28. The substance of this section on training days appeared in Richard P. Gildrie, "De-

emony was also a ritual about social conflicts and communal unity. As with the Sabbath, the ritual itself and its variations, spontaneous or planned, both reflected and shaped the colonists' sense of identity and purpose. Training Day combined the elements of a parade, public holiday, political rally, church service, and sports event with military training. In short, it was a recreational and ideological occasion in which the society displayed itself ceremoniously to its members while preparing them for the necessities of war. In discussing the militia system as a whole, T. H. Breen wrote, "it was as much an expression of Puritan social ideas as were the New England town meeting or the Congregational churches."[29] Training Day was the confirmatory ritual of the militia system, much as Sunday worship affirmed the religious order. In the one, theoretically, the saints were in the pews, and in the other they were under arms.

New England's militia was, of course, a variant of the traditional English system and was a remarkably flexible institution in both organization and military uses.[30] Unlike their English counterparts, the New England trainbands included servants and the poor together with propertied adult males. In England the trend was to disarm the lower classes so as to maintain public order, while in Virginia slaves were excluded on similar grounds. But in New England the requirement to train or at least to maintain arms was virtually universal for the adult male population. With such broad participation came a tendency toward democratic control, a tendency ratified by Puritan covenantal thought. Until 1668 all company and regimental officers in Massachusetts were elected by militiamen, just as church members chose pastors and townsmen elected selectmen. After that date the General Court made appointments on the basis of nominations from local militia committees. Not surprisingly, the command structure of companies and regiments closely resembled the distribution of social and political power in the towns and counties. Men coveted militia ranks as signs of local prestige confirmed by higher colonial authority.[31]

---

fiance, Diversion, and the Exercise of Arms: The Several Meanings of Training Days in Colonial New England," *Military Affairs* (now *Journal of Military History*) 52 (1988): 53–55, and is used with the kind permission of the editors.

29. T. H. Breen, "English Origins and New World Development: The Case of the Covenanted Militia in Seventeenth-Century Massachusetts," *Past and Present* 57 (1972): 82.

30. William L. Shea, "The First American Militia," *Military Affairs* 46 (1982): 18; Lawrence D. Cress, *Citizens in Arms: The Army and the Militia in American Society to the War of 1812* (Chapel Hill, 1982), 5.

31. Breen, "English Origins," 82–87, 92; Douglas Edward Leach, *Arms for Empire: A Military History of the British Colonies in North America, 1607–1763* (New York, 1972), 16–17.

Usually held monthly in wartime and quarterly in peace, Training Day itself was a visual and ceremonial confirmation of the standing order and its worldview. The particular military exercises varied in each session, but the general pattern was constant. Summoned by drum or trumpet, men brought their weapons onto the field and were called into close order by their commander. In their ordered rows, formed up by sergeants, they represented the armed dignity of God's people. The day opened and closed with prayer, usually led by a town's pastor but occasionally in larger places by an officer. Surprised, an English visitor remarked of the Boston exercises in 1686 that he was familiar with the maneuvers, "But solemn Prayer in the field, upon a Day of Training, I never knew but in New England, where, it seems, it is a common custom." After the concluding prayer the whole formation, led again by a cleric or officer, sang a psalm.[32] This practice was a more active demonstration of solidarity than simply listening to a prayer.

Within this explicitly religious framework came the exercises of the day. The morning session usually included roll call, weapons inspection, and rough manual of arms with particular attention to training novices. These were commonly followed by field maneuvers including "facings" and "doublings" for concentrated musket fire. The morning ended with "volley fire." After a noon recess, usually spent in taverns, the formation returned at drum call for transacting unit business such as assessing fines for absence, accepting new colors, or finding volunteers for prolonged service. The remaining portion of the afternoon until roughly 3:00 P.M. saw marksmanship contests, mock battles, or athletic competitions.

Training Day naturally took on a festive atmosphere. Nearly all the adult males left fields and shops to participate. The activities of the day, with the noise and color of a parade and a sporting event, took place on common land in or near the village center, making it even more likely that wives, sweethearts, children, and the elderly would come to cheer, to laugh, to drink, and to be impressed with volley fire and mock battle. The holiday spirit was a traditional element. In the England of James I one Lord Lieutenant contemptuously dismissed the militia musters as a "May Game."[33]

Some forms of recreation—running, wrestling, casting the sledge, shooting at the mark, playing at cudgels—traditionally served military purposes. Also a festal element, athletic contests complete with admiring spectators

32. Leach, *Arms for Empire*, 27–36; John Dunton, *Life and Errors* (London, 1705), 1:114; Thomas, ed., *Diary of Samuel Sewall*, 1:453–54. There were sermons and prayers at English militia training but apparently not so regularly as in New England.

33. Breen, "English Origins," 77–78.

encouraged a sense of individual competition and display as well as communal unity as in an English "May Game." As a Boston matron traveling through Connecticut during King William's War wrote:

> And on training days the Youth divert themselves by Shooting at the Target, as they call it, (but it very much resembles a pillory,) where hee that hitts neerest the white has some yards of Red Ribbon presented him, which being tied to his hatt band, the two ends streeming down his back, he is Led away in Triumph, with great applause, as the winners of the Olympiack Games.[34]

Thus were many of the traditional recreations of the English countryside preserved among American Puritans.

Another vital aspect of the ritual was for officers to demonstrate publicly their claim to be an English gentry, albeit a reformed one, by donating and conferring the prizes as was common in England. To reinforce further the claim to separate and higher status, the officers after training generally withdrew to a dinner to which the clergy but not the common troopers were invited. The men, together with wives and sweethearts, went to a tavern where they could often expect that their officers had earlier arranged for food and drink to be available. If the militiamen were particularly pleased with the day's events and their leaders, they gathered late in the evening outside the place where the officers dined and gave them a few "huzzahs." Officers thus treated had their claim to social as well as military authority joyously affirmed.[35]

The careful cultivation of a deferential relationship between officers and men was not only a military courtesy but a social imperative. Training Day, like the Sabbath and other official ceremonies, provided opportunities for the "counter-rituals of irreverence" in the venting of social tensions and personal animosities. There were acts of defiance. In Hadley during King Philip's War a muster turned into a "riotous assembly" in which a corporal was set upon with cudgels. In Marblehead in 1678 one of two men charged with "refusing to show their armes" and "threatening officers" shouted at his captain, "wee are brought to a brave passe to be ordered by such a pittifull

---

34. Malcolm Freiberg, ed., *The Journal of Madame Knight* (Boston, 1971), 20.
35. Richard L. Bushman, "American High-Style and Vernacular Cultures," in Jack P. Greene and J. R. Pole, eds., *Colonial British America: Essays in the New History of the Early Modern Era* (Baltimore, 1984), 373; Thomas, ed., *Diary of Samuel Sewall*, 1:137–38, 453–54; Francis G. Walett, ed., *The Diary of Ebenezer Parkman, 1703–1782* (Worcester, Mass., 1974), 43, 61, 80.

fellow as thee" (note the contemptuous use of the personal pronoun). A lieutenant refereeing a wrestling match in Topsfield in 1685 suffered pistol wounds to the face for attempting to prevent a man from riding his horse into the ring for a better view. When the trooper saw that the officer was only wounded, he remarked, "then I will goe and make an end of him."[36] Egalitarian and individualistic impatience with restraint found expression here as elsewhere in Massachusetts social life.

More commonly, rowdiness and defiance were fueled by alcohol. Indeed, when trouble did not erupt it was deemed worthy of note. In 1641 Governor John Winthrop, remembering English training debacles, took pride in the fact that in Boston "About 1200 men were exercised in most sorts of land service; yet it was observed that there was no man drunk, though there was plenty of wine and strong beer in the town, not an oath sworn, no quarrel, nor any hurt done." Nearly a century later a Westborough pastor marveled that at a regimental muster of eleven companies "there was so little hurt Done and that there was So little intemperance, Rabblement, and Riot." Indictments for "scurrilous language and riotous behavior, fighting and breaking the peace to the hazard of lives" were frequent. A certain element of bawdiness too was expected, particularly in the late afternoon and the evening when men and women gathered in the ordinaries. Occasionally these episodes escalated from "lascivious carriage" to attempted rape. Festal rowdiness was deemed a traditional right, and attempts by civil and military officers to curb it were resisted. The freedom of the tavern on that day as on others was sacrosanct. One man, for example, claimed that before he and his brother would submit to spending time in the stocks for "abusive carriage" toward a woman in an ordinary, "he would stave the stocks and burn the meetinghouse," those two major symbols of Puritan attempts to discipline the profane.[37]

Not surprisingly, contemporary critics noted the similarity between English and New English conduct on these occasions. "I will tell you how we breed up Souldiers in both Old and New England," fumed Samuel Nowell in an artillery sermon in the aftermath of the catastrophic King Philip's War.

36. *Pynchon Recs.* 284–86; *Essex Recs.* VII, 41–42; IX, 606; Morrison Sharp, "Leadership and Democracy in the Early New England System of Defense," *American Historical Review* 50 (1945): 244–60.

37. Sharp, "Leadership and Democracy," 248; *Essex Recs.* VII, 118–19; VIII, 185–86; IX, 539, 599, 606; Walett, ed., *Diary of Ebenezer Parkman,* 69, 99; Roger Thompson, "Adolescent Culture in Colonial Massachusetts," *Journal of Family History* 9 (1984): 131–33; Lyle Koehler, *A Search for Power: The "Weaker Sex" in Seventeenth-Century New England* (Urbana, Ill., 1980), 207–9.

"Every Farmers son, when he goes to the Market-Town, must have money
in his purse, and when he meets with his Companions, they goe to the
Tavern or Ale-house, and seldome away before Drunk, or well tippled." In
1705 Solomon Stoddard too complained that "When Training is over, men
go to the Taverns, sit tipling till an unseasonable time in the Night, those
exercises end in revelling." He also noted that Training Day was not the only
official ritual so used. "So at Court Times, especially in Country Towns,
there is a great deal of riot; there is more tippling at these times than in a
month before. [Harvard] Commencement are times of riot. So on Lecture
Days many people go from the House of God to the Tavern; Lecture Days
are Market Days for Inn-keepers." The people of provincial Massachusetts
were hardly deprived "of the ritualistic safety valves which other contemporary societies provided."[38]

After 1650, as the population became denser and local traditions had time
to develop, various traditional popular rituals of carnivalesque or satiric
intent emerged independent of the official cycles of church and state. The
simplest of these was the public posting of "libels." In Boston in 1673 two
servants were convicted "of Setting up libells" on a neighbor's "dore &
abusing him therein & other bad actions & carriages towards him & the
neighborhood," including rather noisy "nightwalking." That same year a
physician was charged with "making Verses tending to the reproach of the
late Governor Richard Bellingham, Esq. & of the Ministers." After rebuking
some gamblers on a Sabbath eve in 1699, Samuel Sewall encountered a
variant. "A Pack of Cards are found strewed over my fore-yard, which, 'tis
supposed, some might throw there to mock me, in spite of what I did at the
Exchange Tavern last Satterday Night." Nor was this only an urban phenomenon. In 1727 Mary Bradish, a Westborough church member, penned
a public confession "in Composing a Numb: of verses which hath been very
Scandelous" aimed at satirizing a town committee established "for ye finding
out who Crit [criticized] ye Custom of the Town." Apparently the committee was investigating a string of earlier libels when Mary Bradish responded with some salutary ridicule.[39]

---

38. Samuel Nowell, *Abraham in Arms* (Boston, 1678), 15; Stoddard, *Dangers of a Speedy
Degeneracy*, 20; Roger Thompson, "The Puritans and Prurience: Aspects of the Restoration
Book Trade," in H. C. Allen and Roger Thompson, eds., *Contrast and Connection: Bicen-
tennial Essays in Anglo-American History* (Athens, Ohio, 1976), 52. The problem persisted far
into the eighteenth century. See Fred Anderson, *A People's Army: Massachusetts Soldiers and
Society in the Seven Years War* (Chapel Hill, 1987), esp. 75–78.

39. *Suffolk Recs.* 225, 235, 265; Thomas, ed., *Diary of Samuel Sewall*, 1:81, 411, 2:821;
"Mary Bradish," Parkman Papers, AAS, box 2, folder 2; Laurel Thatcher Ulrich, *Good Wives:*

There were episodes of "rough riding," the English version of charivari, against those whom the perpetrators saw as violating popular sexual or economic mores. In 1675 nine ship carpenters, when charged with taking another "upon a pole & by violence carrying of him from the North end of Boston as far as the Town dock; which occasioned a great tumult of people," explained that "they understood such things were usual in England" as punishment for those seeking skilled work who had not completed an apprenticeship. "Musicke and Dansing" at midnight beneath the windows of newlyweds was not uncommon. But more menacingly, in the countryside south of Boston in 1707 "7 or 8 join'd together" to punish a man suspected of wife-beating, "call'd the Man out of his Bed, quilefully praying him to shew them the way; then . . . tore off his Cloaths and whip'd with Rods; to chastise him for carrying it hardly to his wife." Popular anger was more satisfying than the court system even though a judge that very term had "sentenced a woman that whip'd a Man, to be whip'd; said a woman that had lost her Modesty was like Salt that had lost its savor; good for nothing but to be cast to the Dunghill."[40] Even after three generations of Puritan preaching and legal reform, the honor of families and "modesty" of women were still being enforced in extralegal public ceremonies.

Cotton Mather too was apparently a common target of mockery. "There are knotts of riotous Young Men in the Town," he confided to his diary. "On purpose to insult Piety, they will come under my Window in the Middle of the Night, and sing profane and filthy Songs. The last night they did so, and fell upon People with Clubs, taken off my Wood-pile." A certain rowdy exuberance was a frequent element of these forays. By 1761, after considerable anglicization, it was impossible to distinguish between episodes of "rough riding" in the Massachusetts countryside, which had been occurring in one form or another for a century, and those in the home country. In Westfield a mob, annoyed by a woman's adulteries and "Maltreatment of her husband," forcibly "set her on a rail and carried her on their shoulders, they set her likewise on a sharp back horse, carried her along, hooting at her and ringing Cow Bells and blowing horns." Another traditional vehicle for popular social and moral commentary was informal theatricals. In 1673 ten men of Hampshire County were fined "for theire uncivill Immodest and

Image and Reality in the Lives of Women in Northern New England, 1650–1750 (New York, 1980, 1982), 65.

40. *Suffolk Recs.* 602; Roger Thompson, "Adolescent Culture," 131; Thomas, ed., *Diary of Samuel Sewall,* 1:572.

beastly acting" in an "uncivill play." One suspects that both sexual and social satire account for the court's choice of adjectives.[41]

After the loss of the Charter in 1685 the revival of traditional rituals tied to English ecclesiastical and civil calendars became more pronounced. A Maypole with "a garland upon it" was erected in Charlestown in 1687, and attempts by the watch to cut it down were forcibly resisted. Around Salisbury by 1689 the spring rites had become fairly elaborate. This account also suggests that the ritual had been going on for some years:

> With Bread and Beer, a Duz. or two Come dancing down the Hill the Monday before ascension day; i.e. the two persons last married whom they call the Lord and Lady, but now generally there is a stated Dancer, a merry arch jocose Man, who procures a Lady. A Horse carries about Sixteen Gallons in two tuns, which is worth two pence, to some of the furthest Houses from the Wells. One is for washing, the other for brewing.

A communion in bread and beer, the traditional symbols of Lord, Lady, and Morris Dancer, formed a rite of fertility and cleansing whose essential elements reach back into medieval villages. The complexity of the celebration indicates that it was no mere Elizabethan atavism but an expression of an ancient social and religious sensibility still capable of shaping people's relations to each other, to nature, and to God.[42]

The godly clerics and magistrates, of course, denounced these rites as "superstition" and as examples of "the Vain Conversation received by Tradition," but many of the populace, including the orthodox, happily participated in their preservation and development. The piety and social ethic of the common folk of provincial Massachusetts were more eclectic, more willing to alternate carnivalesque and Lenten moods, and more apt to mock what they sincerely held to be sacred than the reformers could comfortably allow. On Shrove Tuesday in 1712 some forty Bostonians, encouraged by English officials, enjoyed a "Mock Sermon" that was "delivered in costume" at a tavern. The talk was "full of Monstrous profaneness and obscenity," according to Samuel Sewall.[43] One wonders how the laughing spectators interpreted the incident. Is it not conceivable that Rabelais was as much a

41. Ford, ed., *Diary of Cotton Mather*, 2:216–17; Diary of John Ballantine, 21 October 1761, AAS; *Pynchon Recs.* 276–77.
42. Thomas, ed., *Diary of Samuel Sewall*, 1:199.
43. Ibid., 2:680, 680n.

shaper of New England's heritage as Calvin? And might it be that most of the people, had they been directly exposed to both, would have seen no inherent contradiction in that both sought to express and inculcate a sense of individual human dignity over and against the arrogance of church and state?

In their capacity to embrace the Puritan ceremonial cycle, add traditional meanings and practices to it, and also develop independent forms of often ancient provenance, the populace of the region demonstrated that they were not oppressed victims or mindless followers of Puritan pastors and magistrates. They were, on the whole, pious folk who took what suited them (and resisted what did not) from both the Puritan reforms and their popular traditions. The presence of both godly ritual and profane interpretation allowed those whom David Hall has called "horse-shed Christians" to participate in official ceremonies while avoiding full commitment to godly values, a choice that typified the civil conversation.[44] It also provided a forum where profane and godly meanings could conflict and merge publicly into changing understandings of personal liberty and social responsibility. This process, together with the resultant debates, was vital in the formation of New England and American culture.

44. Hall, *Worlds of Wonder*, 130–32.

SIX

Dark Corners and Popular Piety

"We cannot but solemnly bear witness," asserted the members of the Reforming Synod of 1679, "against that practice of settling Plantations without
any Ministry amongst them, which is to prefer the world before the Gospel."[1]
Echoing the ancient Judeo-Christian judgment that "Covetousness is Idolatry," the synod pointed to the dynamism of geographic and economic
expansion as a threat to "Gospel Order" because "farms and merchandising
have been preferred before the things of God."

Unchecked quest for property, the reformers worried, risked creating
the same sorts of "dark corners" bereft of learned ministry and strong congregations that had alarmed their Elizabethan predecessors and contemporaries in the north and west of England. Characteristically they expected no
better of the profane. The heart of their concern was that "There have been
in many professors [church members] an insatiable desire after Land and
worldly Accommodations, yea, so as to forsake Churches and Ordinances, and
to live like Heathen, only that so they might have Elbow-Room enough in
the world." Here too popular and Puritan aspirations overlapped and conflicted, for all favored expansion and yet disagreed over priorities within that
process.

The question of geographic "dark corners" inevitably raises the issue of
popular piety. What were the religious assumptions and resources of New
Englanders bereft of orthodox pastors and regular congregations? Also, in the
imagery of the reformers a geographic wilderness suggested a personal, internal wilderness as well, the "dark corners" of the soul. What many clergy
saw as terrible danger seemed like opportunity to some laity. These differing

1. [Increase Mather], *The Necessity of Reformation* (Boston, 1679), 7; Christopher Hill,
"Puritans and 'The Dark Corners of the Land,'" in his *Change and Continuity in Seventeenth-
Century England* (Cambridge, Mass., 1975), 3–47.

perspectives represent another vital place where the Reformation of Manners engaged the complex folk heritage of the populace.

As usual, the reformers' criticisms of the frontier were both religious and moral. To allow new towns "to set down without Gods Ordinances, which are signs of Gods presence," argued James Allen in his 1679 election sermon, was a violation of the Bay Colony's providential role apt to call down divine wrath. Also, widespread ignorance in these places threatened both orthodoxy and good conduct. Allen hoped that the General Court might find some remedy: "Where persons are not fit to judge for themselves who are fit to administer the holy things of God, provide some way that Heterodox and ungodly ones may not be encouraged; Tares will sooner grow than wheat."[2]

The synod combined religious and moral dangers in the evocative simile "to live like Heathen." This was, of course, both a classical reference to Christian history and a contemporary one to the Indians of New England. King Philip's War was barely over when Increase Mather interpreted that disaster as God's use of this symbolic connection to chastise his wayward people. "No doubt but one reason why the Lord hath let loose the Heathen against us hath been, because some Plantations have been erected and yet no publique acknowledgment of God amongst them, but they have lived like *Heathen,* without Sabbaths, without the Word and prayer." The war had devastated the frontier. Yet, Mather warned the General Court, "People are ready to run wild into the woods again and to be as Heathenish as ever if you do not prevent it." Thus the "Heathen" represented not merely an external threat but a continuing possibility among the English themselves.[3] In the reformers' minds at least, the "heathenism" of the Indians and of their own frontiersmen distinctly resembled the "Old Paganism" of the traditional English popular culture they sought to reshape.

Using the reformers' primary identifying mark as places without settled or adequate churches and ministry, "Dark Corners" were to be found during the late seventeenth century in Maine, Long Island, the inland Massachusetts frontier, and even in some of the more turbulent waterfront towns such as Marblehead. Writing of Long Island in 1677, a Connecticut pastor, John Bishop, observed to Increase Mather that the gospel ought to be preached there, for "the novelty of the thing may bring them to hear." After a visit he strongly suspected that there "may be many young ones grown & growing

---

2. James Allen, *New Englands Choicest Blessing* (Boston, 1679), 13.
3. Increase Mather, *A Discourse Concerning the Dangers of Apostacy* [1677 sermon] (Boston, 1685), 103–4; John Canup, "'The Cry of Sodom Enquired Into': Bestiality and the Wilderness of Human Nature," AAS *Proceedings* 98, pt. 1 (1988): 113–34, esp. 116.

up, that never lived under the meanes, & scarce ever heard sermon in all their lives, some of them." Maine was also notorious. Typical was this observation about a magistrate at Pemaquid in the 1680s: "He was a strict sabbatizer and met with considerable difficulty in the discharge of his office from the immoralities of a people who had long lived lawless." William Phips, the first governor of Massachusetts under the 1691 charter, was born in Maine in 1650 and grew up without contact with a settled ministry. He was baptized as an adult by Cotton Mather.[4]

An English traveler, John Josselyn, remarked on the rowdy egalitarianism of Maine fisherfolk:

> If a man of quality chance to come where they are roystering and gulling in Wine with a dear felicity, he must be sociable and Roly-poly with them, taking of their liberal cups as freely, or else be gone, which is best for him, for when Wine in their guts is at full Tide, they quarrel, fight, and do one another mischief, which is the conclusion of their drunken compotations.

Incidentally, this type of drinking bout, which was virtually a ritual in traditional English popular culture, seemed echoed in Indian conduct. The Indians, however, were more prone to mystic uses as well, a rarity among Englishmen. As James Axtell recently observed, "Inebriation served variously as an inflater of self-esteem in times of social and spiritual pressure from the invaders, as a socially sanctioned time-out in which aggression could be released without consequence, and as a short cut to a dream-like state of religious possession." This coincidence, along with similar ones, was not lost on the reforming clerics.[5]

The social and moral conditions in the Massachusetts fishing towns and their gradual incorporation into the Puritan order in the eighteenth century have been deftly described by Daniel Vickers and Christine Leigh Heyrman. Marblehead had been settled for nearly fifty years before a church was formed in 1681. Needless to say, the influence of the Salem church, which

---

4. "Mather Correspondence," 302, 303; Allen T. Vaughan and Edward W. Clark, eds., *Puritans among the Indians: Accounts of Captivity and Redemption* (Cambridge, Mass., 1981), 95–96; Kenneth Silverman, *The Life and Times of Cotton Mather* (New York, 1984), 80; Charles E. Clark, *The Eastern Frontier: The Settlement of Northern New England, 1610–1763* (New York, 1970).

5. John Josselyn, *An Account of Two Voyages to New England* (London, 1675; reprint, Boston, 1865), 161–62; James Axtell, *The Invasion Within: The Contest of Cultures in Colonial North America* (New York, 1985), 64–65.

had nominal jurisdiction over Marblehead, was minimal and sporadic. In 1714 John Bernard, after reluctantly accepting the Marblehead pastorate, remarked that the people were "as rude, swearing, drunken and fighting a crew as they were poor . . . contented to be slaves that digged the mines, and left the merchants of Boston, Salem, and Europe to carry away the gains." As an example, the enraged assault of Marblehead women against Indian captives during King Philip's War seems reminiscent of the climax of Euripides' *Bacchae*.[6] In not only killing but also dismembering the prisoners, this female mob expressed a profound passion, immediately indulged—the very antithesis of the godly social vision.

The other "Dark Corner," more explicitly on the agenda of the synod, was the frontier. Maine, the fishing towns, and Long Island were not attracting pious, respectable settlers in large numbers. The frontier was, and there the possibility of "apostacy" or "degeneracy" into barbarism seemed strongest while the risk from the other peripheries was merely contamination by bad example. After King Philip's War the peril seemed real indeed. For example, in the experience of the first five towns founded in what became Worcester County there emerged a pattern of the sort that alarmed the reformers.

At first all was normal. Lancaster, incorporated in 1653, had a minister within five years. Mendon had a pastor from the date of its founding in 1667. But badly exposed Brookfield, founded in 1673, was devastated by the war. Nearing recovery by 1692, it still had no church when it was attacked that year and again in 1710. No church was formed until 1717. In Worcester and Oxford the story was similar. Granted to a set of proprietors in 1668, no serious settlement began at Worcester until 1685. For sixteen years the town developed without a settled ministry until it was depopulated by war from 1702 to 1713. With a new population dominated by Irish Protestant immigrants, the town did not form a church until 1719 and held its first formal town meeting in 1722. Oxford's settlement under a grant to Joseph Dudley and William Stoughton began in 1686 with a group of Huguenots soon joined by New Englanders. Its first town meeting was not until 1713, and its first church was organized in 1721. The pressures of war, ethnic differences,

6. Daniel Vickers, "The First Whalemen of Nantucket," *WMQ* 40 (1983): 560–83; Daniel Vickers, "Work and Life on the Fishing Periphery of Essex County, Massachusetts, 1630–1675," in David D. Hall and David Grayson Allen, eds., *Seventeenth-Century New England* (Boston, 1984), 83–117; Christine Leigh Heyrman, *Commerce and Culture: The Maritime Communities of Colonial Massachusetts* (New York, 1984), quote on 107; James Axtell, "The Vengeful Women of Marblehead: Robert Roule's Deposition of 1677," *WMQ* 31 (1974): 647–52; Laurel Thatcher Ulrich, *Good Wives: Images and Reality in the Lives of Women in Northern New England, 1650–1750* (New York, 1980, 1982), 193–94.

and proprietary distance obviously account for these deviations from the standard pattern of Puritan organization, which were nonetheless worrisome to the reformers. No new towns were founded in the region until Westborough east of Worcester in 1717, which took seven years to establish a church. In all subsequent settlements to 1750 churches were formed within five years.[7]

Given this chronology, it is not surprising that the height of expressions of concern over these and similar border settlements came during the period of greatest frontier disruption from 1690 to 1720. In 1702 in *A Letter to Ungospellized Plantations,* Cotton Mather predictably asserted that "A little Village of Believers on the Lord Jesus Christ, with a Good *Minister* of the Gospel among them, is a very Paradise, in comparison of the richest and largest Plantations which are *Ungospelized.*" As support for this proposition the younger Mather succinctly stated the central program of the Reformation of Manners, including its stress on "family government": "Where the Gospel of Christ comes in the power of it, it marvelously rectifies all *Societies;* All *Societies* and particularly *Families,* are brought into more *Excellent* and *Beautiful* Order, where the Gospel has the Regulating of them." The dignity inculcated by Christianity, rightly understood, "*ennobles* mankind, and Advances our Nature into those Flights of Reason, and Goodness, and Comfort, which make one man differ from another, as visibly as any man from a bruit." His trilogy of reason, goodness, and comfort, which were the source and purpose of proper manners in this tradition, marked off civilized persons and societies from the bestial.[8]

Five years later, the colony was still in the midst of harrowing border warfare. Cotton Mather once again stewed over the "many poor People, in a Land of unwalled Villages," an image he meant to be interpreted both literally and morally. The frontier folk he thought generally "to be a very religious People, yett there was much Irreligion and Profaneness and Disorder in many of them." In short, he saw the usual mixture of pious and profane impulses in popular mores as a special danger in the wilderness. As a response he published a sermon of advice to be circulated in the afflicted areas. The burden was "that you would *Watchfully* Avoid and Suppress all Sinful Disorders, which may begin at any Time to appear among you."[9]

7. Peter Whitney, *The History of the County of Worcester in the Commonwealth of Massachusetts* (Worcester, 1793), 25–27, 68–73, 82–84, 328–35; John L. Brooke, *The Heart of the Commonwealth: Society and Political Culture in Worcester Country, Massachusetts, 1713–1865* (New York, 1989), 5–10.

8. Cotton Mather, *A Letter to Ungospellized Plantations* (Boston, 1702), 10.

9. Worthington C. Ford, ed., *The Diary of Cotton Mather* (New York, 1912), 1:593; Cotton Mather, *Frontiers Well-Defended* (Boston, 1707), 22.

His effort was not an exercise in irrelevant and insensitive moralizing to folk in peril but rather a practical observation that a disciplined life meant better preparation to meet danger. Good order was not a luxury but a matter of survival. To be drunk, asleep, or quarreling while on duty in a watch-house was to turn a settlement and its people over to the Indians and French. The first care was "to have *Well-Ordered Families*," the core of community life; then the evils of "Profane Swearing," "Sabbath-Breaking," "Unchastity," "Dishonesty," and "Drunkenness, . . . that worse than Brutish Vice," should be suppressed as sources of contention and weakness as well as violations of religious practice. It seemed clear to him that strong churches and settled ministers were military necessities, signs of civilized life, and pledges to God and the colonists that orthodoxy could survive in the wilderness.[10]

One particularly galling indication of failure on the frontier was the occasional conversion of English captives "into the *Delusions* and *Idolatries* of *Popery*," that most potent symbol and embodiment of the "Old Paganism." Mather urged pious laity and clerics, "Both Publicly and Privately Endeavour that you may have a People of *Well-Instructed Protestants*" on the frontiers. To that end he included two short anti-Catholic catechisms in his pamphlet. "God forbid, That a Popish Priest should outdo a Protestant Minister in his Industry." Of course New Englanders were not the only English prone to defect into Indian or French culture and society. But the ideologically sensitive New England pastors took these conversions particularly to heart.[11]

The weakness that Mather emphasized was not so much doctrinal as ritualistic. The Puritans' best bulwark, he and others thought, was prayer—especially family prayer, that marvelous device for appropriating and reinforcing tenets and rules of conduct while maintaining the solidarity of groups. Mather fumed, "We have been told, That some of our English People never heard a Family-Prayer in their Lives, till they came into the Wigwams of the Indians, who had made Captives of them." He was appalled that the "Common Apology for this more than Common Impiety, is; We know not how to Pray." To be without this essential spiritual technology was to be helpless in the face of the psychological trauma of captivity. Especially

10. C. Mather, *Frontiers*, 26–34, 38–39.
11. Ibid., 49–50; James Axtell, "The White Indians of Colonial America," *WMQ* 32 (1975): 55–88; A. Irving Hallowell, "American Indians, White and Black: The Phenomenon of Transculturation," *Current Anthropology* 4 (1963): 519–31; Alden T. Vaughan and Daniel K. Richter, "Crossing the Cultural Divide: Indians and New Englanders, 1605–1763," AAS *Proceedings* 90 (1980): 23–99; Ulrich, *Good Wives*, 208–13.

horrifying was to hear this "Strange Pretence" from those who came from "gospellized plantations" where they "hear Sermons every Week," together with the benefits of "Psalters and Bibles and Catechisms in their Hands, which lay Matter of Prayers in every Page." The external means for encouraging personal and familial piety and reform broke down in these cases. At this, Mather was reduced to despairing denunciation: "Or can the most Ignorant among you call to mind the Condition of your own *Souls* & of your Families, without breaking forth into Cries to Heaven!"[12]

For their part, many of the Indians grasped the centrality of public and private prayer to the Puritans' cultural power. Those who (largely under the tutelage of John Eliot) converted to English ways called themselves Praying Indians in order to establish a new identity and orientation. Their new societies were called Praying Towns. In their long dialogues and questionings recorded by Eliot they sought to understand for their own purposes the fundamental Puritan notions of sin, salvation, and prayer so as to resolve such perennial issues as child-rearing and community life that beset them as their native culture disintegrated.[13] Similarly, Catholic liturgy and prayer exercised a strong pull on those captive English who experienced the demoralization of a collapsing frontier from 1675 to 1725.

Combining didacticism with stirring melodrama, the Puritan captivity narratives testified as well to the importance of prayer, Sabbath observance, and regular church life. In one of the best of the genre, Mary Rowlandson, a minister's wife taken from Lancaster during King Philip's War, lamented that "On the Sabbath Days I could look upon the sun and think how people were going to the house of God to have their souls refreshed and then home and their bodies also, but I was destitute of both." With the pain of loss came the memories that sustained her sense of identity and commitment to the ways of the godly. "I remembered how on the night before and after the Sabbath when my family was about me and relations and neighbors with us, we could pray and sing, and then refresh our bodies with the good creatures of God, and then have a comfortable bed to lie down on." By vivid examples, she evoked the same standards of reason, goodness, and comfort that Cotton Mather later used to separate wilderness from civil life.[14]

12. C. Mather, *Frontiers,* 45–47.

13. Robert James Naeher, "Dialogue in the Wilderness: John Eliot and the Indian Exploration of Puritanism as a Source of Meaning, Comfort, and Ethnic Survival," *NEQ* 62 (1989): 346–68, esp. 348.

14. Vaughan and Clark, eds., *Puritans among the Indians,* 56; K. Z. Derounian, "Puritan Orthodoxy and the 'Survivor Syndrome' in Mary Rowlandson's Indian Captivity Narrative," *Early American Literature* 22 (1987): 82–93.

Narratives from the "dark corners" made the same point about prayers and Sabbaths while denouncing the "covetousness" that reputedly created such conditions. In a 1690 example, edited by Cotton Mather, Hannah Swarton was provoked by her captivity "to consider of all my sins for which the Lord did punish me." One that "lay very heavy upon my spirit many a time [was] that I had left the public worship and ordinances of God where I formerly lived (viz. at Beverly) to remove to the north part of Casco Bay where there was no church or minister of the Gospel." Having gained "large accommodations in the world," the family was also "exposing our children to be bred ignorantly like Indians and ourselves to forget what we had been formerly instructed in." Then came the judgment: "so we turned our backs upon God's ordinances to get this world's goods. But now God hath stripped off these things also."[15]

New England's "dark corners," often appearing on the agricultural and fishing frontiers, were in their primitiveness something of a refuge not only for religious dissenters but also for those indifferent or hostile to Puritan moral standards. As any reader of colonial southern literature knows, concern over "the slatternly way of life, godlessness, mere brutishness of the frontier" was hardly restricted to New England clerics. These regions, relatively free of institutional controls, were places where the profane life could flourish. But virtually by definition as "frontiers," these "dark corners" were sporadic and ephemeral in comparison with those of early modern England and Europe. For most of the settlers of new places the ultimate goal was to re-create Puritan or English civility, not to escape it permanently.[16]

In comparing the profundity of the "darkness," it is hard to conceive of parallels anywhere in British North America to Increase Mather's experience with a ten-year-old beggar in rural England. After giving some coins, "I asked him how many gods there was. Hee answered, Hee thought there were 8 gods. I asked him who was the son of god. Hee replyed, Hee could not tell. I enquired if he had ever heard of Jesus Christ, Hee told me no. Hee had never heard of that Name before." The only sign of religious knowledge was that "this Lad believed his soul should not dy with his body." In New England, Ebenezer Parkman, the pastor of a newly established church in frontier Westborough, interviewed his "Maid servant of things of an Everlasting Importance" in 1726. He "found she had received but very barely in

15. Vaughan and Clark, eds., *Puritans among the Indians,* 150–51.

16. Richard Beale Davis, *Intellectual Life in the Colonial South, 1585–1763* (Knoxville, Tenn., 1978), 1:9; David D. Hall, *Worlds of Wonder, Days of Judgment: Popular Religious Belief in Early New England* (New York, 1989), 16–17.

her Education, being very unacquainted with the Principles of Religion." His expectations, however, were higher than Mather's, for he was alarmed that the young woman was "not able to so much as to return any Answer to the Catechism taught our Smallest Children." In his concluding lament Parkman also assumed, as Mather had not, that there were sustained efforts to instruct available to these people. "Alas!" he wrote. "The Irreligion and Ignorance of many (professedly Christian) Families among us of this Country, notwithstanding the Care universally taken for their Instruction!"[17]

These places of "Irreligion and Ignorance," however temporary, nonetheless exercised a tremendous pull on the moral imagination. The experience and symbol of wilderness, together with its natural inhabitant, the Indian, became vital elements of the Reformation of Manners, where cultural and moral distinctions far more than geographic ones dominated thought and action. What was most frightening morally about the Indian was not so much the cultural differences as the affinities reformers perceived between Indian attitudes and conduct and those of the profane. In 1642 Thomas Lechford remarked that generally the Indians were "proud and idle, and given much to singing, dancing, and playes," an observation virtually identical to the reformers' criticisms of their own popular traditions. The connection was not merely colonial. As a London reform pamphlet of 1652 noted, "We have Indians at home—Indians in Cornwall, Indians in Wales, Indians in Ireland." The Indian became a human symbol of the "dark corners." "Barbarism" was a cultural, not an ethnic, trait, and it was as communicable as "civility."[18]

As several scholars have explained, the English reaction to American Indians, based on the convoluted experiences in the Elizabethan conquest of Ireland, was both emotionally charged and highly ambivalent. Like the "wild Irish," the Indians were formidable foes requiring subjugation and, at the same time, fit subjects for conversion, even inclusion, into English society. And again like the Irish, Indian mores offered strong temptations to which not a few English succumbed. Notorious examples became a staple of Puritan moral exhortation. William Hubbard in 1677, for instance, told of "one Joshua Tift, a renegado Englishman of *Providence,* that upon some discontent among his neighbours, had turned *Indian,* married one of the *Indian Squaws,* renounced his Religion, Nation and natural Parents all at once, fighting against them" in King Philip's War. Wounded and captured, "he was condemned to die the death of a Traytor." Naturally in the Puritan view, "As to his Religion he was found as ignorant as an Heathen."[19]

As Englishmen became Indians and Indians became Englishmen, the cultural inheritances of both often intertwined in ways confusing and alarming to Puritans. There was no effective line separating the two peoples or cultures. Not only on the frontier but also in the settlements Indians and English mingled freely in the taverns and workplaces. Given these ambiguities in their efforts to reform both Indians and the profane, it is not surprising that New England magistrates never decided whether to treat Indians paternally, equally, or repressively. To their credit, however, the magistrates and clerics never seemed clear on which group was "debauching" the other more quickly.[20]

The Provoking Evils Law of 1675, for instance, denounced "the great abuse & scandall" in the trading houses "where drunkenes and other crimes have binn." Similarly the Connecticut legislature in 1678 noted that there were "some people that doe frequent the meetings of the Indians at their meetings and dances, and doe also joyne with them in their plays, by wagering of their sides." Engaging in Indian sports and gambling not only tempted the English but also "doth much countenance [the Indians] in those fooleries." More profoundly, there was a problem of religious heterodoxy. To attend is to "encourage them in their Divill worship, for some acquainted with their customes doe say their exercises at such times is a principal part of the worship they attend."[21] There was little doubt, of course, that it was the "Divill" that was being worshiped, for Satan in Christian lore was the presiding spirit of all forms of wilderness.

Generally, however, as border wars became more frequent the Indians increasingly were viewed as villains in a drama of moral declension. As Cotton Mather claimed in his popular 1697 collection of captivity tales, "We have too far degenerated into Indian Vices." Those "vices," he asserted, were that

19. Nicholas P. Canny, "The Ideology of English Colonization: From Ireland to America," *WMQ* 30 (1973): 575–98; James Muldoon, "The Indian as Irishman," *EIHC* 111 (1975): 267–89; William Hubbard, *Present State of New England* (Boston, 1677), 59. See also Roy Harvey Pearce, *Savagism and Civilization: A Study of the Indian and the American Mind* (Baltimore, 1953, 1965), 3–49.

20. James H. Merrell, "Some Thoughts on Colonial Historians and American Indians," *WMQ* 46 (1989): 94–119, esp. 96, 117; Yasuhide Kawashima, "Forced Conformity: Puritan Criminal Justice and Indians," *Kansas Law Review* 25 (1977): 361–73; James P. Ronda, "Red and White at the Bench: Indians and the Law in Plymouth Colony," *EIHC* 110 (1974): 200–215.

21. *Mass. Recs.* V, 63–64; Percy A. Scholes, *The Puritans and Music in England and New England: A Contribution to the Cultural History of Two Nations* (Oxford, 1934, 1969), 79.

"they are very lying Wretches, and they are very lazy Wretches; and they are out of measure indulgent unto their Children; there is no Family-Government among them." The latter was to him as to all reformers especially heinous. His point was that "We have shamefully Indianized in all these Abominable Things." Naturally he echoed his father's jeremiad theme from the war of the previous generation. "Now, the Judgments of God have imploy'd Indian Hatchets to wound us, no doubt for these our Indian Vices."[22]

This sense of Indian moral influence for the worse was also common among respectable laity. A Boston matron, Sarah Kemble Knight, traveling through Connecticut in 1704 saw "everywhere in the Towns as I passed, a Number of Indians, the Natives of the Country." She thought them "the most Salvage [savage] of all the salvages of that kind I had ever seen" and was shocked that there was "little or no care taken (as I heard upon enquiry) to make them otherwise," for "they have in some places Landes of theire owne, and Govern'd by Law's of their own making." Like Mather she was particularly sensitive to family organization. "They marry many wives and at pleasure put them away, and on the least dislike or fickle humour, on either side, saying 'stand away' to one another is sufficient Divorce." She then noted that "those uncomely 'stand aways' are too much in Vougue among the English in this (Indulgent Colony) as their records plentifully prove, and on very trivial matters." What she was encountering in Connecticut country towns was an English folk custom at most affirmed rather than caused by Indian contact. Those mores, both Indian and English, also allowed more female initiative than she thought seemly: "some of that foolish sex have had too large a share in the story."[23]

Michael Zuckerman, among others, has well noted that the English denounced Indians for traits they themselves evinced.

> Yet the very individualism they reviled in the Indians still lingered in their own immoderate ambitions. The obstinate antiauthoritarianism that they imputed to the natives still lurked in their own hostility to hierarchy and its pretensions. The mobility that so disconcerted them in the indigenes still survived in their own proclivity to pull up stakes when a better opportunity offered or simply when the spirit moved them.[24]

22. Ford, ed., *Diary of Cotton Mather* 1:210; Cotton Mather, *Great Examples of Judgment and Mercy* (1697), reprinted in *Magnalia Christi Americana* (London, 1702), bk. 6, 35.
23. Malcolm Freiberg, ed., *The Journal of Madam Knight* (Boston, 1971), 21–22.
24. Michael Zuckerman, "Identity in British America: Unease in Eden," in Nicholas P.

As Zuckerman implied, there was more to this notion of cultural parallelism and the sometimes hysterical denunciations of Indian mores than a simple example of hypocritical Freudian projection. To believe that is to overestimate the coherence of English mores and the degree of difference between common English and native attitudes. Within the English and indeed European culture the Indian was a crucial symbol in an internal struggle over values embedded in folk life. Consequently it is not surprising that increasingly in the eighteenth century as European and English intellectuals and reformers developed an appreciation for what they saw as the simpler and more natural elements of their own popular cultures, their estimation of the American Indian (often seen as the Noble Savage) also rose.

The Indian passed from a symbol of degeneracy in wilderness to one of integrity in nature. Yet he always remained a rhetorical device in the attempt to recast European manners.[25] This transition from evil to good was rarer, of course, among colonial Americans who were never free of the horrors of border warfare and rarely had the luxury of contemplating Indian societies from any comfortable distance. But the basic symbolism was present and still is used even in our time to urge such reforms as environmentalism. Surely one of the tragedies of the American Indian is that he or she has always been perceived more as a character in someone else's morality play than as a person.

For New Englanders perhaps more than other English colonists, wilderness was to be found not only in the woods but also at sea. The ocean too had its native, morally dangerous population among the transient deep-sea sailors, who were in their own way almost as culturally distinct as Indians. The waterfronts where sailor met Puritan corresponded to the frontier towns of the interior in the reformers' moral universe. Cotton Mather (with his proclivity for imagery) occasionally thought of the "Sea-faring" folk of Boston as one of "the several Tribes" among his "Flock." Like the people of "ungospellized plantations," those of the maritime population seemed to him at times a "wicked, stupid, abominable Generation." Perhaps inevitably, the Indian captivity narrative had its parallel in the tales of shipwrecks and pirate captures. The pirate, too, was another "heathen" forming a counter-society at war with orderly, respectable standards. Just as the conversion of

---

Canny and Anthony Pagden, eds., *Colonial Identity in the Atlantic World, 1500–1800* (Princeton, 1987), 155.

25. Roger L. Emerson, "American Indians, Frenchmen, and Scots Philosophers," *Studies in Eighteenth-Century Culture* 9 (1979): 211–36; Jay Barrett Botsford, *English Society in the Eighteenth Century, as Influenced from Overseas* (1924; reprint, New York, 1965), 24.

the Indian was both a good work and a security measure, so was the conversion of the maritime population.[26]

The "Ignorance and Irreligion" of the "Dark Corners" where orthodox churches and settled ministers were absent or distant constituted a realm where an eclectic, relatively untutored popular piety held sway. Compared to systematic Puritan theology, this more general piety was a rather inchoate mass of religious and moral principles. By selection and refinement these principles were at various times and places in England and America shaped into Quakerism, Ranterism, antinomianism, separatism, Anabaptism, Arminianism, and even orthodox Nonseparating Congregationalism. As Jon Butler has observed, "The religious choices available in the seventeenth century, though constrained by Calvinism, stimulated diversity and heresy as often as they generated homogeneity and orthodoxy." Popular religiosity was indeed a protean compound. The reformers feared its fecundity and unpredictability. If left uninstructed by orthodox preaching, liturgy, and "family government," a population subject to eccentric stimuli might produce veritable prodigies of heresy and untoward conduct. This piety, they feared, could even respond favorably to "Popery." In 1713, for instance, Cotton Mather thought his congregation prone to "the false Thoughts of *Popery,* and of *Quakerism,* and of *Arminianism.*" This complexity was further deepened by migration and other contacts with a changing homeland, "as new immigrants brought new and old values to new and old settlements," in Butler's deft formulation.[27]

The popular religiosity, however diverse in its impulses, was not bereft of themes. The most important were that piety was essentially personal and that religious truth came largely by intuition or revelation to individuals rather than through tradition developed in communities. Faith was not so much a matter of doctrinal assent or even of ultimate reliance on God's providential acts, but rather "a firm & sure persuasion that Christ dyed for me; and that I shall have life & Salvation by him." The stress on the volitional "persuasion" and on the first person singular pronoun was typical.[28]

26. Ford, ed., *Diary of Cotton Mather* 2: 528; Richard P. Gildrie, "'The Gallant Life': Theft on the Salem-Marblehead, Massachusetts, Waterfront in the 1680s," *EIHC* 122 (1986): 284–96; Marcus Rediker, "'Under the Banner of King Death': The Social World of Anglo-American Pirates, 1716 to 1726," *WMQ* 38 (1981): 203–37.

27. Jim Butler, *Awash in a Sea of Faith: Christianizing the American People* (Cambridge, Mass., 1990), 55; Ford, ed., *Diary of Cotton Mather,* 2:207.

28. "Errors held by Separatists at this Day," ca. 1685, Curwen Family Manuscripts, AAS, box #1, folder #4; Hall, *Worlds of Wonder,* is the best and most recent study of popular religion in early New England.

Private experience implied individual judgment, which in turn threatened the charitable sense of communion sought by Nonseparatist clerics. "The strict Legalist, who trusts in himself that he is Righteous, despiseth others," complained Samuel Moody in 1710. "If he be in Church-Fellowship, he thinks any scarce Good enough for his Communion. . . . If a Non-Communicant, he thinks the Churches so Corrupt that he must not hold Communion with them." This preference for the private over the communal helps explain the oft-noted "neglect of the ordinances." As Cotton Mather wondered in 1713, "There are People in my Flock, who have arrived unto a considerable Age, and are of good Esteem for their Piety. And yett these People never have come to the Table of the Lord. Nay, some of them are not baptised unto this Day." Obviously these "dilatory Christians" did not share Mather's sense of intimate connection between piety and communal sacraments.[29]

Also, some concluded that if faith were a private matter then the individual might be able to control the timing and substance of God's grace. As a "dying Woman" confessed to the younger Mather in 1711, "Syr, I was once under the Power of a foolish and wicked Persuasion, that it was in my own power to Repent at my Pleasure. With this presumption, I went on in my Sins." This problem of the role of individual will and initiative in conversion was one of the knottiest in a Puritan theology that shared the popular interest in personal experience but also insisted on God's absolute sovereignty. The continual stress on individual experience also led to divergent assessments of the significance of the Bible in religious life. Some who believed that they were "Expert in the letter of the Scriptures," asserted Moody, denigrated the "Poor, Weak, tho' True Believers," claiming, "This people who knoweth not the Law are Cursed." More commonly, however, the ministers complained of those "Barren even of Common Knowledge in Religious Matters" who nonetheless presumed to hold that "their Hearts (they profess and verily think) are as Good as the best Professors of them all."[30]

One source of the popular tendency to downplay the significance of the Bible and of churches as guardians of its meaning was the common assumption "That God hath more light to reveal . . . than is already revealed in Scripture." Religious experience, then, was not to be evaluated solely in

---

29. Samuel Moodey, *The Doleful State of the Damned* (Boston, 1710), 103; Ford, ed., *Diary of Cotton Mather,* 2:251; see Norman Pettit, *The Heart Prepared: Grace and Conversion in Puritan Spiritual Life* (New Haven, 1966), for the role of the sacraments.

30. Moodey, *Doleful State,* 103; Ford, ed., *Diary of Cotton Mather,* 251.

terms of biblical precedents because "in many things [believers] are guided by immediate Revelation from Heaven." Such "immediate Revelations" and their possible consequences were, of course, difficult for churches or governments to control. Puritan thinkers asserted that the Bible provided the only proper criteria for evaluating and shaping religious thought and conduct and that a highly learned tradition was essential to its interpretation. While usually granting that the Bible was an important source of religious knowledge, popular tradition usually assumed that a deep understanding of Scripture was not a learned monopoly. One common formulation was that beneath "the plain sense" of the text open to any reader, "a Spiritual Meaning lyes hid under all passages of Scripture, which no man can come to the knowledge of but by the special Revelation or opening of the Spirit of God." It followed "that all *annotation* & human aide to understand the Bible are Useless."[31]

This view of biblical interpretation clearly implied that "*Education* is needless for a Minister" and that "all Christians have a right to preach according to the Measure of Faith, if perswaded that the Spirit of God moves them thereto." Deprived of sacramental significance and special instructional authority, pastors properly had "no more Power of Rule in the church than any private Brother." Some groups arising out of this popular milieu reached the logical conclusion that an organized ministry was a hindrance and, like the Quakers, tried futilely to abandon formal religious leadership. Most, however, recognized the practical benefits, if not the special authority, of an organized, well-trained ministry. On occasion even this grudging acceptance led to bitter denunciations of clerical presumption. In 1682, for example, a Salem Village farmer, Jeremiah Watt, explained that "Christians are to exhort & edify one another by speaking often one to another . . . & help one another" and that "the minister should be the leading man in the worke." But instead of this egalitarian ideal, "I doe perseive that ministers doe aim to bring all to pulpit preaching & there they may deliver what they please & none must object: & this we must pay largely for." This "lording of it & trampling under foot" of "our Christian priviledge" seemed so egregious to him as to constitute one of "the Marks of the beast Antichrist which prevaille in our times."[32] Goodman Watt may have become overwrought amid the village's chronic factionalism, but his underlying sense of the pastor's role in a democratic church organization was not unusual.

31. "Errors held by Separatists at this Day"; Harry S. Stout, *The New England Soul: Preaching and Religious Culture in Colonial New England* (New York, 1986), 105–6.
32. "Errors held by Separatists at this Day"; *Essex Recs.* VIII, 294–95.

A common inheritance of the English people, anticlericalism was (as David Hall has felicitously described it) "a constantly shifting and evolving language" not restricted to the powerless or uneducated. Congregational New Englanders became annoyed with their pastors, while Quakers denounced them as "hirelings." But Puritan clerics too defined themselves in contrast to the "dumb dogs" of Anglican and Catholic churches who reputedly hid their incompetence and laziness behind rote performances of liturgy. In a faint echo of the recurrent Donatist heresy of the early church, popular tradition—particularly in its antinomian forms—tended to hold that the effectiveness and authority of ministers rested more on their presumed spiritual state than on their formal training or official ordinations. Although obviously an opening to disorder and even demagogic fraud, this ancient Christian impulse was a counter to authoritarianism and excessive formalism. Despite its variety, the direction of English anticlericalism was toward a more egalitarian, flexible sense of church order. Ministers were to be leaders in a loving Christian community, not rulers and judges over a cowed populace. Some New England folk, among others, made the egalitarian principle apply to the cosmos. As Cotton Mather complained of untutored opinion evident in some "ungospellized" places, "Foolish men will sometimes say, God Almighty never made men to Damn them."[33]

As participants in as well as critics of traditional piety, Massachusetts's orthodox pastors were in an ambiguous position. Through their ordinations they were to be among the saints, giving evidence of saving grace and chosen by their congregations to lead. At the same time they were to be certified by their superior education and by recognition from their clerical peers as men set apart and above their people. Seen as an ideal, this compromise was impressive and effective; but the tensions, both theoretical and practical, were enormous. Church members and townspeople were rarely certain whether their pastors were employees, companions in the spiritual quest, or officials from some nebulous and distant ecclesiastical authority.[34]

33. David D. Hall, "Religion and Society: Problems and Reconsiderations," in Jack P. Greene and J. R. Pole, eds., *Colonial British America: Essays in the New History of the Early Modern Era* (Baltimore, 1984), 329–32, esp. 331; C. Mather, *Letter to Ungospellized Plantations*, 13.

34. James F. Cooper, Jr., "'A Mixed Form': The Establishment of Church Government in Massachusetts Bay, 1629–1645," *EIHC* 123 (1987): 233–59; Robert F. Scholz, "Clerical Consociation in Massachusetts Bay: Reassessing the New England Way and Its Origins," *WMQ* 29 (1972): 391–414; David D. Hall, *The Faithful Shepherd: A History of the New England Ministry in the Seventeenth Century* (Chapel Hill, 1972); J. William T. Youngs, Jr., *God's Messengers: Religious Leadership in Colonial New England, 1700–1750* (Baltimore, 1976), esp. 26–37.

The related problems of the propriety of lay or itinerant ministries were illustrative of the ambivalent relationship between popular tradition and Puritan reform. "Lay Prophecying" was an important Puritan practice, having medieval roots in England. Yet during the early 1650s Massachusetts clerical and political leaders, alarmed by the proliferation of sects at home and the appearance of various sorts of "Opinionists" in America, attempted to impose a licensing law on a recalcitrant populace. A swift repeal was the predictable result, followed late in the decade with another ringing denunciation in the prologue to a law with no serious definition or means of enforcement.[35]

Looking back on the 1650s in his *Magnalia,* Cotton Mather wondered at the "*Libertine* and *Brownistick* Spirit then prevailing among the People" of Plymouth Colony and the "strange Disposition to Discountenance the *Gospel-Ministry* by setting up the *Gifts of Private Brethren* in Opposition thereunto." In his effort to denigrate this old tradition while establishing the respectability of New England practices to a largely English audience, he also retailed the story of a "Godly Minister of a certain Town in Connecticut" who "employ'd an honest Neighbour of some small talent for a Mechanick to read a Sermon out of some good book" while he was away. "This Honest, whom they ever counted also a Pious Man, had so much conceit of his Talents that . . . to the Surprize of the People, fell to preaching" on the text "Despise not Prophecyings." In his effort "he betook himself to bewail the Envy of the Clergy of the Land, in that they did not wish all the Lord's People to be Prophets, and call forth Private Brethren publickly to prophesize." As Mather would have it, "in the midst of his Exercise, God smote him with horrible Madness," and the "People were forc'd with violent Hands to carry him home." A ranting style, in the respectable view, was a sign of insanity or chicanery. Apparently the congregation took the charitable option, for, as Mather reiterated, "he was reputed a Pious Man."[36] The moral was clearly that "Mechanicks," even "pious" ones, should not "bewail" their clergy from pulpits.

Yet in a system where ordination depended largely on public affirmation the line between clergy and laity was not easy to define. During the drive for the Reforming Synod Increase Mather urged "that none but faithful ones (as far as men can judge) be employed as Publick Preachers: Though the just

---

35. Stephen Foster, "English Puritanism and the Progress of New England Institutions, 1630–1660," in David D. Hall, John M. Murrin, and Thad W. Tate, eds., *Saints and Revolutionaries: Essays in Early American History* (New York, 1984), esp. 35.

36. C. Mather, *Magnalia Christi Americana,* bk. 2, 6, bk. 6, 31.

Liberty of Churches should not be infringed." However, this essential free-dom "may be in time a great Inlet to ignorance, error, & profaneness." Committed to both popular authority and reformed standards, he could only hope that members of the General Court "would think of some Ex-pedient" to reconcile the contradiction. The problem was never resolved, despite the growing influence of ministerial associations and church councils during the eighteenth century. In 1702 some thirty of the "Ministers of the Province" meeting in Boston suggested criteria for mutual enforcement to the churches, including educational standards, doctrinal orthodoxy, mem-bership in "a particular church," a narrative of "evangelical principles," a "probationary sermon," and testimonials of fitness from "at least Four or Five Settled Pastors."[37] Although these came to constitute the common practice, some churches and factions within towns tended to "stand to their liberties."

Given the popular milieu, defining the "settled ministry" was difficult—but controlling itinerancy was impossible. In 1700, long before the Great Awakening made the problem a cause célèbre, Cotton Mather noted that "a Good Order has never yet been provided among us, that no Untryed and Unfit shall set up for a Preacher, and run about from Town to Town." Popular tolerance for and interest in wandering prophets of varying degrees of orthodoxy was high, and "Men are too insensible of the horrible Villany and Blasphemy in the Crimes of these Fellows who set up for Teachers to the People of God, when God knows they are wicked Vagrants and Varlets, designing to abuse the honest people." Many assumed that they had a right to hear diverse religious ideas and styles and to debate their merits regardless of the views of their "settled" clergy. In such conflicts the reformers usually agreed on the right while trying to limit the sources and method of its exercise. As Mather explained, "The Apostolick Injunction, *To Prove all Things,* does not invite Unstable people to *Run after all Preachers* (as they too often pervert the sence of it) but it only directs people to *Examine* by the Word of God, the Doctrine, which they hear from those that in an orderly way are to be heard as their Teachers."[38]

Mather's worries were not hypothetical. For instance, his father in 1682 was asked by some parishioners to allow an itinerant to preach in his church at a particular Sunday afternoon service. The elder Mather refused the

<hr>

37. I. Mather, *Dangers of Apostacy,* 103; [Cotton Mather], *Proposals for the Preservation of Religion in the Churches by a Due Trial of them that Stand Candidates of the Ministry* (Boston, 1702), 1–3.

38. Cotton Mather, *A Warning to the Flocks* (Boston, 1700), 6–7, 12.

specific request as being on too short notice and said he would consult "with some of my church before [I] would consent to his preaching at all." With crucial lay support Mather denied the use of his pulpit. A week later an irate communicant "spoke to me in the street wishing that God would reward those according to their Workes" who had opposed the itinerant's appearance in the town's churches. Her sense of personal freedom had been so violated that "she prayed God to revenge those that are not free to have him here." When Mather objected "that her expressions were sinfull & scandelous, she Sayd, I might be angry at her if I would. She cared not."[39]

Both the right to hear itinerants and the clerical ambivalence were deeply rooted in traditional popular culture. Wandering preachers of questionable antecedents were a vital feature of late medieval religious life. Puritanism itself had a "pilgrim" view of Christian experience evidenced in the *Book of Martyrs* and the works of John Bunyan, to say nothing of their own New England "errand into the wilderness." Cotton Mather himself in 1717 speculated on the practicality of sending "a couple of itinerant Ministers" from Scotland to "the Plantations to the South-ward of us" in order to serve the Scotch-Irish immigration. The itinerant imagery was potent for both the populace and the reformers. As one scholar of English Puritanism has noted, "When the Puritan encounters a displaced person, he sees a prerationalized type of himself; the wayfaring Christian walking the strait path is a rationalized and regenerate version of the displaced and degenerate persons wandering aimlessly."[40]

The common assumption that a "displaced person" might have insight and perspective not readily available to the "settled" and respectable encouraged the notion "that *Illiterate Men* may be Serviceable and Admirable Preachers," a medieval idea the younger Mather claimed was defended in his time by "Jesuits." It might even apply to the insane. Mather himself was grateful for the puncturing of his complacency in 1724 by "a poor Mad woman" of Charlestown. Having addressed her condescendingly, "Is this not a pretty Damsel?" she gave "this wise and sober and pungent Answer, *The Crow thinks so, Syr!*" Mather regarded this "Rebuke and Satyr" as a "useful . . . Admonition" on the universality of death.[41] In both Puritan and popular thought religious wisdom came from many directions. Orthodox

39. Diary of Increase Mather, 10 October, 12 October, and 19 October 1682, AAS, box 3, folder 3.

40. Edmund Leites, *The Puritan Conscience and Modern Sexuality* (New Haven, 1986), 6; Ford, ed., *Diary of Cotton Mather* 2:471; James Holstun, *A Rational Millennium: Puritan Utopias of Seventeenth-Century England and America* (New York, 1987), 38.

41. C. Mather, *Warning to the Flocks*, 8–9; Ford, ed., *Diary of Cotton Mather* 2:804–5.

efforts not only to evaluate the messages authoritatively but also to discipline their delivery and reception among the folk were doomed to frustration.

Some of the wanderers openly espoused Ranter or other blatantly heretical views. In Salem in 1680 a couple whom the county court found "to be wandering vagabond persons" were arrested at the home of a prominent Quaker for "disturbing the family and using very threatening and railing words of fire, sword, and divisions." A wanderer from Salem, according to Cotton Mather, appeared in New Haven "being Cloathed in Black, was taken for a Minister, and was able to Ape one, and Humored the mistake." Invited by the local pastor to preach both Sunday services, he completed the first "to Acceptation, but in the last Exercise, he plentifully shewed himself to be a whymsical Opinionist; and besides Railed . . . and Reviled the Magistrates, Ministers, and Churches at such a rate, that the people were ready to pull him out of the pulpit."[42] Apparently, however, the congregation heard him out.

On rare occasions after the famous Quaker "invasions" of the mid-seventeenth century these itinerants appeared in groups and found other means of expression besides preaching. There was some continuation of the flamboyant Quaker protests against Puritan church services. As Samuel Sewall recorded in 1677, "In Sermon time there came in a female Quaker, in a Canvas Frock, her hair disshevelled and loose like a Periwigg, her face as black as ink, led by two other Quakers, and two followed. It occasioned the greatest and most amazing uproar that I ever saw."[43]

But more spectacularly and more obviously echoing the pilgrim revels of Europe was an episode in Plymouth Colony in 1683 that became a staple orthodox horror story into the Great Awakening. A group of Ranters known as "Case's Crew" apparently purged from a Quaker band, flourished on Long Island, a noted "dark corner." In Carla Pestana's recent description, "This group, obviously possessed, cavorted in the wilderness and accepted singing and dancing as a sign of conversion. Those who were seduced into their ranks were either murdered, driven mad, inspired to dance naked, led to believe that they were the risen Christ, or urged to participate in ritual blood sacrifices."[44]

Some turned their attention to Plymouth. Led by a "Jonathan Dunham alias Singleterry," the small party of men and women made a convert of "a

42. *Essex Recs.* VII, 328; C. Mather, *Warning to the Flocks*, 21–22.

43. M. Halsey Thomas, ed., *Diary of Samuel Sewall, 1674–1719* (New York, 1973), 1:44.

44. Carla Garinia Pestana, "'The City upon a Hill under Siege': The Puritan Perception of the Quaker Threat to Massachusetts Bay, 1656–1661," *NEQ* 56 (1983): 338.

younge woman named Mary Ross" who "made herself naked, burning all her clothes, and with infinite blasphemy, said that she was Christ." After giving names to her "Apostles" and preaching on the necessity of her death and resurrection, she ordered a Last Supper that required her disciples "to sacrifice a Dog." So they killed a farmer's dog, broke into the man's house, forcibly evicted him from the premises, "and according to their anticke trickes and foolish powers, made a fier in the said house, and threw the dogg upon it, and shott of a gun several times, and burnt some other things in the house to the hazard of burning his house and younge children, keeping the dores and not opening them" to the enraged farmer "when he come with some of his naighbours to rescue" his household. Dunham was also charged with abandoning his family, "wandering about from place to place as a vagabond in this collonie, also deseminating his corrupt principles, and drawing away another man's wife." He was whipped out of the colony. Mary Ross, for her part, compounded her crimes by "uncivell and outrageous railing words and carriages" before the judges and was whipped and banished "toward Boston, where her mother dwells." As late as 1704 around Milford, Connecticut, there was still a band of Singing Quakers who practiced "Humming and singing and groneing after their conjuring way" and were inclined to thrust their way unwanted into houses. But they seem to have become objects of exasperated humor rather than fear.[45]

Of course most itinerant preachers were not so bizarre in their conduct or opinions. Some were profiteering charlatans, such as the notorious Samuel May, an Englishman who at various times passed as an Anglican priest, a Puritan pastor, and an Anabaptist preacher. In Boston he made the mistake of trying to start off as an orthodox minister, was caught plagiarizing Scottish sermons, and then took up with a "Congregation of Anabaptists" in Cotton Mather's "Neighborhood." Mather was astonished that "Multitudes of the giddy People are as much bewitched with him, as if hee were another Simon Magus." After six months he was driven out of town, having sexually "affronted" several "sober, modest, and virtuous women" of various persuasions who swore out complaints in December 1699. Even so, his supporters raised money enough for his passage to England and peppered Mather's windows with pebbles. It turned out that his real name was Samuel Axel, a brickmaker who "left a Wife and Family in deplorable Circumstances" in England to bring "a whore with him hither, under the name of Wife!"[46]

45. *Plymouth Recs.* VI, 113–14; Freiberg, ed., *Journal of Madam Knight*, 35–36.
46. C. Mather, *Warning to the Flocks*, 24–27, 31–32; Ford, ed., *Diary of Cotton Mather*, 1:313–16, 318, 323–24, 329, 351.

Samuel May or Axel was a picaresque rogue who added itinerant preaching to the traditional inventory of cozening skills.

The majority of the itinerants of diverse and often eclectic views were pious "mechanick preachers" following an old and (to their mind) honorable tradition. Their influence was greater in the larger ports, frontier towns, and other "dark corners" where orthodox, settled ministries were absent or inadequate, but clearly they appeared elsewhere as well. They were a common experience in the lives of New Englanders. They functioned within a popular religious milieu that overlapped but was not fully congruent with Puritan orthodoxy. These differences, which sometimes aroused passion or factionalism, could also lead to seriocomic puzzles. For instance, the "cryptomaterialism" so often apparent in popular thought raised such questions as "Will there be any use for bellies?" after the Resurrection. In places where orthodox churches were strong, conversion narratives, catechisms, and other devices served to clarify and reconcile these divergences, as well as to adapt both Puritan and popular heritages to new American environments.[47]

The religious climate of provincial Massachusetts was not one of bland uniformity nor of a welter of competing, self-conscious sects necessarily at war with Puritan dominance. Rather, it was a general matrix rooted in English common life within which various movements, some ephemeral and some not, emerged. The general matrix was more fundamental than the specific groups or opinions. Persons could move from one to another rather easily or simply experiment with attractive positions much as in modern American denominationalism—but with less of a sense that sects or groups were formal or permanent entities. This situation, of course, created openings for some bizarre religious expressions. Puritan orthodoxy in Massachusetts was what the Church of England was at home, an established institutional focus or spinal cord for this volatile religious culture. As "reformed" churches, the Puritan congregations and ministers were anxious to do a better job in both disciplining and accommodating popular religious themes and impulses.

Within this context itinerant and lay preaching in houses, taverns, fields, and churches followed naturally, as did orthodox ambivalence about these phenomena. This perspective may also cast light on the New England

---

47. Bob Scribner, "Cosmic Order and Daily Life: Sacred and Secular in Pre-Industrial German Society," in Kaspar von Greyerz, ed., *Religion and Society in Early Modern Europe, 1500–1800* (London, 1984), 24–26; Thomas, ed., *Diary of Samuel Sewall*, 2:747; Patricia Caldwell, *The Puritan Conversion Narrative: The Beginnings of American Expression* (Cambridge, 1983), 26, 35.

Quaker experience. The Society of Friends, along with the New England Baptists, was among the few groups to transcend charismatic form into institutional permanence, albeit an often tenuous achievement. By fervently combining the popular themes of intuitive personal religious experience with antiauthoritarianism expressed in compelling theatrical and verbal witness, the earliest Quaker messengers were guaranteed an audience throughout the English world. In New England they had the greatest impact or attracted the most converts where orthodox Puritanism was virtually nonexistent (as in Maine or Rhode Island) or was heavily compromised by separatist attitudes (as in Plymouth Colony or Salem). The converts, while not exclusively the poor or politically disadvantaged, were disaffected either from stricter Puritan standards generally or from specific churches. But they were not aliens within the region's religious ethos, a condition that helps explain why orthodox neighbors and kin could rise readily and easily to their defense and why some Friends were uncertain of their allegiance or opinions even in periods of relative toleration.[48]

Although, as a popular movement often distant from Puritanism, Quakerism tended in its early history to embrace such profaneness as a looser commitment to "family government" and proclivities to bizarre public conduct, over time the society evinced similar trends toward personal and social discipline as those which typified Puritan and popular culture generally during the late seventeenth and early eighteenth centuries. The process led to debate and schism within the movement as it had in others. In contrast to, say, Gortonism or Ranterism, Quakerism was not only an identifiable but also a fairly permanent phenomenon whose New England history reflects the broader, complex character and development of popular piety in the region.[49] Thus Quaker accommodation and dissent, like itinerancy or even strict orthodoxy, were neither monolithic nor merely a product of specific social settings or local conflicts. It was a matter of traditions interacting with circumstances in people's lives.

The existence of "dark corners" in Massachusetts and its peripheries, as well as Puritan concern about them, constitutes another arena in which the reformers engaged traditional English popular culture. They worried about "covetousness" and individualism, which they saw creating "ungospellized

48. Jonathan Chu, *Neighbors, Friends, or Madmen: The Puritan Adjustment to Quakerism in Seventeenth-Century Massachusetts Bay* (Westport, Conn., 1985), passim.

49. Carla Gardina Pestana, "The Social World of Salem: William King's 1681 Blasphemy Trial," *American Quarterly* 41 (1989): 308–27; Pestana, "City upon a Hill under Siege," 349; Philip F. Gura, "The Radical Ideology of Samuel Gorton: New Light on the Relation of English to American Puritanism," *WMQ* 39 (1982): 78–100.

plantations" on a morally as well as militarily vulnerable frontier. The parallels in fishing areas and major ports did not elude them. They wrestled with the issues of itinerancy and even formal dissent, which seemed a particularly important challenge in those places. In the process, the complexity of the interaction between reformed aspirations and traditional patterns of thought and conduct emerges here too as both ambivalent and creative.

SEVEN

Visions of Evil:
Witchcraft and the Occult

The Massachusetts witchcraft crisis of 1692 was the most spectacular, notorious, and perhaps revealing episode in New England's experience with the Reformation of Manners in the aftermath of the Reforming Synod of 1679.[1] Both the severity of the crisis and its meaning for New England rest in part in the differing but overlapping interpretations of witchcraft and the occult among the clergy, magistrates, and populace. Witch lore embodies rich traditions about the nature of evil, a concept with cultural and religious significance as well as social and psychological implications. There was no more fundamental issue in the Reformation of Manners than the nature of evil and possible responses to it.

Nor was the question an abstraction. A convoluted system of belief and action, witch lore was a vital force in daily life. It provided explanations, some influence over others, and modes of expression beyond the limits of respectability. Having grave practical as well as cosmic significance, witch lore was as crucial to the moral imaginations of late seventeenth-century New Englanders as it was to other early modern European peoples. Indeed, one traveler to Boston in 1680 claimed "that I have never been in a place where more was said about witchcraft and witches."[2]

1. The substance and much of the wording of this chapter appeared as Richard P. Gildrie, "Visions of Evil: Popular Culture, Puritanism, and the Massachusetts Witchcraft Crisis of 1692," *Journal of American Culture* 8 (1985): 17–33, and is reused with the kind consent of the editors.

2. B. B. James and J. Franklin Jameson, eds., *Journal of Jasper Danckaerts, 1679–80* (New York, 1913), 290. The best studies include Chadwick Hansen, *Witchcraft at Salem* (New York, 1969); Paul Boyer and Stephen Nissenbaum, *Salem Possessed: Social Origins of Witchcraft* (Cambridge, Mass., 1974); John Putnam Demos, *Entertaining Satan: Witchcraft*

Essential to the folk understanding was magic. Healing by charms or spells, "conjuring" or "divination" to gain information or occult power, and fortune-telling by palmistry and astrology were widely practiced in early modern Europe and America.[3] In England people skilled in these arts, whether amateur or professional, were termed "cunning folk" and were quite common. In fact, one historian has claimed that they were "at least as numerous in sixteenth-century England as the parish clergy." Although less conspicuous in seventeenth-century Massachusetts, cunning folk were certainly present.[4]

By popular repute cunning folk were foes of witches. Witch practices commonly took the same forms as popular magic but with malicious intent. For instance, where cunning folk used spells to heal people or animals, witches "cursed" them. Given this enmity of purpose, magic to counter witchcraft was an important facet of cunning lore. Yet the struggle between cunning folk and witches was often ambiguous. Obviously the relationship was symbiotic. Cunning men and women indulged in witchcraft to best rivals. In popular lore this occult combat was between good and evil, but it was not a simple one.[5]

---

and the Culture of Early New England (New York, 1982); Richard Weisman, Witchcraft, Magic, and Religion in Seventeenth-Century Massachusetts (Amherst, Mass., 1981); Carol F. Karsen, The Devil in the Shape of a Woman: Witchcraft in Colonial New England (New York, 1987); Richard Godbeer, The Devil's Dominion: Magic and Religion in Early New England (New York, 1992). Excellent bibliographies are in Weisman, Witchcraft, Magic, and Religion, 251–62, and Paul Boyer and Stephen Nissenbaum, eds., The Salem Witchcraft Papers (New York, 1977), 1:43–46 (hereafter Witchcraft Papers).

3. Richard Kieckhofer, European Witch Trials: Their Foundation in Popular and Learned Culture, 1300–1500 (Berkeley and Los Angeles, 1972), esp. 27–46; Norman Cohn, Europe's Inner Demons: An Enquiry Inspired by the Great Witch-Hunt (New York, 1975), 252–55; Christina Lerner, Enemies of God: The Witch-Hunt in Scotland (London, 1981). The distinction between "theological" and "popular" views in Massachusetts is central to Weisman, Witchcraft, Magic, and Religion, esp. 5–11, 98–105.

4. Demos, Entertaining Satan, 61, 80–84, 356–58; Jon Butler, "Magic, Astrology, and the Early American Religious Heritage," American Historical Review 84 (1979): 317–46; Jon Butler, "Magic and the Occult," in his Awash in a Sea of Faith: Christianizing the American People (Cambridge, Mass., 1990), 67–97. Descriptions of cunning lore and its practitioners can be found in Keith Thomas, Religion and the Decline of Magic (New York, 1971), 177–211, 222–52, and Ronald Horsley, "Who Were the Witches? The Social Roles of the Accused in the European Witch Trials," Journal of Interdisciplinary History 9 (1979): 689–715, quote on 697.

5. Ronald Horsley, "Further Reflections on Witchcraft and European Folk Religion," History of Religions 19 (1979): 71–95, esp. 92; Thomas, Religion and the Decline of Magic, 265–76, 427, 514; Demos, Entertaining Satan, 138–39, 182–84, 390–91; Robert Muchembled, "The Witches of Cambresis: The Acculturation of the Rural World in the Sixteenth and Seventeenth Centuries," in James Obelkovich, ed., Religion and the People, 800–1700 (Chapel

Learned observers knew that cunning lore, particularly healing by spells, conjuring, and fortune-telling, was prevalent in New England. Cotton Mather worried over these "little Sorceries," while John Hale, the minister at Beverly during the Salem trials, was perplexed by their survival in a Puritan environment. Thomas Brattle, wealthy Boston merchant and member of the Royal Society, found the subject acutely embarrassing. John Dunton, an English bookseller, was alternately amused and titillated by experiences with fortune-telling and a "reputed witch" of Boston. Indeed, in 1686 poor Dunton nearly won himself an avid clientele by toying with fortune-telling as a joke. But, as he remarked, "I refused to meddle any more, for the reputation of a Conjuror is not so desirable."[6]

The Salem witchcraft transcripts are replete with references, some quite detailed, to the lore of witches and cunning folk in the English mode. For instance, Samuel Shattuck, a Salem cooper and Quaker, related how in 1680 a fortune-telling "stranger" convinced him that his neighbor, Bridget Bishop, had bewitched his son and then attempted vainly to break the spell by countermagic. For several years prior to 1692, Roger Toothaker, the "French Doctor" of Billerica who crossed the vague line between medicine and cunning lore, built up a practice handling witchcraft cases and taught his daughter, Martha Emerson, something of the art. He bragged to some Beverly mariners in a tavern that at his direction his daughter had once killed a witch by boiling the urine of the bewitched in a pot overnight. The war between witches and cunning folk was waged in Massachusetts just as it was in England.[7]

In its worries over witchcraft the populace was most concerned about "maleficium," or evil deeds done by occult means, and viewed cunning folk as potent if at times unreliable allies. Considered together with the bewildering variety of magical practices to heal or harm, to gain love or wealth, to tell the future, or to influence the behavior of animals and people, popular cunning and witch lore constituted a lively ingredient of daily life. It helped define good

Hill, 1979), 221–76, esp. 260; A.D.J. Macfarlane, *Witchcraft in Tudor and Stuart England: A Regional and Comparative Study* (London, 1974), 115–34.

6. John Hale, *A Modest Enquiry into the Nature of Witchcraft* (Boston, 1702), 67–70, 143–44; "Letter of Thomas Brattle, F.R.S., 1692," in George L. Burr, ed., *Narratives of the Witchcraft Cases* (New York, 1914, 1956), 181–82; John Dunton, *Letters Written from New England, A.D. 1686*, ed. William H. Whitmore (Boston, 1867), 138–40, 186.

7. *Witchcraft Papers* I, 98–99, 125, 308–09; III, 772–73, 821, 847–48; Demos, *Entertaining Satan*, 80–84; Hansen, *Witchcraft at Salem*, 72–81.

and evil, provided explanations and remedies for the ills of life, and even offered entertainment and catharsis.[8]

For the well-educated ministers, magistrates, and merchants of Massachusetts too, witch lore was an important fact of life. But although familiar with the folk version, their interpretation differed significantly. They were less interested in incidents of maleficium and more concerned with the moral and religious implications of occult activity. The core of the learned tradition was the notion that witches and indeed cunning folk derived their powers, knowingly or unknowingly, from Satan. The devil's purpose was not only to ensnare tempted souls but also to use these people to sow chaos throughout Christian society and thereby establish his satanic rule.[9]

This profound sense of dread, this fear of moral and social anarchy inspired by Satan himself, was a highly symbolic theological version of the spirit animating the more general Reformation of Manners. The vision of the chaotic potential of evil permeated the reformers' analysis of other elements of folk culture as well. The catalog of "Provoking Evils" and the fear of corrupting the "rising generation" so prominent in the results of the Reforming Synod of 1679 were dangers closely related to the learned version of witch lore on both sides of the Atlantic. With witch lore the movement had a cosmic, indeed potentially Manichaean, dimension that provoked debate as well as passionate commitment.

To elaborate on this learned lore, the clergy and other English reformers developed a prolific literature. Stimulated by the great witch-hunts of 1560–1630 and by the continuing possibility of satanic conspiracies, most of the authors sought first to comprehend the occult theoretically, next to collect instances illustrating the powers of good and evil spirits, and finally to discover means of identifying and deterring humans who acted in collusion with evil. New Englanders both read and contributed to the debate.[10]

8. Demos, *Entertaining Satan,* 128, 172–78, 300–309.

9. Stuart Clark, "Inversion, Misrule, and the Meaning of Witchcraft," *Past and Present* 87 (1980): 98–127; Horsley, "Who Were the Witches?" 690–98. These should be considered in conjunction with William Bouwsma, "Anxiety and the Formation of Early Modern Culture," in Barbara Malement, ed., *After the Reformation: Essays in Honor of J. H. Hexter* (Philadelphia, 1980), 215–46.

10. Weisman, *Witchcraft, Magic, and Religion,* 23–38, 53–78; Wallace Notestein, *A History of Witchcraft in England from 1558 to 1718* (New York, 1911, 1965), 227–312; Clark, "Inversion," 109–10. The most famous New England works in this genre are Increase Mather, *Essays for the Recording of Illustrious Providences* (Boston, 1684; London, 1686, 1687), commonly known as *Remarkable Providences;* Cotton Mather, *Late Memorable Providences Relating to Witchcraft and Possessions* (Boston, 1689; London, 1691); and John Hale, *A Modest Enquiry into the Nature of Witchcraft* (Boston, 1702).

One reason for this Anglo-American literature was considerable disagreement over whether Satan needed the conscious collaboration of the reputed witch, especially in "afflicting by specters," and whether the effects of witchcraft and cunning lore were real or "mere delusions of Satan." Those thinkers most out of sympathy with popular conceptions held that Satan needed no human assistance or permission and that the only limits on the devil's power were those imposed by God. Satan merely duped witches and victims into believing that the witch had occult initiative in order to wean both from Christianity.

This view, with its strong insistence on God's ultimate control, had obvious allure for Puritan intellectuals. The two most famous Bay Colony critics of the Salem investigations, Thomas Brattle and Robert Calef—angered by what they saw as the authorities' pandering to popular ignorance and falling for the devil's snare—held this version of learned witch lore. Neither doubted Satan's existence. Brattle grumbled of the trials "that all is perfect Devilism, and an Hellish design to ruin and destroy this poor land." Calef, convinced that spectral evidence was Satan's trick to confuse and distract, asserted that the true test of a witch "is a maligning and oppugning the Word, Work, or Worship of God, and, by an extraordinary Sign, seeking to seduce any from it." He would have executed such people without hesitation, not for occult evil deeds that they could not have accomplished anyway, but for "diabolic" apostasy.[11]

The witchcraft theory advocated by New England clerics, particularly Increase Mather, was closer to Calef's and Brattle's view than to that which animated many of the magistrates and the populace in 1692. In fact, Brattle had nothing but praise for the elder Mather's approach. Likewise, Calef's famous criticism of Cotton Mather's *Wonders of the Invisible World* (1693) was based on Calef's belief that the younger Mather had dishonestly compromised a position they both shared in order to vindicate questionable court procedures. Mather undoubtedly did so in order to preserve the momentum of moral reform. In Calef's eyes the need to shore up the shaky legitimacy and popularity of the new regime under the 1691 charter in time of war was not sufficient justification for Mather's actions. Mather's hysterical reaction indicates that the criticism hit home.[12]

11. "Letter of Thomas Brattle," 188–89; Robert Calef, *More Wonders of the Invisible World,* excerpted in Burr, ed., *Narratives,* 330–31, 389–90.
12. "Letter of Thomas Brattle," 180; Calef, *More Wonders,* 300–301, 307, 378–80, 388–93; Richard H. Werking, "'Reformation Is Our Only Preservation': Cotton Mather and Salem Witchcraft," *WMQ* 29 (1977): 281–90.

The ministers' approach was not so pristine. Unlike Calef and Brattle, they were under pastoral constraints to deal with the common lore rather than merely deride or ignore it. Manifestly people were suffering long before, but most spectacularly during, 1692 because of widespread belief and indulgence in occultism. Brattle's advice was that "civil leaders and spiritual teachers . . . should punish and preach down such sorcery and wickedness."[13] The ministers had been doing that, perhaps too energetically, but they also had to compromise with some aspects of occultism in order to discipline it.

In this arena of reform as in others the contrasts should not be drawn too starkly. There were, after all, points of contact between learned and popular witch lore. Few doubted Satan's existence or his character defects, no matter how much they debated his powers and initiative. That popular lore concentrated more on specific occult deeds did not preclude assimilation of much of the learned version. Also, both theories agreed that one basic motive behind witchcraft was malice. As one New England minister wrote in 1640, "And it is commonly observed, that men and women who have turned Witches, and been in league with the Devil, thereby to do mischief, are never given over so to do, till they begin to have an evil eye, which grieveth at the prosperity, and rejoiceth at the misery of others." Such malice, most agreed, expressed deep-seated "discontent," which could derive from many sources: envy, thwarted ambition, unjust treatment by family or neighbors, unsuccessful courtship, and so on. In the reformers' psychology, malice was a particularly wicked result of wounded pride, whose pretensions and pain were heightened by the spirit of competitive individualism. Malice was, in short, a syndrome recognized by both the learned and the populace as inherently dangerous on a potentially cosmic scale.[14]

Another point of contact was that both understood witch attitudes and activities as malicious parodies of proper conduct. In common lore witches perverted healing spells or prayers into sickness-inducing curses, fortune-telling into "foreknowledge," and gratitude into "muttering." Witches were bad neighbors thwarting rather than aiding those around them. They were bad mothers, suckling familiars and blasting children. They were wicked fathers, perverting "family government." In the learned version, as one might expect, these themes were taken most seriously and then engrafted onto a

13. "Letter of Thomas Brattle," 179.

14. Christina Lerner, "Crimen Exceptum? The Crime of Witchcraft in Europe," in V.A.C. Gatell, Bruce Lenman, and Geoffrey Parker, eds., *Crime and the Law: The Social History of Crime in Europe since 1500* (London, 1980), 49–75, esp. 51, 63–65; William Hookes, *New Englands Tears for Old Englands Fears* (London, 1641), 6–7; Thomas, *Religion and the Decline of Magic,* 437–45, 514, 522.

more comprehensive theory. As one recent historian has argued, "Renaissance descriptions of the nature of Satan, the character of hell, and, above all, the ritual activity of witches shared a vocabulary of misrule, that they were in effect part of a language conventionally employed to establish and condemn the properties of a disorderly world."[15] The theme of perverting the most sacred institutions of Puritan society played a major role in the Salem investigations.

Thus, despite significant differences, the two traditions were congruent enough to allow ministers—if they downplayed the more astringent elements of the learned interpretation—to speak credibly to those more sympathetic to popular lore. The most sensible pastoral approach was to distinguish between "little Sorceries" and more overt diabolism, even though in learned theory both ultimately derived from Satan. John Hale, for instance, could not bring himself to condemn "those that ignorantly use charms, spells, writings of forms of words." He knew from experience that "those who use them are not sensible that they are but various ceremonies to invoke the Devil, and that the effects following these charms, etc., are done by the Devil." He noted sadly that practitioners "have an implicit faith that the means used shall produce the effect desired, but consider not how."[16] This opinion was general among the New England clergy and reflected their willingness to accept the distinction between cunning lore and witchcraft, albeit on their terms.

To overcome such ignorance, education rather than heavy-handed suppression was the preferred solution. If they were to pursue the campaign effectively the ministers needed information and examples presented popularly in their "plain style" of exposition. That was the primary motive behind Increase Mather's *Remarkable Providences* (1684). This treatise was another of his efforts to carry out the program of the Reforming Synod. As he explained, "My design in writing these things is, that so I might bear witness against the superstitions which some in this land of light have been found guilty of, and that (if God shall bless that which has been spoken to convince men of the errors of their way) the like evils may no more be heard of amongst us."[17]

15. Clark, "Inversion," 99–110; Demos, *Entertaining Satan,* 172–210. For a good account of shared beliefs in the supernatural, see David D. Hall, *Worlds of Wonder, Days of Judgment: Popular Religious Belief in Early New England* (New York, 1989), 213–32.

16. Hale, *Modest Enquiry,* 131–32.

17. I. Mather, *Essay for the Recording of Illustrious Providences,* 196 (hereafter *Remarkable Providences*); I used the 1856 edition. For a feminist perspective on this work, see Ann Kibbey, "Mutations of the Supernatural: Witchcraft, Remarkable Providences, and the Power of Puritan Men," *American Quarterly* 34 (1982): 125–48.

The work was immediately inspired by Mather's discovery of a collection of occult incidents among the papers of the deceased John Davenport, Connecticut's most influential divine. The papers were discussed "at a general meeting of the ministers of the colony, May 12, 1681," where it was decided that Mather would gather more examples from correspondents and publish the whole along with commentary and casuistry in a section entitled "Several Cases of Conscience Considered." The organization of *Remarkable Providences* followed the tradition exemplified by the most respected English commentator on witch lore, Joseph Glanvill, an Anglican priest with whom Mather maintained a correspondence. However, he included the casuistical section to meet more explicitly his reformist and pastoral purposes.[18]

In his examples and casuistry Mather marked out a clerical consensus on the interpretation and treatment of witchcraft. Essentially, the skepticism of the learned tradition was confirmed: pastors should remember "that the world is full of fabulous stories concerning some kind of familiarities with the Devil, and things done by his help, which are beyond the powers of creatures to accomplish." Mather also thought it likely that most accusations, confessions, and cures effected by cunning lore were "delusions" caused by Satan, ignorance, or "Melancholia."

Prescriptions for treatment arose out of both skepticism and pastoral concern. The afflicted persons should be isolated as much as possible from their audience and then carefully encouraged to examine their experiences rationally with a minister. Fasts and prayers (both public and private) seemed to dampen hysteria. If an afflicted person accused someone explicitly, it often helped if the accused would pray with the afflicted, particularly if the accused were "sincere" and "holy." Finally, New England experience suggested to Mather that witches, if involved at all, usually acted alone or in small groups. "Apparitions" too were rare. "Nevertheless," Mather reminded his readers, "that spirits have sometimes really (as well as imaginarily) appeared to mortals in the world is amongst sober men beyond controversy."[19] Thus, *Remarkable*

18. For an introduction to the character and importance of casuistry to English thought and moral reform, see Camille Wells Slights, *The Casuistical Tradition in Shakespeare, Donne, Herbert, and Milton* (Princeton, 1981), esp. 3–34.

19. I. Mather, *Remarkable Providences*, 25–26, 101–11, 134–35, 143, 180–81, 190–91. Three cases were especially important to Mather's analysis: the Morse poltergeist (Newbury, 1679–80), Anne Cole (Hartford, 1662), and Elizabeth Knap (Groton, 1671), who was closely studied by the brilliant Samuel Willard. The literature on these cases is vast, but see the accounts in Demos, *Entertaining Satan;* Samuel Drake, *Annals of Witchcraft in New England* (Boston, 1869), 258–96, for the Morse depositions; "Samuel Willard's Account of the Strange Case of Elizabeth Knap of Groton," Massachusetts Historical Society *Collections*, 4th ser., 8 (1868): 555–70.

Providences should be read as a collection of instances and arguments for a concerted clerical campaign to suppress witchcraft and discredit cunning lore. The other famous pre-1692 witch book, Cotton Mather's *Late Memorable Providences Relating to Witchcraft and Possession* (Boston, 1689; London, 1691), which was an update of his father's work, should be approached similarly.[20]

Well before 1692 the more astute of the clergy were keenly aware of witch and cunning lore. As part of the reforming drive after King Philip's War they had studied it, classified its elements, and developed devices for coping with the practices within the general confines of learned witch lore. Their approach was skeptical, moderate, and pastoral. Sensational witch-hunts fueled by spectral evidence and resulting in mass prosecutions did not fit their theory or practice. The weak link in their armor of skepticism was the pact theory. In 1692 they encountered evidence of a vast satanic conspiracy, and some of their favorite techniques for control failed. This led to moments of confusion as some ministers succumbed to the worst implications of their position. But after initial shock they tended to revert to the prescriptions explicated in *Remarkable Providences.*

After the panic at Salem was well under way Cotton Mather wrote in protest to one of the magistrates, "it is worth considering whether there be a necessity always by extirpations by halter or faggot of every wretched creature that shall be hooked into some degree of witchcraft." Was it not possible, he asked, to impose "some lesser punishments, and also put upon some solemn, open, public, and explicit renunciation of the Devil?"[21] Yet despite such objections from the younger Mather and others, reliance on the threat and the reality of the "halter" governed events from April to October 1692. One way to understand the situation is to examine the experience of the magistracy during the years when the clergy were developing their approach to the occult.

The Salem cases were not Massachusetts's first experience with witchcraft trials. Nor indeed was the Bay Colony alone. Beginning in the 1640s a spate of trials spread throughout the English mainland colonies, the bulk of them in Massachusetts and Connecticut. By 1663 there had been some sixty-eight cases in New England. The interpretation used by judges and legislators was the learned version. As Frederick Drake observed, "Colonial leaders became increasingly concerned during the 1640s with the emergence of witchcraft activity as a manifestation of the Devil's desire to subvert God's Commonwealth. Puritan, Anglican, Pilgrim, and Catholic alike took steps to arm

20. Extensive excerpts are in Burr, ed., *Narratives,* 89–143.
21. "Cotton Mather to John Richards, May 31, 1692," "Mather Correspondence," 396.

themselves with legal protection against his agents." In the colonies some 40 percent of those tried were executed from 1647 to 1662, a rate similar to England's during the 1637–46 scare. Then, after 1662, the pace of trial and execution declined in both England and America.[22]

The English courts before 1660, having adopted the learned interpretation of witch lore, were hostile to most forms of magic, although cunning folk were usually lightly punished. Meanwhile the continuing debate over the nature and efficacy of occult actions gradually narrowed the range of admissible evidence and made conviction more difficult. After 1660 judges became increasingly indifferent, regarding the problem largely as one of vulgar superstition. Similarly, in America after 1662 the courts—caught between the popular desire to prosecute and the narrowing theological definition of the crime—temporized wherever possible, thereby avoiding executions.[23]

In the Bay Colony caution was also encouraged by the failure to suppress Quakerism, another great enemy of the "godly commonwealth."[24] The heightened political tensions of the era further inclined magistrates to avoid disciplining manifestations of popular culture, turning the task increasingly over to the clergy. The courts after 1662 showed no intense desire to control servants, the poor, or the profane generally. Instead the magistrates tended to concentrate on policing the respectable population and were especially interested in such crimes as "contempt for authority." The courts also tended to be lenient with such offenders, relying on the shame of public humiliation and the capacity of churches and towns to rehabilitate offenders. This trend was not welcomed by the clergy and helped give rise to the agitation for the Reforming Synod. During the 1680s the courts (as we have seen) evinced renewed interest in such matters as tavern regulation, but enforcement was often sporadic and lax.[25]

22. Demos, *Entertaining Satan*, 401–5; Frederick C. Drake, "Witchcraft: The American Colonies, 1647–1662," *American Quarterly* 20 (1968): 711; Richard Beale Davis, "The Devil in Virginia in the Seventeenth Century," in his *Literature and Society in Early Virginia, 1608–1840* (Baton Rouge, La., 1973).

23. Thomas, *Religion and the Decline of Magic*, 256–63; Drake, "Witchcraft," 724; Weisman, *Witchcraft, Magic, and Religion*, 105–12; Godbeer, *Devil's Dominion*, 153–78.

24. Quakers in both England and New England from the 1650s through 1692 were frequently suspected of witchcraft or other forms of diabolism, largely because of their belief in immediate revelation and the conduct that arose from such belief. See Godbeer, *Devil's Dominion*, 194–98.

25. Eli Farber, "Puritan Criminals: The Economic, Social, and Intellectual Background to Crime in Seventeenth-Century Massachusetts," *Perspectives in American History* 11 (1977–78): 102–12, 116–25, 135–44; David H. Flaherty, "Law and the Enforcement of Morals in Early America," *Perspectives in American History* 5 (1971): 228–33; Roger Thompson, "'Holy

But the magistrates, particularly William Stoughton and Samuel Sewall, could not remain indifferent once the crisis of the Dominion of New England struck directly at the legitimacy of social and political authority. The trauma of those events and the fear of unrest and agitation among the populace were palpable among the civil leaders who held office under the various regimes from 1686 to 1692.[26] They learned to be wary of plots originating not only from English royalists, French courtiers, and Indian sagamores but also from their own people and even from the "vulgar," whose care they had earlier consigned to the clergy. If danger could come from all those directions, why not from Satan himself? The magistrates lacked the ministers' sophistication, but they understood enough of the canons of learned witch lore to fear "hellish conspiracy."

In 1692 the nightmares of magistrates, the clerical campaign for "reformation," and popular witch lore collided in a crisis complicated by local social tensions. Given this complexity, interpreting the event—then or now—has not been simple. The timing is the easiest thing to understand. King William's War, the first serious contest with the French and their Indian allies, was in its third year and was going poorly in northern New England. The Maine and New Hampshire frontier had virtually collapsed. There were rumors of impending attacks on the exposed Essex County villages. The fishing and commercial fleets of the coastal towns, particularly Salem and Marblehead, had been decimated. The entire economy of the region was disrupted. After the overthrow of the Dominion of New England in 1689 the provisional government was weak and uncertain as it coped with war and awaited the king's pleasure on new political forms for the colony and its neighbors. Early in 1692 the populace of Essex County, the colony's magistrates, and its ministers all faced an uncertain, turbulent future. Hysteria was near the surface.

The fact that panic first erupted in Salem Village rather than in one of the more exposed frontier towns or disrupted ports is something of a mystery. Perhaps, paradoxically, people require a modicum of safety in order to indulge hysteria. But be that as it may, rural Salem Village—with its entrenched factionalism and its long, intimate but contentious relationship with highly

---

Watchfulness' and Communal Conformism: The Function of Defamation in Early New England Communities," *NEQ* 56 (1983): 504–22.

26. T. H. Breen, "War, Taxes, and Political Brokers: The Ordeal of Massachusetts Bay, 1675–1692," in his *Puritans and Adventurers: Change and Persistence in Early America* (New York, 1980), esp. 103–5; Richard P. Gildrie, "Salem Society and Politics in the 1680s," *EIHC* 114 (1978): 185–206.

commercialized Salem Town—was certainly prone to disturbance.[27] The fact that many of those accused early on were respectable folk around whom clung no aura of the occult was a source of great confusion and played no small part in accelerating the crisis.

Yet there is risk in concentrating exclusively on the village. Accusations spread quickly through most of the county and into nearby areas. Once launched in the village, the 1692 witchcraft investigations had a dynamic, a logic, that transcended the peculiar social and political configurations of Salem Village.[28] One way to approach this inner logic is to note the geographical and chronological phases of the investigations.

The investigation proceeded in essentially three phases. The first, from 29 February to 22 April, centered on Salem Village with strong attention being paid to neighboring Salem Town and Topsfield. Village factionalism was at the heart of the disturbance. In Salem Town the focus was on the Proctor family and other connections that straddled the village-town boundary, while in Topsfield interest was on the Hobbs family, whose deviant family life was notorious. The first phase culminated in the accusation of George Burroughs, which, as we shall see, gave this stage a coherence satisfying to the clerics and magistrates committed to learned witch lore.

In the second phase, from 22 April to 2 July, the populace and the magistrates collaborated in a general investigation of suspicious characters, many of whom had established occult reputations before 1692. Zeal was fueled by suspicions rekindled in the earlier phases and by preparations for the opening of formal trials in the Court of Oyer and Terminer early in June.

The third phase centered strongly on Andover. This least-studied aspect of the 1692 crisis is in many ways the most perplexing. The pattern of accusation and investigation was controlled not so much by the afflicted as by the accused of Andover, most of whom (thirty-five of forty-three) made lurid confessions that blended popular and learned witch lore in ways which, taken together, fit none of the contemporary paradigms. Through all three phases the interplay between learned and popular witchcraft was crucial. In 1692 the perennial struggle for the Reformation of Manners got out of hand as clerics, magistrates, and the populace grappled with their various visions of the evils that afflicted their society.

Fittingly, the Salem Village stage began with some elementary cunning lore that went awry. A band of girls who habitually met in the Reverend Samuel Parris's house for conjuring became "afflicted." After a baffled physician

---

27. Boyer and Nissenbaum, *Salem Possessed*, 80–109, 179–216.
28. Breen, "War, Taxes, and Political Brokers," 238 n. 99.

suggested witchcraft, Mary Sibley, a church member and aunt of one of the girls, had Parris's servants, Tituba and John Indian, bake "a cake of rye meal, with the children's water" and feed it to a dog. According to popular lore, this was to allow the victims to "see" their afflicters. It worked, and Tituba herself along with two others who fit the popular witch stereotype, Sarah Good and Sarah Osborne, were duly named.[29]

Once accusations arose out of popular lore, recourse was to learned investigation. Warrants were sworn on February 29, and two magistrates from Salem Town, John Hathorne and Jonathan Corwin, came out the next day to examine the accused. Their approach was, of course, strictly learned. Hathorne's first question to Sarah Good was the classic, "Who do you serve?" She knew the routine and responded, "I serve God." But she fit the prediction of malice perfectly: "her answers were a very wicked, spiteful manner, reflecting and retorting against the authority with base and abusive words, and many lies she was taken in." Sarah Osborne too said little to disrupt expectations. For instance, she avoided worship, she said, because "a voice" told her she "should go no more to meeting."[30]

With the arrest of these three the episode should have ended. Instead, Tituba made a confession that triggered the worst nightmare of learned witch lore: explicit satanic pacts made by a cabal of witches including, beyond Good and Osborne, at least two unknown women and a man who met in the village. Satan himself had appeared to Tituba: "he tell me he god, and I must believe him and serve him six years and he would give me many fine things."[31] Here was the theme of inversion in stark form: Satan, using a standard indenture period and claiming to be God, was seeking worshipers and servants through promises of material reward.

Tituba's vision was probably influenced in part by relations with her master, Samuel Parris, a minister who had played a strong supporting role in the crusade for moral reform. A pastor of mediocre talents, Parris was floundering in the complexities of Salem Village factionalism. Now his own household was "afflicted." Lacking the sophistication of an Increase Mather and being personally embroiled, he leapt quickly to the worst conclusions of the pact theory. Tituba's confession may have been her translation of his worries not only about witchcraft but also about apostasy.[32] Indeed, her

29. Calef, *More Wonders,* 342; Boyer and Nissenbaum, *Salem Possessed,* 193–94, 203–8.
30. *Witchcraft Papers* II, 357, 611.
31. *Witchcraft Papers* III, 746, 747, 753–54.
32. Larry D. Gragg, "Samuel Parris: Portrait of a Puritan Clergyman," *EIHC* 119 (1983): 228–29; James E. Kences, "Some Unexplored Relationships of Essex County Witch-

statement seems prime evidence of the extent to which the clerical crusade for reformation had been assimilated by the lowliest into their witch lore.

Despite signs that this was an uncommon case, the magistrates refused to panic. Tituba's alarming confession seemed confirmed by the fact that the afflictions continued even after the examinations, which was unusual in New England. Nonetheless Hathorne and Corwin were wary. Even after the girls in their hallucinations settled on Rebecca Nurse and Martha Cory on 12 March, the court waited a week to issue warrants. Nurse and Cory apparently attracted the girls' fears for local factional reasons and decidedly not because they fit any witch image.[33] That pattern of accusing the probably innocent was not unknown; and so the magistrates waited for clarification, undoubtedly hoping that the problem would resolve itself.

Meanwhile during March the techniques developed by the clergy were tried and failed, which naturally compounded the fear. On the eleventh a prayer service led by "several neighboring ministers" held in the presence of the afflicted only stimulated them to "act and speak strangely and ridiculously."[34] Martha Cory, a pious churchwoman certain that witches "were idle, slothful persons and minded nothing good," determined "to open the eyes of the magistrates and ministers" by following the common remedy of visiting and praying with her chief accuser, young Ann Putnam. The result was worse affliction. The unfortunate Rebecca Nurse, when later asked by Hathorne why she did not try the same device, answered, "Because I was afraid I should have fits too."[35]

On 19 March, the day a warrant for Cory was issued, Deodat Lawson, a former village minister, arrived hoping to calm the situation. Instead he became convinced (as had Parris) that Satan, aided by witches, had opened an assault on Christian society. Lawson witnessed a part of the attack when he tried to preach at the regular Sunday services. "In the beginning of the sermon, Mrs. Pope, a woman afflicted, said to me, Now there is enough of that. And in the afternoon, Abigail Williams, upon referring to my doctrine, said to me, I know no doctrine you had. If you did name one, I have forgot it."[36] Pandemonium at Martha Cory's examination the next day indicated that Satan was disrupting courts as well as churches.

---

craft to the Indian Wars of 1675 and 1689," *EIHC* 120 (1984): 187; *Witchcraft Papers* I, 607.

33. Boyer and Nissenbaum, *Salem Possessed,* 146–47, 173–74.

34. Calef, *More Wonders,* 342.

35. *Witchcraft Papers* I, 262, 264–65; II, 586.

36. Deodat Lawson, "A Brief and True Narrative," in Burr, ed., *Narratives,* 145–46.

These demonstrations of satanic power went beyond previous clerical experience. Lawson worked out his analysis in a lecture-day sermon given on the twenty-fourth.[37] The village had become "the rendezvous of devils, whence they muster their infernal forces." The fact that "visible members of the church are under the awful accusations and imputations of being the instruments of Satan" triggered his worst fears. Satan "insinuates into the society of the adopted Children of God, in their most solemn approaches to him, in sacred ordinances . . . for it is certain he never works more like the Prince of Darkness than when he looks most like an angel of light." Even so Lawson refused to panic. He was certain that some of the accused were innocent, and he suspected that village animosities played a role. "Give no place to the Devil by rash censuring of others, without sufficient grounds, or false accusing any willingly." He reminded the faction-ridden village church that "Surely his design is that Christ's Kingdom may be divided against itself." Lawson was giving symbolic clarity to their experience.

Even yet amid a flood of accusatory visions and rumors, restraint was the rule. By the end of March only Cory, Nurse, and Rachel Clinton of Ipswich were newly indicted.[38] But the element of subversion by parody was growing. The afflicted had hinted at witch meetings resembling church services almost from the beginning, but on 31 March and 1 April their premonitions blossomed into explicit visions. On the thirty-first, while a "public fast" (another clerical staple for dampening disturbances) was "kept at Salem," Abigail Williams claimed "that the witches had a sacrament day at an house in the Village, and that they had red bread and red drink." While the people of God mourned, the people of Satan held communion! The next day Mercy Lewis explained that she had spurned the "red bread like man's flesh" and was rewarded with a vision of heaven, "a glorious place, which had no candles nor sun, yet was full of light and brightness where there was a great multitude in white glittering robes."[39]

The number of indictments increased markedly after Deputy Governor Thomas Danforth and other magistrates joined the proceedings in mid-April. The persons accused throughout the remainder of this first phase generally

---

37. Sermon notes are in Paul Boyer and Stephen Nissenbaum, eds., *Salem-Village Witchcraft: A Documentary Record of Local Conflict in Colonial New England* (Belmont, Calif., 1972), 124–28.

38. Clinton had a well-established witch reputation. See Demos, *Entertaining Satan*, 19–35.

39. Lawson, "Narrative," 160–61. Mercy Lewis's vision seems another reflection of Parris's concerns. He was particularly apt to castigate the Mass and stress the importance of the Lord's Supper. See Gragg, "Samuel Parris," 213, 221–22.

fit the factional alignments within the village. But the logic of the hallucinations was governed by visions of a witch church, an alternative society. Sarah Cloyse and Elizabeth Proctor, for instance, "were their deacons" at the witch sacrament. To end the crisis, a convincing agent of the devil capable of raising such havoc had to be identified.

Who better to perpetrate subversive parodies of church order, complete with sacraments and deacons, than an alienated cleric? The magistrates found their man in the Reverend George Burroughs, a former village pastor who, Cotton Mather came to believe, "had the promise of being a King in Satan's Kingdom, now going to be erected."[40] On 21 April two fathers of the afflicted, Jonathan Walcott and Thomas Putnam, wrote to the magistrates "of what we conceive you have not heard, which are high and dreadful." Ann Putnam had a vision explicitly of Burroughs. The warrant was drawn on 22 April.

His examination early in May rendered the Salem Village outbreak comprehensible within the clerical tradition. Burroughs was treated with the close attention his place in the drama required. Once arrested and brought to Salem, he was questioned privately by four magistrates at length before he was brought into court, where the heightened sufferings of the afflicted confirmed all suspicions. In camera the magistrates concentrated on Burroughs's religious indifference. He was pastor at Wells, Maine, and yet despite the vast distance he remained "in full communion at Roxbury." Maine, the area most thoroughly devastated by recent Indian attacks, was also noted for its religious and moral laxity. To those who feared God's judgment, the conclusion was obvious.

Yet Burroughs made no attempt to allay suspicion. When asked when last he took communion, "he answered it was so long since he could not tell." He also admitted "that none of his children, but the eldest was baptised." His conduct was indeed odd for a Puritan cleric. The magistrates had what they needed, but they did not forbear asking questions out of popular lore. "He denied that his house at Casco was haunted, yet he owned there were toads." Having uncovered their apostate, their mention of spirits and familiars was just icing on the cake. There was also strong evidence that Burroughs had been dabbling in the occult and that he had made claims to magical powers in order to intimidate others, particularly his wives and their friends and relatives.

Burroughs was executed in August. All through the crisis and even in death he continued to play his assigned role, which further confirmed the leaders'

---

40. Cotton Mather, *The Wonders of the Invisible World* (Boston, 1693; London, 1862), 120; Hansen, *Witchcraft at Salem*, 74–77; *Witchcraft Papers* I, 151–78. Boyer and Nissenbaum, *Salem Possessed*, 21, suggest Burroughs may have been a surrogate for Parris.

sense of his significance. The theme of parody deepened as he became the witches' surrogate Christ. Several confessing witches claimed "that the night before Mr. Burroughs was executed that there was a great meeting of witches . . . that Mr. Burroughs was there and they had the sacrament and after they had done he took leave and bid them stand to their faith and not own [admit] anything."[41]

The arrest of Burroughs marked the climax of the first phase of the investigation. The crisis now made sense within the context of learned lore. Together with some continuing echoes of the village phase, the logic governing the second from 22 April to 2 July 1692 was largely that of popular witch belief, which greatly expanded both the numbers and the geographic range of the accusations.

Generally those accused in this phase fit well into the "collective portrait" of reputed witches emerging in recent scholarship.[42] Most were women, middle-aged or older, of quarrelsome disposition who had histories of conflict with neighbors or relations. Some were deranged. Susannah Roots, for instance, was an impoverished Beverly widow placed in the household of another family for support. She had gained a reputation prior to 1692 as a "bad woman" by pointedly refusing to join in family prayers and by wandering about alone in the night speaking "as if there were five or six persons with her." Such persons taxed the charitable resources of their communities and generated feelings of guilt among those who felt obligated to assist but who also resented the burden. Witchcraft accusations could discharge the guilt. Apparently this was a common situation in both Old and New England.[43]

Yet alongside and within this general rubric of struggle between communal and individualist impulses, the accusations reveal something of the diversity of these conflicts and the complexity of the profane conversation through which they were expressed. Both Dorcas Hoar of Beverly and Wilmot Reed of Marblehead, for example, were aggressive women living on the edge of subsistence.[44] Yet they were hardly innocent victims. Both cultivated occult reputations in order to intimidate others and to cover fencing operations. Wilmot Reed, the fiftyish wife of a fisherman, encouraged neighboring servants to steal linen—a practice tolerated, however grudgingly, by those who

41. *Witchcraft Papers* II, 624–28.
42. See especially Demos, *Entertaining Satan,* 57–94.
43. *Witchcraft Papers* III, 722; Macfarlane, *Witchcraft,* 172–76; Demos, *Entertaining Satan,* 292–329.
44. *Witchcraft Papers* II, 389–404; III, 711–17; *Essex Recs.* VI, 81; VIII, 41–55.

knew her. But when a woman newly arrived in Salem Town threatened to charge her before the magistrates, the fisherwife "told her . . . that she wished she might never mingere, nor cacare." The unfortunate newcomer naturally developed "the distemper of dry bellyache" and could not relieve herself "so long as she was in Town." Dorcas Hoar, a widow, ran an illegal alehouse, practiced fortune-telling to intimidate as well as to amuse, and developed a reputation for maleficium in order both to encourage young people to steal and to prevent them from divulging the crimes. She had an unsavory reputation stretching back twenty years before 1692. Clearly, for some witch lore and popular magic were a career that opened into wider realms of criminality.

Other cases of persons with established reputations prior to 1692 indicate the variety of occult activity and suspicion that dominated this phase of the investigation.[45] Ann Pudeator, a widow of Salem Town who used "threatenings" to gain services she could not afford, may also have been experimenting (judging from the strange "ointments" found in her house) with what was called the "Devil's Grease" in Europe. Then, too, there had been swirling about her since 1680 suspicions that she had aided her late husband in poisoning his first wife.[46] Arrested as well was Alice Parker, a reputed "sea witch" able to control weather, founder ships, and forecast the fate of voyages. Given her fame along the waterfront it would have been a hardy captain indeed who refused her husband a berth. An occult reputation was at times cultivated by those who simply had little other claim to notoriety. For instance, Job Tookey, a chronically poor but profligate laborer and sailor, sought status by claiming "that he had some learning and could Raise the Devil." The court, more impressed with his talents as a braggart than a wizard, turned him loose.[47]

Nor were all of the accused in this second phase poorer people. Mary Bradbury was a church member, the wife of one of Salisbury's leading citizens, and among the mariners a reputed sea witch. First accused in 1679, Bradbury fought the designation and earned among many a reputation as "a goodly, godly wife." Stout denials and strong support from the members of her church eventually led to her vindication.

<hr />

45. "Established reputations" were determined by selecting cases from *Witchcraft Papers* in which there was evidence from persons other than the afflicted and referred to suspicions of occult activity prior to 1691. Twenty-six cases fit these criteria. Compare with Demos, *Entertaining Satan*, 66.

46. *Witchcraft Papers* III, 702–3, 709; *Essex Recs.* VIII, 59–60. For the importance of the Devil's Grease, see Edward Bever, "Old Age and Witchcraft in Early Modern Europe," in Peter N. Stearns, ed., *Old Age in Preindustrial Society* (New York, 1982), 168.

47. *Witchcraft Papers* II, 624–28; III, 759–62; *Essex Recs.* VIII, 336.

Meanwhile, suspicions that she violated godly economic ethics dogged her. A sailor testified that in 1681 she had sold spoiled butter to the captain of a vessel bound for Barbados, "which made the men very much disturbed about it and would often say that they had Mrs. Bradbury was a witch and that they verily believed she was or else she would not have served the captain so." To her malignancy they attributed the storms and apparitions that plagued them. Among the landsmen of Salisbury her occult reputation arose out of rumors of love potions, frustrated courtship, and the remark of a cunning man "that Mrs. Bradbury was a great deal worse than Goody Martin," Salisbury's most stereotypical witch—who incidentally was also arrested in this second phase.[48] Mrs. Bradbury clearly was more victim than exploiter of the witch designation.

Philip English, a wealthy Salem merchant, was another whose unsought occult fame was tied to perceptions of sharp economic practice. A supporter of the Andros regime, English was engaged in challenging the old town grants on Marblehead during the Dominion of New England. Because of his "threatenings" and attempts to suborn witnesses, some of the fishermen became convinced that he was responsible for various accidents that befell them. When the afflicted of the village mentioned his name in their fits the Marblehead fishing folk brought their fears to court, and English fled the colony.[49]

Worries about maleficium and the conflicts between communal and individualist impulses governed the second phase of the witch-hunt. Old suspicions and quarrels crystallized into formal accusations. Candidates, likely and not so likely, were examined and imprisoned to await trial or released as the evidence seemed to dictate. The authorities were no longer uncovering a satanic conspiracy but rather sifting through the region's accumulated witch lore.[50] By 2 July the process of examination seemed to be concluding as the trials before the Court of Oyer and Terminer were already under way.

But in mid-July the situation changed dramatically. The Andover phase erupted, and before it ended nearly one out of every fifteen residents in that town had confessed to or been formally accused of practicing witchcraft. It began as had the village phase with an exercise in popular counterwitch magic.

48. *Witchcraft Papers* I, 117–20, 125–26; Demos, *Entertaining Satan,* 58, 66, 74.
49. *Witchcraft Papers* I, 313–21; David T. Konig, "A New Look at the Essex 'French': Ethnic Frictions and Community Tensions in Seventeenth-Century Essex County, Massachusetts," *EIHC* 110 (1974): 167–80.
50. For a different view attributing more consistency, initiative, and intentionality to the magistrates throughout the crisis, see Weisman, *Witchcraft, Magic, and Religion,* 132–35, 148–59.

Joseph Ballard, a substantial Andover farmer worried over his wife's ailments, suspected witchcraft, an understandable notion in 1692. Yet Andover's most likely suspect, Martha Carrier, had been arrested during the second phase. Perplexed, Ballard went to the afflicted of Salem Village to determine if maleficium was involved and, if so, to uncover the culprit. Two of the girls came to Andover to apply the traditional "touch test": if the afflicted relaxed their fits when touched by another, then that person was probably a witch. That large numbers of persons quickly became suspect by this method is hardly surprising.[51]

According to clerical witch lore the device was anathema. In similar circumstances Increase Mather berated a Bostonian who had sought out the afflicted girls, "asking him whether there was not a God in Boston, that he should go to the Devil in Salem for advice." The Andover magistrate Dudley Bradstreet, seeing the scope of the accusations, refused to sign warrants resting on that evidence. In this view he was supported by the town's two pastors.[52]

Learned skepticism, however, did not dampen popular hysteria. Rather, some of the magistrates came to share the fear. The preliminary hearings on the new cases began with a spectacular four-day confession by Ann Foster, a widow, that revived the learned nightmare. Foster claimed that Martha Carrier had coerced her into joining the witches, numbering over three hundred, who sought "to set up the Devil's Kingdom." The conspiracy was led, she hinted, by other satanically apostate clergymen "besides Mr. Burroughs . . . and one of them had gray hair." One of the Andover ministers, Francis Dane, was an elderly man with an impressive mane of gray.[53]

Thus the Andover phase, animated by a renewed convergence of learned and popular lore, developed two major facets. First, its direction came more from confessions than from hallucinatory accusations, and second, its logic dictated the search for at least one other leader of a demonic conspiracy as convincing as Mr. Burroughs. The latter effort was futile. The confessions pushed closer and closer to Mr. Dane, implicating a deacon's wife and then his own daughters and granddaughters. Several of these women confessed as well, but no one explicitly accused the minister. The process obviously reflected tension between Dane and his people, or even within his family. An autocratic man, he had been pastor at Andover since 1649. In 1681 a dispute

51. Claude M. Fuess, *Andover: Symbol of New England* (Andover, Mass., 1959), 86–87; Marion Starkey, *The Devil in Massachusetts: A Modern Enquiry into the Salem Witch Trials* (New York, 1949), 180–83; Philip J. Greven, Jr., *Four Generations: Population, Land, and Family in Colonial Andover, Massachusetts* (Ithaca, N.Y., 1970), 84–85.
52. "Letter of Thomas Brattle," 180–82.
53. *Witchcraft Papers* II, 341–44; Fuess, *Andover*, 91.

over his "maintenance" had been serious enough to be settled by the General Court, which ordered the town to render adequate support but also suggested hiring an assistant. Yet in 1692 Dane could not credibly be accused of witchcraft, even if that had been a conscious wish of any of the confessors. The weakening patriarch, however cantankerous, did not have about him the aura of an occult apostate. Thus the investigation whirled about with no clear point of resolution. Finally all had to settle for the substitute first suggested in one of the early confessions—that Martha Carrier had been promised that "she would be Queen in Hell."[54]

The other major facet of this final phase, the confessions, testifies to the psychological impact of, first, the long-standing campaign for moral reform and, second, the preceding witchcraft investigations. The people of Andover, a relatively isolated farming town in the northwest corner of the county, were particularly vulnerable to a communal and personal sense of impending judgment. Unlike other Essex towns, Andover suffered Indian attacks in King Philip's War and again in 1689–90. The villagers knew that they would see more. Also, they were experiencing the first signs of land shortage. To compound this sense of unease, the community faced internal divisions. Having two pastors and a growing population, the town was debating forming two precincts—a move Mr. Dane and his supporters resisted. Meanwhile, they were disturbed by a militia reorganization that separated them from the neighboring unit at Boxford, a move that, some felt, left both towns even more open to attack.[55]

Rather than strike out at each other as had the people of Salem Village, the people of Andover turned on themselves and confessed en masse to "discontent" and "temptations" that recent events and old pressures transmuted into guilts and fears. Confession allowed communal purgation of anxieties about "impiety."[56] Ann Foster, who began the process, hungered improperly for "prosperity." But more than that, "she formerly went frequently to the public meeting to worship God, but the Devil had such power

54. *Witchcraft Papers* I, 327–34; II, 335–37, 347–48, 499–506, 523; *Mass. Recs.* V, 343–44; *Essex Recs.* VIII, 100; C. Mather, *Wonders,* 159.

55. Fuess, *Andover,* 51–56, 69–74, 114; Greven, *Four Generations,* 103–24; Kences, "Some Unexplored Relationships," 197–98.

56. Chadwick Hansen argued in "Salem Witchcraft and DeForest's 'Witching Times,'" *EIHC* 104 (1968): 100, that the "majority" were "hysterics," and thus by implication had the initiative. Richard Weisman, in contrast, believes that the village afflicted controlled the Andover cases, which "no longer bore any discernible relationship to local discontents." From the wording of the confessions the latter seems unlikely. Yet he is astute on the symbolic importance of confession in the reform movement. See Weisman, *Witchcraft, Magic, and Religion,* 97, 144, 159.

over her that she could not profit there and that was her undoing." If not Puritan worship, then Satan's. Mary Lacey, Sr., cried out on the last day of Foster's marathon confession, "We have forsaken Jesus Christ, and the devil hath got hold of us. How shall we get clear of this evil one?"[57]

Satan, his deeds, and the ceremonies he enjoined were metaphors for temptations, attitudes, and practices that they felt were separating them from Puritan standards and endangering their lives and souls. Mary Toothaker, Martha Carrier's sister and the wife of the "French Doctor," was plagued by nightmares about Indians and devastated by her inability to internalize Puritan religious experience. Her baptism, which Satan desired her to renounce, was a burden "because she had not improved it as she ought to have done." She failed at private prayer too, "but sometimes she had been helped to say, Lord be merciful to me, a sinner." Even the Bible was a snare because the devil "deludes also by Scripture." Having no place in God's kingdom, she assumed that she had joined Satan's. In contrast, Hannah Bromage of Haverhill, being urged to confess by an Andover confessor ("that being the way to eternal life") could only uncover "some deadness with respect to the ordinances for the matter of six weeks." Not being directly involved in Andover passions, she in her perplexity came close to the problem: "She being asked what shape the devil appeared to her, answered, she believed the devil was in her heart."[58]

Evil wishes, malice, guilt for past deeds and present hopes that threatened the standing order were what had to be confessed. Learned and popular witch lore became a kind of Rorschach test to elicit inner visions. One of Francis Dane's daughters, Abigail Faulkner, being angry that "folks laughed" at pious families brought low, admitted that "she did look with an evil eye. . . . She knew not but what the Devil might take that advantage." Rebecca Eames feared her son was a wizard "because he used dreadful bad words when he was angry and bad wishes." She came to suspect that she had been a witch "for twenty-six years" because in 1666 "She was then in such a horror of conscience that she took a rope to hang herself and razor to cut her throat by reason of the great sin in committing adultery and by that the Devil gained her, he promising she would not be brought out or ever discovered." William Barker, a middle-aged farmer, was discontented. "He said he had a great family, the world went hard with him." Satan promised to pay his debts "and he should live comfortably." The devil explained that his "design was to set up his own worship, abolish all the churches in the land . . . that his people

57. *Witchcraft Papers* II, 513; Thomas, *Religion and the Decline of Magic*, 520–21.
58. *Witchcraft Papers* I, 143–44; II, 767–68.

should live bravely, that all persons should be equal, that there should be no day of resurrection or of judgment, and neither punishment nor shame for sin." Barker's dream was as old as Piers Plowman and an integral part of traditional English radicalism. But in Massachusetts in 1692 the farmer, certain that Puritan standards came from God, was forced to conclude that his aspirations were from Satan.

From the confessions of this phase a multitude of similar examples could be elaborated, ranging from the use of "Venus glasses" to attempted murder and swimming nude in front of persons of the opposite sex; but through all the underlying point was the same. Within the rubric of pacts, witches' sabbaths, and afflictions, the people of Andover were confessing their deepest, most personal worries and temptations. They were under enormous pressure so to do.[59] The afflicted cried out at them. Their own neighbors, friends, and kin who had confessed urged them to do likewise. Magistrates assumed that they had something to tell. There was even physical pressure, bordering on torture. And so most confessed. They were admitting to the "provoking evils" the clergy had been denouncing since the Reforming Synod of 1679. The drama of the last phase was that the confessing witches were delivering personal jeremiads and purging themselves, much the way those sermons purged the whole society.

Yet the drama had to end, even if the magistrates could find no logical conclusion. Judicial institutions were exhausted. There were too many accusations, examinations, and incarcerations. The Court of Oyer and Terminer, which opened on 2 June, spent its first week on Bridget Bishop alone. Even though the pace increased markedly, the court was unable to try persons as expeditiously as they were being examined and arrested from late April to mid-October.

Even more important was the exhaustion of the witch paradigms used in the investigations. The chief weaknesses were the pact and conspiracy aspects of learned lore, which, once provoked by Tituba's confession and abundantly confirmed by disruptions and hallucinations, undermined the moderate prescriptions developed earlier by the clergy. Also, some of the accused did not fit the emphasis on "malice." The only acceptable explanation was a deeper satanic plot to subvert church and society than the leaders had hitherto encountered. The failure of standard clerical cures also helped cast doubt on the whole moderate clerical position. In fact, William Stoughton, the chief

59. *Witchcraft Papers* I, 280, 282, 328; Calef, *More Wonders*, 355–56. For the role of confessions generally, see Mary Douglas, ed., *Witchcraft Confessions and Accusations* (London, 1970), esp. xxxiv–xxxv.

judge on the Court of Oyer and Terminer, was convinced that the ministers, led by Increase Mather, had misinterpreted witch lore consistently since the 1670s.[60]

Thus, the full-blown conspiracy theory dominated the investigations during at least the first and third phases. But this explanation too had potent critics who were vocal at least as early as Cotton Mather's letter in May. On 15 June, their confidence restored by Increase Mather's return from England, the ministers rallied and publicly attacked both the theory and the practice of the investigations in a statement urging that in "prosecution . . . there is need of a very critical and exquisite caution."[61] Particularly, the magistrates were admonished to show "an exceeding tenderness towards those that may be complained of; especially if they have been persons formerly of an unblemished reputation." In court they recommended "as little as possible of such noise, company and openness, as may too hastily expose them that are examined." If these procedures had been followed, the Andover phase would not have occurred. In the Court of Oyer and Terminer the jury too initially had problems with the magistrates' approach. On 30 June in the first set of trials after the easy condemnation of Bishop, the jury first found Rebecca Nurse innocent—a verdict William Stoughton could not accept. Even so, the jury might have stood by their decision had not the ever unfortunate Nurse made a cryptic remark that seemed a near confession.[62]

The conspiracy theory worked only so long as it was confirmed by the example of Burroughs (whose execution, incidentally, was the only one Increase Mather ever explicitly condoned)[63] and by the "confessing witches." Mather and other clerics undermined the latter by visiting the confessors in jail and eliciting accounts of how they had come to confess. The magistrates' interpretation collapsed when they failed to find anyone in the last phase who resembled Burroughs.

The theory of popular witch lore was also unable to sustain the investigations credibly. Long before 1692 the popular approach had been badly compromised through its gradual assimilation of learned lore. Traditionally it had held that suppression of occult evil by countermagic or court action was effective and legitimate. But to conclude, and to have it abundantly confirmed in confessions, that all sorts of cunning lore (including defensive

---

60. "Letter of Thomas Brattle," 183–84.
61. "The Return of Several Ministers . . . ," reprinted in Kenneth B. Murdock, *Increase Mather: The Foremost American Puritan* (Cambridge, Mass., 1926), 405–6.
62. Calef, *More Wonders,* 358–59; *Witchcraft Papers* II, 607–8.
63. Hansen, *Witchcraft at Salem,* 138; Boyer and Nissenbaum, *Salem Possessed,* 13n.

magic) were of satanic origin utterly undermined the theory. Also, judging by the confessions, even the desire to defend oneself or others against witch attacks by such means could be "a devil's snare." The only solution was a general purge of guilt and a wholesale defection to the ministers' position on the dangers of popular magic.

Briefly put, the Salem crisis erupted when the carefully forged clerical interpretation of witch lore failed to account adequately for what was happening in Salem Village. The crisis ended when the magistrates and populace concluded that they had no intelligible substitute.[64]

The witchcraft crisis of 1692 not only graphically illustrated some of the important differences between English folk lore and Puritanism but also indicated the degree of interpenetration of these traditions. The populace was not immune to clerical views of the dangers of witch lore or, by extension, to other elements of "the Vain Conversation received by Tradition from our Fathers," to use Cotton Mather's notable formulation.[65] Nor were the advocates of moral reform insensitive to the nuances of thought and feeling among their people. The central link in the crisis was the problem of evil, a basic moral and theological question of enormous significance to both. Enflamed by unprecedented political, military, and social pressures, the tensions erupted into a sustained crisis. Yet amid the tragedy and confusion the reformers won a partial victory and in the process maintained their moral influence and initiative. As the Glorious Revolution altered fundamentally the institutional order of New England, the clergy's continued prestige was a vital element of continuity. The campaign for the Reformation of Manners endured, even becoming reinvigorated as its advocates adapted to the new order after 1691.

64. There was a witchcraft incident in 1720 in Middleton involving "afflicted" girls and complaints of a specter that neighbors "pronounced a piece of witchcraft, as certain as that there ever had been any at Salem." Yet the episode never evolved into a crisis, possibly because the only woman accused died and because the local ministers applied the usual remedies. Thomas Hutchinson, *The History of the Colony of Massachusetts Bay,* ed. Lawrence Mayo (Cambridge, Mass., 1936), 2: 20–22.

65. Cotton Mather, *Advice from the Watchtower: In a Testimony against Evil Customs* (Boston, 1713), 27–28.

THE MEASURE
OF CIVILITY

EIGHT

Adjustment to a New Order

The witchcraft crisis of 1692 occurred amid a longer political and ideological transformation of Massachusetts from a virtually independent Puritan commonwealth into a royal province. It was a time of revolution in England and English America with tensions aggravated by the onset of prolonged warfare against the French and their Indian allies. The last years of the century saw a sustained effort to reconsider New England's covenantal mission and its essential moral component, the Reformation of Manners. By adapting to the political changes wrought by revolution and by incorporating and emphasizing elements of English Whig ideology, the American reformers prolonged and even reinvigorated their campaign to reshape popular attitudes and conduct. The outcome, as Harry S. Stout has summarily explained, was that "New England's mission would continue even though the Puritan state did not."[1] This result required commitment, careful thought, prudent action, and great flexibility on the part of the clergy in particular.

As the relationship with England became increasingly ominous in the early 1680s, Weymouth pastor Samuel Torrey in an election sermon reasserted in traditional covenantal rhetoric "That we henceforth transact with God, and one with another" to forward "that great and most important business of *Reformation,*" not only "in suppressing all the great and general Sins" but "That we also labour to retrieve and raise the visible Interest of Religion, and advance it." Not surprisingly, Increase Mather wrote the introduction for the

---

1. Harry S. Stout, *The New England Soul: Preaching and Religious Culture in Colonial New England* (New York, 1986), 119. Two excellent general studies are David S. Lovejoy, *The Glorious Revolution in America* (New York, 1972), and Richard R. Johnson, *Adjustment to Empire: The New England Colonies, 1675–1715* (New Brunswick, N.J., 1981).

published version.[2] Whatever the political portents, the clergy was determined to pursue the agenda of the Reforming Synod of 1679.

The question was one of means, and on that the ministers were divided. At first the issue was whether to resist the impending loss of the founding charter, the legal bulwark that allowed the Bay Colony near immunity from English imperial interference as well as clear title to the land and government. Increase Mather, with his knowledge of and extensive connections in England, initially favored negotiations and compromise. However, by late 1683 he became alarmed by what he judged to be the corrupt and arbitrary royal government of New Hampshire, established in 1679. Not the least of the sins of the governor, Edward Cranfield, was the arrest of Joshua Moody, a Puritan cleric and student of Mather's who had been a vociferous critic of the new regime. With that precedent in mind, Mather addressed a special meeting of Boston's freemen and, to "a General Acclamation," urged resistance. In the April elections those magistrates most strongly advocating accommodation were dropped from the Court of Assistants, while their less outspoken allies barely kept their seats.[3]

Meanwhile, Salem's John Higginson, a respected elder statesman among the clergy, was beginning to separate ideologically the colony's government from "the cause of Religion, which is our praedominant interest & cause." "For though we are many wayes obliged to do our duty, to preserve our Civil Rights according to the Charter of this Colony, yet they are not to be confounded with, but distinguished from our Religious Rights which we have (not from men, but) from the Charter of the Gospel." Higginson advised Mather to remember that "good men differ in their apprehensions about the way & manner of keeping our Charter" and that the best course was to spread the word "throughout New England of the cause of God . . . which many do not understand." In that way the clergy would be better able to encourage the godly in their faith, and to "be of good report among the churches & people of God abroad." The best defense of the charter, he thought, was to "stand firm for religion" without becoming distracted by "worldly" controversy.[4]

However theologically sound, Higginson's distinction between civil and religious rights seemed implausible to Mather and a majority of their colleagues. As Mather's brother in Ireland, Nathaniel, wrote him of conditions

---

2. Samuel Torrey, *A Plea for the Life of Dying Religion* (Boston, 1683), 23.

3. Johnson, *Adjustment to Empire*, 40, 52–53; "The Autobiography of Increase Mather," ed. Michael Hall, AAS *Proceedings* 71 (1961): 307–8.

4. "John Higginson to Increase Mather, 5 February 1684," "Mather Correspondence," 283–84.

in the British Isles, "At present I see no place that is like to bee quiet, unless you in New England bee. But if your Charter bee gone, & other Governors appoynted, I expect not any other but that your Ministers must conform [to the Church of England] or bee packing." The danger seemed real enough. The crisis came in the summer of 1685 when an English frigate arrived with word of the charter's annulment and orders to establish a temporary government under Joseph Dudley, the foremost advocate of obedience to the crown.[5]

Ominously, the frigate also brought an Anglican priest. At the request of the old government some thirty ministers met at Boston and advised that "the Government ought not to give way to another till the General Court had seen and judged of the Commission." This policy meant not only delaying for the arrival of a permanent royal governor but also asserting the right of consent. Higginson, his Salem colleague Nicholas Noyes, and three others objected strenuously. Higginson "gave in his Opinion for Submission" immediately and without conditions in writing. Samuel Sewall thought the meeting "uncomfortable" and might "breed great animosities."[6]

The old charter government determined, despite the majority opinion of the ministers, to turn authority over to Dudley and his appointed council. An Anglican priest of the Church of England regularly conducted services in his surplice according to the Book of Common Prayer and preached in the Boston Town House, much to the scandal of many. John Dunton, the English bookseller who remained friendly with all sides, was understanding, if condescending. "But I could easily forgive them, in regard the Common Prayer and the Surplice were Religious Novelties in New England." Quakers too saw the old order giving way. With their cultivated sense of symbolism, some Friends asked the outgoing governor, Simon Bradstreet, for "leave to enclose the Ground the Hanged Quakers are buried in under or near the Gallows, with Pales." The day after Bradstreet and the magistrates unanimously refused "the monument," a Quaker came to the governor and spoke of "a Message he had which was to shew the great Calamities of Fire and Sword that would suddenly come in New England." He would have delivered his prophecy "in the Meetinghouse, but was prevented."[7] In Boston at least it was a time of outrage for orthodox Puritan sensibilities.

5. "Nathaniel Mather to Increase Mather, 5 February 1684," "Mather Correspondence," 57.

6. M. Halsey Thomas, ed., *Diary of Samuel Sewall, 1674–1709* (New York, 1973), 1:71–72.

7. John Dunton, *Life and Errors* (London, 1705), 1:111–12; Thomas, ed., *Diary of Samuel Sewall*, 1:67.

Although unpopular in the countryside, Dudley's provisional government enjoyed support among the merchants and maritime populations of Boston, Salem, and Marblehead. Salem's ministers remained "steady for Submission" and were backed by the port's militia companies, often commanded by leading merchants and political figures who could profit from the new regime. Boston's militia also showed a willingness to defend it. These bands ceremoniously declared their support by training together in Boston in May 1686, while the capital's militia provided Dudley with a ceremonial escort to and from his home in Roxbury. Such ceremonial military displays were essential because the rural trainbands continually evinced signs of unrest. Topsfield's captain, for instance, was arrested in August 1686 "for Treasonable Words spoken about the change of Government" and held without bail.[8]

As long as there was no consensus supporting the legitimacy of the colony's government, the town meetings and local militia exercises continued to offer forums for political debate and organization. The fear of revolt remained palpable even after a settlement was reached in 1691. Once Sir Edmund Andros arrived in December 1686 he attempted to solve the problem by restricting town meetings and gaining strict control over militia appointments. In the long run, however, his main contribution to eventual political stability was his success in alienating all factions and thus uniting the Bay Colony's populace and leaders against him. Authoritarian in temperament, Andros presided over a Dominion of New England that combined all the settlements from Maine to New Jersey, with no elected assemblies or guarantees of civil liberties. The new government was charged with frontier defense over a vast area and manned by people eager to make the most of fees and land speculations. By traditional New England standards the new government appeared both lavishly expensive and utterly unaccountable.[9]

As Andros busily generated an opposition, two incidents involving Massachusetts ministers took on political and ideological significance. At the urging of John Wise, the Ipswich town meeting refused to pay rates to the Dominion on the grounds that "no taxes shall be levied on the subjects without consent of an assembly chosen by the freeholders for assessing the same." The town was forced to pay, and Wise was imprisoned for several months. The cleric remained a heroic symbol of the combination of Whig

8. Theodore B. Lewis, "Land Speculators and the Dudley Council of 1686," *WMQ* 21 (1974): 255–72; Thomas, ed., *Diary of Samuel Sewall,* 1:114, 119.
9. Johnson, *Adjustment to Empire,* esp. 64; T. H. Breen, "War, Taxes, and Political Brokers: The Ordeal of Massachusetts Bay, 1675–1692," in his *Puritans and Adventurers: Change and Continuity in Early America* (New York, 1980), 84–89, 96–102.

and Puritan defense of liberty into the 1770s. The other episode involved John Higginson, the minister most apt to assist the Dominion. Andros and some of his council met with the pastor at Salem in March 1689 and asked him about land claims. Higginson presented biblical warrant and evidence of Indian purchases in Salem. Having heard the claims, Andros "said with indignation, Either you are Subjects or you are Rebels." Higginson took that to mean "that if we would not yield all the Lands of N.E. to be the Kings, so as to take Patents for Lands, and to pay Rent for the same, then we should not be accounted Subjects but Rebels, and treated accordingly." Both property rights and civil liberties were at hazard in ways that the old minister had not foreseen when he stood "steady for Submission."[10]

The political battle was of necessity a ceremonial struggle as well because the underlying issue was the identity and purpose of the public order. Such ideological positions traditionally were expressed in ritual as well as words. Both Dudley and Andros attempted to assert an Anglican ceremonial hegemony in Boston. Supporters of the new government occasionally chose to "drink Healths, curse, swear, talk profanely and baudily to the great disturbance of the Town and grief of good people." There were Anglican weddings and funerals, which Dudley, Andros, and other officials pointedly attended while avoiding Puritan equivalents. Within a week of his arrival Andros—escorted by a "Red-Coat" and a Royal Navy captain—went to Christmas services held at the Town House in both the morning and afternoon while Puritans kept their shops open and some country folk carried firewood to market as usual. Andros did not attend lecture days. In 1686 the queen's birthday was celebrated on a Sabbath evening by "beat of drum," cannon fire from Royal Navy frigates, bonfires, and a raucous tent party on Noddles Island. This episode led Samuel Willard during the Sunday services to express "great grief in [his] Prayer for the Profanation of the Sabbath last night." The king's birthday fell on a Thursday lecture, and so "before Lecture the guns fired; some marched throw the Streets with Viol and Drums, playing and beating by turns." In January 1687 Church of England services were held "forenoon and afternoon" together with the ringing of bells "respecting the beheading of Charles I." One is pressed to imagine a more direct affront to the Puritan sense of identity. On all sides there were emotionally charged, highly symbolic acts designed to express and shape conflicting conceptions of New England's meaning and future.[11]

10. Stout, *New England Soul,* 112; William H. Whitmore, ed., *The Andros Tracts* (Boston, 1868–74), 1:88–91.

11. Thomas, ed., *Diary of Samuel Sewall,* 1:114, 119, 121–24, 127–28, 132; Richard P.

Until after the Glorious Revolution these conceptions were seen as mutually exclusive. The possibility of blending and compromising them, as roughly suggested by John Higginson in 1684 and 1685, was lost in the passions and struggles of the late 1680s. However, even in these turbulent years the outlines of such an accommodation were emerging in England and Massachusetts.

Perhaps in part because of Higginson's arguments, the ministers did not as a rule interpret the loss of the Charter and subsequent political events as calamitous judgments of God. Such restraint implied a flexibility, an openness to the future. At the height of the Dominion's power in 1687 Increase Mather began a lecture series on the New Jerusalem from Revelation 3:12. He argued the "premillennial" position that the New Jerusalem, appearing at Christ's Second Coming, would be on earth, not in heaven, and would thus be a culmination rather than a repudiation of historical societies already existing. His hopes for New England were high because of the continuing influence of the "written word of god" and "the word preached." There was no mention (beyond the usual invocation of the godly magistrate) of any particular political order.[12]

In another sign of continuing orthodox élan, Samuel Willard, who was one of the leading intellectual figures in eastern Massachusetts, began a series of 226 monthly lectures in 1688 and lasting until his death in 1707. These sermons addressed the major points of Calvinist thought as suggested in the Westminster *Shorter Catechism*. These well-respected public performances, clarifying the doctrinal heritage of New England orthodoxy, were an impressively ambitious, creative response to pressure from the Church of England and various dissenting sects. Not surprisingly, they were finally published in 1726 as *A Compleat Body of Divinity,* a massive undertaking completed during another time of renewed Anglican competition in New England.[13]

The leading ministers were not plunged into despair or hysteria. Their belief in providential history as expressed through Mather's lectures helped sustain them, as did their perception of the failures of the old regime. Even in their moments of near panic they had recognized the need for changes. John Bishop of Stamford, for example, wrote a lament to Increase Mather shortly

---

Gildrie, "The Ceremonial Puritan: Days of Humiliation and Thanksgiving," *NEHGR* 136 (1982): 13–15.

12. Stout, *New England Soul,* 102–3.

13. Ibid., 111.

after Connecticut was absorbed into the Dominion. Fearing an Anglican establishment, he wryly admitted that "Many are gospel-glutted, & growing weary, & so may be shortly eased of that their burden." Even worse was "that worldly, earthly, profane, & loose spirit up & down in the country," which he prayed the "Lord rebuke." But even he saw the judgment of God not in the loss of Connecticut's political independence but in some possible future catastrophe. This sense of the moral failure of the former semitheocratic states was not restricted to clergymen. John Dunton in 1686 observed of Massachusetts, "Their Laws for the Reformation of Manners are very severe, yet but little regarded by the People, so at least as to make 'em better, or cause 'em to mend their manners."[14]

In England the sense of impending change and moral failure among Nonconformist ministers was also intense. Samuel Petto of Sudbury, England, wrote to Mather of his fear for the loss of "civil & religious liberties" and his alarm at "the open prophaneness of multitudes here, & the height of their opposition against the power of godliness, yea, against the very form of it."[15] There was a consensus emerging on the necessity of reinvigorating, not abandoning, moral reform regardless of political changes. There was also a growing sense that public morality was connected to civil as well as religious liberties.

The ideological and civil framework of reform had to be altered. The opportunity came in 1689 with the Glorious Revolution and the subsequent overthrow in April of the Dominion of New England in Boston. Justifying revolution and underlying a new order were the Whig themes of liberty and property. Prior to the 1680s the dominant view of the role of government was profoundly religious. As John Eliot of Roxbury explained in 1659, "The Office and Duty of all the Rulers is to govern the people in the orderly, and seasonable practice of all the Commandments of God, in actions liable to Political observation, whether of piety and love to God, or of justice and love to man with peace." Their function was to defend the orthodox worship of God and enforce morality as outlined in the Ten Commandments, of which "they are keepers . . . as to compel men to their undoubted duty, and punish them for their undoubted sins, errors, and transgressions." That ideal had obviously failed.[16]

---

14. "John Bishop to Increase Mather, 18 October 1687," "Mather Correspondence," 314–15; John Dunton, *Letters Written from New England A.D. 1686*, ed. William H. Whitmore (Boston, 1867), 71.

15. "Samuel Petto to Increase Mather, 8 October 1684," "Mather Correspondence," 349.

16. T. H. Breen, *The Character of the Good Ruler: A Study of Puritan Political Ideas in New*

Fortunately the overtly Whiggish alternative was not alien to Massachusetts political thought. A decade before the Glorious Revolution Samuel Nowell, a chaplain in King Philip's War who became a magistrate in the 1680s rather than a settled minister, argued in a 1678 artillery election sermon that "There is such a thing as Liberty and Property given to us, both by the Laws of God & Men; when these are invaded, we may defend ourselves." Governments not only existed to defend these rights but also were limited by them. "God hath not given great ones in the world that absolute power over men, to devour them at pleasure, as great fishes do the little ones; he hath set Rulers their bounds & by his Law hath determined peoples libertyes and property." Nowell joined Mather's mission to England in 1688, where the latter lobbied the Lord President of the Board of Trade against Andros so "that liberty & property might be secured to us."[17]

Once the revolution occurred in Massachusetts in April 1689, it was justified in the London pamphlet wars as a "casting off the Arbitrary Power of those ill men who invaded Liberty and Property." This explanation was meant to solidify support not only in England but in New England as well. Although the revolt had been virtually unanimous, the Council of Safety, led by the aged former governor Simon Bradstreet and composed of twenty-two prominent citizens dominated by the Boston mercantile community, was uncertain of its popularity. There was a fear that unrest, particularly in the countryside, might engender an uprising. To gain advice and support the council called a convention of town representatives in May.[18]

The convention swiftly demonstrated in two turbulent sessions the depth of rural distrust. The delegates asserted that since the charter annulment was illegal and void the only real question was whether there should be immediate elections or whether the officials in office in 1686 should simply resume power. Although members of the council argued that either act might be construed as defiance by the new English government, the old government was restored, together with a newly elected lower house. The delegates also insisted that any new charter or frame of government sent from England be "signified to the respective Towns of the colony that they may be consulted

---

England, 1630–1730 (New Haven, 1970), esp. xii; John Eliot, *The Christian Commonwealth: Or, the Civil Policy of the Rising Kingdom of Jesus Christ* (London, 1659), 21.

17. Samuel Nowell, *Abraham in Arms* (Boston, 1678), 10; Diary of Increase Mather, 21 June 1688, Mather Papers, AAS, box 3, folder 4; Michael G. Hall, *The Last American Puritan: The Life of Increase Mather, 1639–1723* (Middletown, Conn., 1988), 216.

18. Whitmore, ed., *Andros Tracts,* 1:128; Robert Earle Moody and Richard Clive Simmons, eds., *The Glorious Revolution in Massachusetts: Selected Documents* (Boston, 1988), 6–7.

with in order to their approbation and compliance." In their view the locus of sovereignty was not in London or Boston but among the people of the towns. As a defender of the revolution insisted, "an Election or Free Choice in Government by the People . . . was one thing aimed at." Nor could this power be limited to orthodox church members. In February 1690 the General Court—controlled by the rural towns—granted the franchise to all adult males of good character who paid four shillings in a single country rate and who owned house and lands worth at least six pounds. As one historian has noted, the new law "opened a floodgate of political participation in Massachusetts Bay."[19]

This closer reliance on the populace, always an inherent possibility in Puritan political thought, was a necessity in the 1690s. The border war was going badly and expensively. An attempt to end it in 1690 by capturing Quebec resulted in a debacle profligate of life and resources. In Plymouth Colony the towns refused to pay rates that in some cases had increased 2,000 percent from August 1689 to November 1690. This reduced the colony's central government to impotence and helped lead to the merger with Massachusetts Bay under the 1691 charter. Neighboring New York was rapidly slipping into civil war. The problem was aggravated by a marked, albeit temporary, deterioration of the agricultural base as the colder climate of the 1680s and 1690s reduced harvests for a population that had quadrupled from 1641 to 1691. Many towns ceased to produce a surplus, and some areas (notably in eastern Massachusetts) were forced to switch from mixed farming to dependence on pastures and orchards. By the 1690s the entire New England region was becoming a net importer of food. The possibility of famine was serious, particularly in 1691, 1697, and 1698. This danger along with the imminent collapse of social and political order drove the ideological shifts and internal institutional adjustments of the final decade of the seventeenth century.[20]

Under these circumstances the defense of "Liberty and Property" had a virtually universal appeal. The forms of property that seemed most at hazard were the freehold farms and the towns' right to control their common lands. As Increase Mather argued, the Dominion policy of "forcing them to take Patents" for the land "would have squeezed more out of the poorer sort of

---

19. Moody and Simmons, eds., *Glorious Revolution*, 6–7; Breen, "War, Taxes, and Political Brokers," 82–83, 95–96.

20. Richard LeBaron Bowen, "The 1690 Tax Revolt of Plymouth Colony Towns," *NEHGR* 112 (1958): 4–14; Karen Ordahl Kuppermann, "Climate and Mastery of the Wilderness in Seventeenth-Century New England," in David D. Hall and David Grayson Allen, eds., *Seventeenth-Century New England* (Boston, 1984), 30–31, 35.

people there, than half their Estates are worth." That Dominion officials had begun with the larger farmers and the town commons did not mitigate the affront. "And if their boldness had madness would carry them out to oppress the Rich after such a manner . . . , what might the Poor look for?" The Puritan regimes may have proved expensive, but comparatively they seemed neither corrupt nor rapacious.[21]

A Dominion apologist made clear the connection between popular political rights and the defense of property by complaining that "Persons of Ability" in Massachusetts sought to "improve" lands left "vacant under the notion of Commons" but "cannot because they are less numerous than the poorer sort of the Town, whose advantage is that the Lands should so lie, and who manage their Affairs by a majority of voices."[22] Despite the ravages of war and taxation, then, the "poorer sort" were told that they had a strong economic stake in the success of the revolution in Massachusetts.

Nonetheless, the overt defense of property rights presented moral problems. The reforming clergy and more pious laity feared that property, seen as an end in itself, was a spiritual and moral peril—including even the modest holdings of small farmers. Cotton Mather lamented in a fast sermon of 1692 that "Men employ themselves as if they had nothing in the world to do, but build and fill a little Nest made of Straw & Clay, wherein after they themselves have been Merry for many years, their young ones may be comfortably Lodged after them." The dangers of commerce were even greater, increasing the possibility of corruption through luxury. Back in 1684 William Hubbard thanked God for "turning us into a way of Trade and Commerce, to further our more comfortable subsistence"; but he also denounced "Commodities to make fuel for Lust," which "called young people not to the mountain of the Lords House, but to our own private recesses to offer sacrifices to Bacchus and Venus."[23]

In these warnings the tensions between communal piety and private indulgence were strong. Yet it was "covetousness" and not the personal and familial drive to economic security that alarmed Puritan thinkers. The quest for property and the freedom to control it, inherent in traditional popular aspirations, was respected by many English and American moral reformers as a means not only to a "more comfortable subsistence" for the whole society

21. Whitmore, ed., *Andros Tracts*, 1:50; Daniel Vickers, "Competency and Competition: Economic Culture in Early America," *WMQ* 47 (1990): 3–29.

22. Whitmore, ed., *Andros Tracts*, 1:97–98.

23. Cotton Mather, *A Midnight Cry* (Boston, 1692), 38; William Hubbard, *The Benefit of a Well-Ordered Conversation* (Boston, 1684), 97–98.

but also to a subduing of the profane. John Blackwell, a former commonwealth layman who came to Massachusetts from Ireland in the 1680s, argued in favor of a land bank to increase currency in part because the economic opportunity thus generated "helps to civillize the Ruder Sort of people, & encourages . . . industry & civillity." This moral argument was prominently discussed in seventeenth-century England and became increasingly important in eighteenth-century New England.[24] In America the Puritan approach to the moral dimensions of wealth remained ambivalent. But the defense of property rights in the 1690s by such ministers as Increase Mather was no anomaly, nor was it insincere. They saw no necessary conflict between communal well-being and private economic striving in a properly ordered society.

Their thinking on "Liberty" during the 1690s experienced a similar shift of emphasis but not of substance. There were no problems with most of the civil liberties, such as trial by jury, which were encased in common law and confirmed in Massachusetts's own Body of Liberties of 1641. The most troublesome question was religious toleration. Thomas Danforth, a conservative layman and strong defender of the Old Charter, wrote to Increase Mather in London in 1687 begging "that no mention may be made of [James II's] Proclamation for a generall tolleration," for he saw the old "paenall lawes" of England and Massachusetts against dissent as "the only wall against Popery." In England, many Congregationalists and Presbyterians saw the royal proclamation of toleration, without recourse to Parliament, as both tyranny and a subterfuge under a Catholic king. But for Massachusetts Bay and Plymouth the issue was more symbolic than practical. Since the late 1660s laws for religious conformity had been dead letters. Quakers and Baptists underwent only sporadic official and unofficial harassment. Mather exaggerated only slightly when he claimed that "*New-England*, long before the Questioning of their Charters, had come to an Intire *Tolleration* of the Sectaryes crept in among them, having by Experience found that their *Tolleration* prov'd their *Dissipation*." He could also point to the fact that the 1689 convention of towns had voted "That any Laws which might seem Repugnant to the Laws of England, *or Contrary to a due liberty of Conscience never should be Executed in the Territory*."[25]

24. Joseph Dorfman, *The Economic Mind in American Civilization, 1606–1865* (New York, 1946), 1:100–101; Joyce Appleby, *Economic Thought and Ideology in Seventeenth-Century England* (Princeton, 1978); J. E. Crowley, *This Sheba, Self: The Conceptualization of Economic Life in Eighteenth-Century America* (Baltimore, 1974). Because this issue became more significant after 1700, it will be more fully treated in the chapter on Augustan civility.

25. "Thomas Danforth to Increase Mather, October 9, 1687," "Mather Correspondence," 507–8; Whitmore, ed., *Andros Tracts,* 2:58.

In 1692 after the arrival of the new charter the Massachusetts legislature passed a "Bill for the General Rights and Liberties" to replace the Body of Liberties. In eliminating all reference to church or religion, the law confirmed the substance of England's postrevolutionary Toleration Act of 1689 as well as the colony's drift toward grounding constitutionalism explicitly on the rights of Englishmen. These were now conceived in terms of liberty and property, rather than in a sense of covenantal rights derived from a special religious identity. This shift perforce weakened the separate or sectarian view of American Puritanism as an opposition to the Church of England. Correspondingly it strengthened the Nonseparatist interpretation of New England orthodoxy as a continuing reform movement within the national church. The elder Mather reminded his English and American audiences that Massachusetts was "A Protestant Country . . . and of the Church of England too (whatever is blathered to the Contrary) in that they acknowledge the Doctrinal *Articles of Religion.*" Indeed, he claimed "a greater sincerity" for Massachusetts orthodoxy in its commitment to the Articles because, unlike some English clergy, New England's ministers had not "preached up *Pelagian, Arminian,* and *Socinian Heresies* (not without a spice of Popery)." Dissent, he insisted, was not in doctrine or faith but in "their Liturgy and form of *Church-Government.*"[26] This view remained dominant until the American Revolution.

In the long run, a renewed stress on this interpretation encouraged a growing anglicization of New England's religious life culminating in a crisis during the 1720s when some Yale tutors and students took episcopal orders. But more immediately the effect was to ratify a long-standing trend toward a latitudinarian and ecumenical approach not only within Massachusetts churches but also in their relation to other Reformed bodies in the British Isles and western Europe. Increase Mather claimed in a pamphlet aimed at English Whig opinion that orthodox congregations in New England had been following a policy of fairly open admissions roughly in the manner of the national church. "In the same Church there have been *Presbyterians, Independents, Episcopalians,* and *Antipaedobaptists,* all welcome to the same Table of the Lord when they have manifested to the Judgment of Christian Charity a work of Regeneration in their souls."[27]

26. M. Hall, *Last American Puritan,* 264; Kenneth Silverman, *The Life and Times of Cotton Mather* (New York, 1984), 70, 140; Whitmore, ed., *Andros Tracts,* 2:21–22. See also a Boston pamphlet by two prominent laymen, Edward Rawson and Samuel Sewall, "The Revolution in New England Justified" (1691), in Whitmore, ed., *Andros Tracts,* 1:68, to the same point.
27. Whitmore, ed., *Andros Tracts,* 2:22.

A later generation of Great Awakening pietists came to regard that "Christian Charity" as so generous as to constitute "Arminianism," but for the time being it served to confirm New England orthodoxy's place within a national, not sectarian, definition of church life. This view also encouraged a renewed sense of the international and interdenominational character of Calvinism. While Increase Mather was in London, his brother Nathaniel joined in efforts to combine Presbyterian and Congregationalist resources into a "General Fund" that was to be a step toward creating a common Calvinist front. Increase was also active in producing the 1691 "Heads of Agreement" on doctrine between the two groups. Although the English negotiations collapsed in 1694 New Englanders, particularly Cotton Mather, remained intrigued with the idea of ecumenical cooperation and even union. He endorsed the term "United Brethren," as used in English discussions, not only a means of joining Presbyterians and Independents, but also as an opening to the European Reformed groups. Closer to home, he and Benjamin Colman of the Brattle Street Church attempted to work out a pattern of more formal cooperation among local ministerial associations. Viewed as a threat to congregational autonomy and lay influence, the "Proposals of 1705" were not adopted in Massachusetts but were, with modifications, by Connecticut's clergy in 1708.[28]

A common goal in all these shifts was to further the Reformation of Manners. In this too the revolutions in Massachusetts and England were similar. "To many Englishmen," wrote a recent scholar, "this reformation was the most important aspect of the revolution, since only through a reformation of manners could the revolution endure." In attempts to legitimize their reigns, William and Mary, Queen Anne, and even James II issued proclamations calling for better enforcement of laws suppressing vice and crime. Read quarterly in churches and court sessions and posted prominently in public places, these declarations were intended to encourage order and sobriety among a people feared for their fickle turbulence and independence. Early in his reign William instructed Archbishop John Tillotson to urge clergy to more thorough catechising, preaching, observing of sacraments, and alleviating of social ills. For his part Tillotson requested that the crown assist in calling a formal convocation to consider "the Union of Protestants" by removing barriers to Nonconformist participation in the national church and

---

28. Silverman, *Life and Times of Cotton Mather,* 140–41; Carl Bridenbaugh, *Mitre and Sceptre: Transatlantic Faiths, Ideas, Personalities, and Politics* (New York, 1962), 32–33, 60–61.

a revision of the canons, "especially those regarding the reformation of manners" and the procedures of ecclesiastical courts.[29]

Opposition from the High Church faction prevented reform along these lines. The parallels with New England trends toward association in the name of efficiency and moral reform are striking. On the role of secular courts Tillotson preached that justice meant the enforcement of sound laws "which are the guard of private property, the security of publick peace, and of religion and good manners." Provoked by a common sense of political instability and personal insecurity in the midst of revolution and international war, and beset by the moral confusions of communal and individualist impulses reflected in passionate debate and even violence, reformers in England and New England responded similarly. This occurred not only because their circumstances were alike but also because they remained in communication and believed that they shared a mutual identity and mission.[30]

In reply to William's proclamation as well as to its own situation, the restored Massachusetts government declared in March 1690 "that the Laws of this Colony against *Vice* and all sorts of *Debauchery* and *Prophaneness* (which Laws have too much lost their edge by the late Interruption of the Government) be now faithfully and vigorously put in Execution." Explicitly, "the LAWS against *Blasphemy, Cursing, Profane Swearing, Lying, unlawful Gaming, Sabbath-breaking, Idleness, Drunkenness, Uncleanness,* and all the Enticements and Nurseries of such *Impieties*" were declared still in force so that "we may approve ourselves a *peculiar People, zealous of good works.*" In this renewed crusade civil officers were "enjoyn'd to perform their Duty in finding and bringing out Offenders against the aforesaid *Laws*" in the interest of "the Justice of *Exemplary Punishment.*" Churches were urged "to reflect seriously and frequently on their Covenants, to sharpen their Discipline against those that *walk disorderly;* and immediately to compose their *Differences* and *Contentions* . . . that so they may become *Terrible as an Army with Banners.*"[31]

29. Dudley W. R. Bahlman, *The Moral Revolution of 1688* (New Haven, 1957, 1968), 16–21, 40–41, historian's quote on 40; Harry Grant Plum, *Restoration Puritanism: A Study in the Growth of English Liberty* (Chapel Hill, 1943), 74–75, 83.

30. Richard B. Schlatter, *The Social Ideas of Religious Leaders, 1660–1688* (New York, 1940, 1971), 90, for Tillotson on justice; Roger Thompson, "The Puritans and Prurience: Aspects of the Restoration Book Trade," in H. C. Allen and Roger Thompson, eds., *Contrasts and Connection: Bicentennial Essays in Anglo-American History* (Athens, Ohio, 1976), 53; Francis J. Bremer, "Increase Mather's Friends: The Trans-Atlantic Congregational Network of the Seventeenth Century," AAS *Proceedings* 94, pt. 1 (1984): 59–96.

31. The proclamation is appended to Cotton Mather, *The Present State of New England* (Boston, 1690), 47–51.

Clearly the new stress on liberty did not mean freedom from the reformers' moral code. Indeed, to them as to their English counterparts the success of the revolutions depended on the discipline the code embodied. In seconding the proclamation that he may very well have written, Cotton Mather charged, "I will in one word express the most considerable thing that is to be done for us: Tis Reformation! Reformation! Reformation!" After praising the "Admonition from our Honourable Rulers, to *reform* our many *Provoking Evils*," he was forced to add, "O that all ranks and kinds of people among us were in earnest about the universal *Reformation of our Manners*."[32]

The younger Mather's wish for general popular participation was not a mere rhetorical flourish. Church discipline, however well functioning, did not embrace all—and the political institutions beyond the towns were weak reeds indeed. Mather believed that the magistrates were "doubtless perswaded that a Feeble Executor of the Laws is more Criminal than a Direct Violater of them," yet they were hobbled by "murmurings" and "the Disrespect cast upon Government" amid continuing war and uncertainty over a constitutional settlement. "We have been giving our little scratches to one another while we have been managing the Debates that the unsettlement of our Government has furnished us withal." He asked, "Shall they turn into Gangrenes with us?"[33]

Cotton Mather's father-in-law John Philips, who served on the Council of Safety and as a member of the upper house and treasurer under the new charter, complained in a 1691 pamphlet written between the overthrow of the Dominion and the reception of the new charter that "peoples Heads were Idly bewhizled with Conceits that we have no Magistrates, no Government, And by Consequence that we have no Security for any thing which we call our own." These "foolish conceits" limited the provisional government's effectiveness, in particular in establishing the credit of its currency. He suspected that people were using this notion to increase their own freedom of action. However, the "consequence they will be Loth to allow" but which seemed inevitable to him was that "once we are Reduced to Hobs his state of Nature which (says he) is a state of war, and then the strongest must take all."[34] In calling up the Hobbesian vision Philips was explicitly tapping one of the most basic sources of the Reformation of Manners while asserting that the feeble government of Massachusetts was virtually helpless without it. He

---

32. Cotton Mather, *The Serviceable Man* (Boston, 1690), 47.
33. C. Mather, *Serviceable Man,* 60; C. Mather, *Present State,* 39–41.
34. John Philips, "Considerations on the Bills of Credit" (Boston, 1691), in Andrew M. Davis, ed., *Colonial Currency Reprints, 1682–1751* (Boston, 1910–11), 1:191–92.

was implying that moral reform was not merely a defense of political stability but its precondition.

In its proclamation of 1690 the General Court, despite its recurrence to earlier conceptions of legal power, also noted that there were "*Spiritual Sins,* which fall not so much under the cognizance of Humane Laws" but whose suppression was vital because they "are the *Roots* of *Bitterness* in the midst of us." These underlying sources of trouble were "*Unbelief, Worldliness, Heresy, Pride, Wrath, Strife, Envy,* and the Neglect" of both "Natural and *Instituted Worship.*" All were connected of course to a "shameful want of due Family-Instruction."[35] The earlier Puritan state had at least claimed some jurisdiction over these "Spiritual Sins" and had passed laws to curb them. After 1689 that approach was no longer deemed possible or proper. Few denied the significance of these sins or their potential to disrupt social and political order. But what was being denied was the capacity of government to counter them. Other institutions and individual self-discipline would have to meet this crucial need. This conclusion—that the state could treat only the symptoms and not the underlying causes of its own diseases and those of society—marked a milestone in the development of an Anglo-American conception of limited government.

As the new royal charter went into effect in 1692, Cotton Mather preached to the General Assembly and ratified this change in the relation of religion to government. Regardless of belief, "A Man has a Right unto his Life, his Estate, his Liberty, and his Family" that the state is bound to foster and protect. The "spiritual sins" were not its concern. This definition of authority was in marked contrast to his father's 1677 exhortation to the General Court, which helped spur the Reforming Synod of 1679. But it must be remembered that this shift was not so much a liberation of the state as a recognition of its practical as well as theoretical limitations. In this process the orthodox churches were not losing power but gaining social influence, prestige, and responsibilities. As Harry Stout has observed, the Puritan mission "continued to define New England's identity at the deepest social and cultural levels. The language of rights and liberties continued to be understood mainly in an instrumental sense as the liberty to pursue New England's covenant." The covenantal obligations that undergirded society and political order were the special preserve of the reforming clergy and the churches until the American Revolution.[36]

35. C. Mather, *Present State,* 50.
36. M. Hall, *Last American Puritan,* 264–65; Stout, *New England Soul,* 119–21, quote on 121.

Now deprived of the arm of the magistracy, the clerics and churches had to find other means. As Cotton Mather meditated in his diary on what became his 1692 address to the General Assembly, it was essential to pursue "the Suppression of Heresy by Endeavours more Spiritual and evangelical." One strategy, with roots in the Half-Way Covenant and confirmed (albeit ambiguously) in the Reforming Synod of 1679, was what David Hall has called "sacramental evangelism." By practicing near-comprehensive baptism, ministers could assume a wider audience in whom grace could be nurtured. The sense of the appearance of grace as gradual rather than cataclysmic had wide ecclesiological, theological, and ethical ramifications that the clergy and interested laity debated heatedly for more than a century.[37]

If grace could be cultivated, did that imply more human initiative and control over conversion? Then what were the proper uses and forms of conversion narratives? Should they be required for admission to the Lord's Supper? Could it be, as Solomon Stoddard argued, that even that sacrament was more a means of grace than a seal of it? In New England polemics this trend of thought was often termed "presbyterian"—which also implied greater ministerial authority, increasingly independent of lay control, as the congregations came to embrace a more "mixed multitude" and had no serious role in evaluating candidates.

A further complication developed when the General Assembly ordered churches to gain the agreement of townsmen regardless of church membership in the choice of ministers because the ministers' support came from general town taxation. This law ratified a tendency toward town participation that dated from the 1670s. In effect, the distinction between town and congregation, and thus between church and society, was becoming more difficult to sustain. The formation of the prestigious Brattle Street Church in Boston in 1698, which called Benjamin Colman without benefit of local ordination in 1699, was based on open communion without requiring any tests of grace. The new church also adopted such Anglican practices as scriptural readings without commentary and regular public recitations of the Lord's Prayer.[38]

At bottom these latitudinarian trends were part of the shift toward a more national, universal sense of church life as opposed to a sectarian one. Although the Mathers played a major role in stimulating and fostering this tendency,

37. Worthington C. Ford, ed., *The Diary of Cotton Mather* (New York, 1912), 1:149; David D. Hall, *The Faithful Shepherd: A History of the New England Ministry in the Seventeenth Century* (Chapel Hill, 1972), 199, 207, 217–18, 253.

38. M. Hall, *Last American Puritan*, 292–93; Stout, *New England Soul*, 130–31; John Corrigan, *The Prism of Piety: Catholic Congregational Clergy at the Beginning of the Enlightenment* (New York, 1991), 27–31.

they (the elder in particular) opposed this view of the sacraments and con-version. In the first decade of the new century Increase Mather, Solomon Stoddard, and the Brattle Street group became embroiled in a fierce—some thought scandalous—pamphlet debate on these themes. Mather's objections were threefold. The first was that open communion seemed a betrayal of the Reformation's emphasis on the separation and empowerment of the "godly." The second was that he saw the stress on nurture as "Arminianism," em-phasizing morality over conversion. As he intoned in 1704, "Men are told that they must Reform their Lives, Believe the Gospel, Observe Holidays appointed by the Church; but nothing said to them of a *Justifying Faith.*" The third, a matter of strategy as well as principle, was his concern that a lessening of genuine (as opposed to formal) lay participation in church government meant a loss of support as well. Explicitly referring to the delay in convening the Synod of 1679 until laymen arrived, he warned in 1700 against "admitting anything that should look an infringement of that Liberty and priviledge which does by the Institution of Christ belong to the *Brotherhood* in particular churches."[39] Although Mather's objections were largely futile during the early eighteenth century, they were revived and recast during the Great Awakening, particularly by Jonathan Edwards.

Nonetheless, there were alternative ways of furthering moral reform and piety that directly encouraged lay participation and initiative in an ecumen-ical, evangelical spirit. The most prominent were voluntary associations, which had the added advantage—in the eyes of the Mathers, for instance—of preserving the Protestant distinction between the "godly" who were at work and the "unregenerate" who were to be reformed. These also enjoyed the prestige of English origin and Anglican blessing, no small matter at the turn of the eighteenth century. As Cotton Mather excitedly noted in his diary in 1692, "Some admirable Designs about the Reformation of Manners have lately been on foot in the English Nation in pursuance of the most excellent Admonitions which have been given for it by the Letters of their Majesties." To carry it through there "have been started a Proposal for the well-affected people in every Parish to enter into orderly Societies."[40]

Beginning in 1690 the Society for the Reformation of Manners spread with the encouragement of the Anglican hierarchy through the London parishes.

---

39. Ford, ed., *Diary of Cotton Mather* 1:325–26, 329–30, 332–33; Increase Mather, *Practical Truths Tending to Promote Holiness* (Boston, 1704), 3; Increase Mather, *The Order of the Gospel* (Boston, 1700), 83; Paul R. Lucas, *Valley of Discord: Church and Society along the Connecticut River, 1636–1725* (Hanover, N.H., 1976), 169–87.

40. Ford, ed., *Diary of Cotton Mather,* 1:144–45.

Including both Nonconformists and Anglicans, the societies involved clergy members, justices of the peace, and tradesmen in attempts to spur enforcement of laws against such evils as "Apostacy," Sabbath-breaking, prostitution, assault, and public drunkenness. By 1725 the London groups claimed credit for securing some ninety thousand prosecutions. They were also interested in public and private poor relief and in education, particularly for lower-class children. The reform groups were related to and grew out of the religious societies of "young men" who met together for mutual edification and, according to a contemporary observer, commonly appointed "two stewards as Managers of their Charity." This movement apparently began in the city during the late 1670s and was more strictly Anglican, stressing a renewed sacramentalism as the root of good works. The proliferation of voluntary pious and reform associations also spawned in 1697 the Society for the Promotion of Christian Knowledge and later the Society for the Propagation of the Gospel in Foreign Parts. Surviving well into the 1730s, the religious societies and the societies for the Reformation of Manners were a bridge between the Puritan impulses, both Anglican and Dissenter, of the late seventeenth century and the Methodist movement.[41]

Cotton Mather's enthusiasm was only mildly premature. Formal societies for the Reformation of Manners did not appear outside of London in any numbers before 1698. Yet their existence together with the religious societies, their pattern of organization, and the excellent prospects of using such forms in New England greatly strengthened the Mathers' argument against the Stoddardean approach and proved to be part of a rapprochement with the Brattle Street leaders. As Increase Mather wrote in 1700, "I thank the Lord in that there are at this day in London, several *Religious Societies* of the *Communion of the Church of England,* whose design is to promote Religion in the Power of it. Now these Societies require of such as joyn to them, that they give the Society a Solemn account of their sence of Spiritual things." Demanding conversion narratives clearly did not weaken these groups in either numbers or influence and indeed may have enhanced them. In comparing Stoddard's and Mather's attempts to recast the relation of church to

41. J. C. Curtis and W. A. Speck, "The Societies for the Reformation of Manners," *Literature and History* 3 (1976): 46–64; Bahlman, *Moral Revolution,* 31–32, 37–39, 66–70, 83; Edward J. Bristow, *Vice and Vigilance: Purity Movements in Britain since 1700* (Dublin, 1977), 11–31; Plum, *Restoration Puritanism,* 89–90; Tina Isaacs, "The Anglican Hierarchy and the Reformation of Manners, 1688–1738," *Journal of Ecclesiastical History* 33 (1982): 391–411; Josiah Woodward, *An Account of the Rise and Progress of the Religious Societies of the City of London and of Their Endeavours for Reformation of Manners,* 4th ed. (London, 1712), quote on 23.

society Stephen Foster felicitously observed, "The former's church sounded like the old conception of civil society, and the latter's civil society sounded like the older conception of the church."[42]

Increase and Cotton Mather argued that moral reform embracing the whole of society and even the cultivation of piety among such hard-to-reach groups as youths and mariners would have to take place largely outside of the institutional churches. Their approach was no less universalist than Stoddard's. Building on his father's premillennial optimism, Cotton Mather put social reform and "Reforming Societies" within an eschatological context. "There is a World to Come; a World wherein there will be no Disorders, a World wherein the People will all be Righteous; a World wherein Holiness to the Lord will be written on all Persons and on all Affairs. The Aspirations of Reforming Societies are to raise this World, as far as ever they can, toward that Desirable State." He gave as evidence the claim that such societies were already formed or forming in Ireland, Scotland, Holland, Switzerland, and Germany as well as England and British North America. In short, the international Calvinist network, together with elements of the Church of England, was once again using similar means toward similar ends deliberately, a fact that further isolated Stoddard and cemented Massachusetts's adjustments to the Glorious Revolution within a wider Atlantic framework. Ironically, however, given their opposition to Arminianism, the Mathers' fostering of the societies provided another opening to that heresy, which was also part of that wider framework. Cotton Mather himself wrote of those who joined the effort, "Let them think that the Zeal which is now flaming in them is a most comfortable Token and Symptom of their Title to the future Felicity, wherein God will bring Every Work to Rights."[43]

Preferring the term "Societies to Suppress Disorders," the younger Mather published a prospectus in 1703 suggesting that each group contain seven to seventeen members, including a minister, a magistrate, and "a couple of stewards" for secretarial and financial work. New members should be admitted by unanimous vote. The parallel to strict congregational polity was obvious. However, he also urged "that the Society Study Secrecy; and oblige every Member to divulge neither *Who* they are, nor *What* they do, one jott further than the whole Society shall allow them." Using biblical warrant, he

---

42. I. Mather, *Order of the Gospel*, 36; Stephen Foster, *Their Solitary Way: The Puritan Social Ethic in the First Century of New England* (New Haven, 1971), 60–63, quote on 63.

43. Cotton Mather, *Methods and Motives for Societies to Suppress Disorders* (Boston, 1703), 4–5, 11–12.

believed that such discretion was both tactically sound and spiritually edi-fying.[44]

Intriguingly, he also hinted that "such a Society consisting of more than Twice Seven Persons" had been active "in a very populous place," presumably Boston, "for diverse years together; and yet nothing at all that while divulged." The goals were to repair "what is defective in the by-laws of the Town," to "influence" elections and political appointments, to direct "admonitions and Remonstrances at those notoriously Defective in their Duty," and to consult with local ministers on the "Condition of the People . . . for the Advancement of Piety in the Flock." Being laymen with broad social contacts, members could discover families without "Family Worship" and be able to get clerics to visit them or even "Exhort them" on their own. Attention should be paid to support for schools and the distribution of books among the poor. More efficiently than pastors, "the Society may find out who are in Extream Necessities and may either by their own Liberality, or by that of others to whom they shall commend the matter, obtain Succours."[45]

In 1705 Mather wrote in his diary that "Our Society for the Suppression of Disorders" contained members from "each of our three Churches" and was becoming so large that "two or more such Societies; one for the North End of the Town; one for the South" were formed under his direction. Together with the reform groups, "a Number of religious private Meetings," or reli-gious societies, were established. Mather claimed that by 1702 there were "at least thirteen or fourteen" in Boston by which he thought "that the Spirit of Religion was mightily preserved and promoted." From 1705 to 1725 there were religious societies for specific groups including blacks, mariners, "devout women," "People of the Scotch Nation," those with a special interest in millennialism, and a "Society for our superiour and principal Gentlemen" who met not only to worship but also to "project Methods for the Deliverance of the Countrey from the dreadful Distresses, which it is running into." Attempts were made, especially after 1715, to coordinate activities of both reform and religious societies in Boston through an executive committee made up of "a Delegate or two" from each, with only sporadic success.[46]

As usual with voluntary organizations, their effectiveness and membership fluctuated. Generally the religious societies, based as they were on old tra-ditions of "private meetings" for pious purposes reaching back to the found-ing decade of the Bay Colony, functioned better and longer than the reform

44. Ibid., 7–8.
45. Ibid., 7–9.
46. Ford, ed., *Diary of Cotton Mather*, 1:411, 516–17, 2:49, 364, 395, 439, 532, 573, 580.

groups, whose influence peaked in the last years of Queen Anne's War, 1711 to 1713. Overwhelmed by "Calamities" of war-related poverty and a measles epidemic in the winter of 1713–14, the charitable arm collapsed. But by 1724 both poor relief and moral reform efforts through the Societies to Suppress Disorders revived. They largely died out again after 1728, as Cotton Mather's death removed their main inspiration. To fill the gap Boston churches established that year a formal "pious and evangelical treasury," governed by laymen, to use donations from fast and thanksgiving days for both relief and religious instruction among the poor.[47] With their flexibility, diversity, and overlapping memberships, religious and reform associations were effective means of coping with Boston's urban complexity. They functioned in ways and in places the established congregations could not and thereby extended the impact of the Reformation of Manners in the port town.

As in England, it took longer to establish such organizations in the countryside; and once present, they were not so diverse in membership or interests. In 1708 John Norton, the pastor of Hingham, delivered a council election sermon to the royal governor and General Assembly in which he evoked the reformers' theory of the moral basis of social dynamics ("If we are not Reforming, we shall be Deforming, Sinning") and urged that a recent crown pronouncement on the Reformation of Manners be "follow'd in *New England,* as it was in *Old England,* with REFORMING SOCIETIES" throughout the region as an essential engine of continual social renewal. By the 1720s societies combining reformist and pious purposes were common even in the smaller towns, although the emphasis was more on the latter in those areas where congregational discipline and small-town life made special reform groups redundant. In 1721 even tiny Wenham had more than one "private Societies of Religion." So too did the small township of Needham in 1723. Frontier Westborough also had one for adult males and presumably for other groups as well in 1739. After 1721 Cotton Mather's hopes "for the reviving and preserving of Piety, by *religious Societies,* well animated and regulated in every Plantation" were generally realized as these institutions became a routine part of New England's religious and social order.[48]

47. Charles E. Hambrick-Stowe, *The Practice of Piety: Puritan Devotional Disciplines in Seventeenth-Century New England* (Chapel Hill, 1982), 140–41; Ford, ed., *Diary of Cotton Mather,* 2:110, 131, 156, 275–76, 767; Christine Leigh Heyrman, "The Fashion among More Superior People: Charity and Social Change in Provincial New England, 1700–1740," *American Quarterly* 34 (1982): 109–11.

48. John Norton, *An Essay Tending to Promote Reformation* (Boston, 1708), 27; Ford, ed., *Diary of Cotton Mather,* 2:602, 634; Diary of Nathan Bucknam, 1722–67, AAS, 29 July

Just as in England where these organizations connected Puritan tradition to an emerging Methodist movement in the eighteenth century, so in New England they were an institutional bridge to the Great Awakening. Functioning as "gathered saints" amid an increasingly "mixed multitude" within society and the congregations, the religious societies were in effect a revival of one of the earliest forms of Puritan organization in Elizabethan England. They were also similar in purpose and form to the confraternities of reformed Catholicism in seventeenth- and eighteenth-century France. As one French statute forming such a group in 1653 explained, "The confraternity joins us together in such a way that all our affections, which without it would be isolated, are through it mingled and reunited in bonds of brotherly love." These varying types of religious societies connected laity and clergy more intimately than even congregations could. By changing in form, influence, and specific interests over time, the societies illustrated the continuity of both Catholic and Protestant reform throughout the social transformations of the early modern era.[49]

A stress on cultivating the piety and discipline of youths and mobilizing them for general moral reform was another element of this continuity across time and religious affiliations. Within the popular tradition the heritage of youth groups reaching back into the Middle Ages was rich and convoluted. With or without official sanction or formal organization, bands of the young—usually unmarried males of varying ages—functioned as both defenders and critics of communal mores. Their celebrations, plays, and revels were not only boisterous but often derisive of those in authority or those who seemed to violate their codes of conduct. Given the fact that in many times and places unmarried young men were the backbone of the local militia, their potential influence was enormous and their discipline both important and problematic. These young men often exhibited, particularly in the English tradition, "ideals deeply hedonistic and antiauthoritarian, associated with youth and summed up in those two outlets of sex and drink."[50]

1723; Francis G. Walett, ed., *The Diary of Ebenezer Parkman, 1702–1782* (Worcester, Mass., 1974), 66–67.

49. George W. Harper, "Clericalism and Revival: The Great Awakening in Boston as a Clerical Phenomenon," *NEQ* 57 (1984): 554–66, esp. p. 562; Francois Lebrun, "The Two Reformations: Communal Devotion and Personal Piety," in Robert Chartier, ed., *A History of Private Life,* vol. 3, *Passions of the Renaissance,* trans. Arthur Goldhammer (Cambridge, Mass., 1989), 87–89.

50. Susan Brigden, "Youth and the English Reformation," *Past and Present* 95 (1982): 37–67; Natalie Z. Davis, "The Reasons of Misrule: Youth Groups and Charivaris in Six-

Massachusetts's worries over the "rising generation" were, as we have seen, central to the Reforming Synod of 1679 and to subsequent efforts to strengthen "family government." For the usual reasons, disorderly assemblages were commonplace throughout the colony's history. The formation of pious youth groups to counter these tendencies was common as well by the 1670s. Cotton Mather while at Harvard belonged to a "society of pious young men" who met every Sabbath night (a traditional period of disorder) for worship and religious studies. In 1677 in Boston's North End a group began weekly Sunday night sessions and drew up elaborate by-laws. Their purpose was "to avoid those Temptations & abandon those Courses that by Sad Experience we find our Youth to be Exposed or Inclined to." This society lasted at least until January 1715. In 1693 Cotton Mather urged youngsters of Reading, "why should you not Associate yourselves with such young People as have their Pious Meetings every week?" He was delighted in that time of trouble "that we have so many such meetings amongst us" in Boston. In the rural areas it seemed otherwise to him. "Tis an Extreme Sleepiness in our Churches abroad in the Country that they no more Consult their own Hopeful Growth by encouraging their Young People" to form societies. "Such Praying Meetings of Young People, I am sure, will turn to better Account than those Husking Meetings [harvest festivals] whereat so many of our young People in the Country do debauch themselves." During the early eighteenth century religious youth groups became virtually ubiquitous in Massachusetts and played a significant role not only in furthering the Reformation of Manners but also in fostering the Great Awakening.[51]

The Glorious Revolution transformed the formal relation of church and state in Massachusetts as well as the colony's borders and constitutional position within the empire. Although tensions and the sense of danger from foes (some even satanic) ran high in the 1690s, the Puritan ethos persisted and even experienced renewal as expressed in increased church membership and reinvigorated theological and ethical thought. The transition was successful partly because the new English governments under William and Mary

teenth-Century France," *Past and Present* 50 (1971): 41–75. Quote is Ronald Paulson, *Popular and Polite Art in the Age of Hogarth and Fielding* (Notre Dame, Ind., 1979), 9.

51. Silverman, *Life and Times of Cotton Mather,* 23; "The Orders of the Young Men's Meeting," in Parkman Family Papers, AAS, box 2, folder 4; Cotton Mather, *Early Religion* (Boston, 1694), 31; Walett, ed., *Diary of Ebenezer Parkman,* 3, 29, 44, 48, 90, 95, 107, 121, 126–27; Ford, ed., *Diary of Cotton Mather,* 1:67–68, 80, 399, 2:44, 200, 365, 499, 544, 614–15, 633; Jonathan Edwards, *A Faithful Narrative,* in C. C. Goen, ed., *The Works of Jonathan Edwards: The Great Awakening* (New Haven, 1972), 146.

and Queen Anne were more sympathetic, libertarian, and latitudinarian than those of Charles II and James II. By furthering moral reform and cultivating personal piety, dominant opinion within the Church of England encouraged New England orthodoxy's commitment to a universal Protestant Reformed movement. Within Massachusetts itself the changes seemed more a codification of trends dating back to the 1670s than a stark rejection of the past. During the late 1690s Cotton Mather confidently embraced both "a Revolution and a Reformation" that he thought might even bring on the millennium. "Now I live to see in 1697," he wrote, "greater Tendencies to the new Reformation than there were to bee seen in 1517 for the Half-Reformation, then begun."[52]

To carry it to a conclusion, he explained in a 1696 election sermon, it was necessary to choose (as usual) men who "will do all they can for the Reformation of the Country from Ignorance, from Idleness, from Dishonesty, from Uncleanness, for all Profaneness and Paganism." This must be done, he had learned, through "an English Tenderness of our Liberties" essential "in all we call to Serve the Publick." Nor could the burden be left to magistrates and ministers. Reform remained a popular crusade. "In pursuing the Designs of Reformation, why should not Every man, even Every one, concern himself, according to the capacities of the Station wherein God has placed them?" To urge recommitment he had recourse to the agenda of the "Synod of our Churches near Seventeen Years ago" without any sense of discontinuity.[53]

All that was required was to adapt the means, not the ends. With that notion came renewed thought and energy. Beginning in 1690 the pastors of the Boston region held "stated meetings for the Help of each other." Together they debated such questions as the meaning of ordination, the secrecy of confessions, the function of synods and associations, the use of "Instrumental Music" in services, and the extent of church discipline among baptized persons. They also took up such social issues as divorce and usury. In 1699 Cotton Mather published the questions and arguments in short casuistical form so as to further debate and consultation.[54] Puritanism in America had passed through the furnace of revolution with its rationale and impetus intact.

52. Cotton Mather, *Things for a Distressed People to Think Upon* (Boston, 1696), 33–35; Ford, ed., *Diary of Cotton Mather,* 1:262–63.

53. C. Mather, *Things for a Distressed People,* 10–11, 50.

54. Cotton Mather, *Thirty Important Cases* (Boston, 1699).

NINE

Augustan Civility and the Great Awakening

The Massachusetts advocates of the Reformation of Manners skillfully weathered the demise in 1684 of the Puritan state, which had become as much a liability as an asset after King Philip's War. They readily incorporated Whig conceptions of liberty, for which they had sympathy in any case, and embraced voluntarism to create pious and reform associations within and beyond the established orthodox churches. As Harry Stout has noted, these adjustments "were turned to a traditional defense of inherited religious beliefs and values that would hold New England to the covenant."[1]

In 1702 Increase Mather put his imprimatur on the interdependence of Whig and Puritan aspirations by observing that "Next to Religion, the happiness of a People consists in Civil Liberties." That same year the Connecticut government issued a bill of rights, entitled "General Privileges of the Inhabitants," that explicitly linked a disciplined conception of freedom with both religious and social order. The "free fruition" of "Liberties," the preamble held, "hath ever been and ever will be the Tranquillity and Stability of Churches and Commonwealths, and the Denyal or deprival thereof the Disturbance, if not ruin, of both." It is not difficult to conclude from such rhetoric, as does Professor Stout, that "finally, English rights and liberties came to mean nothing more than the old covenant duties of obedience and submission to the dictates of *Sola Scriptura,*" the clergy's reading of biblical imperatives.[2]

1. Harry S. Stout, *The New England Soul: Preaching and Religious Culture in Colonial New England* (New York, 1986), 140.
2. Ibid.; Increase Mather, *The Excellency of a Publick Spirit Discoursed* (Boston, 1702), 18; *Acts and Laws of His Majesty's Colony of Connecticut in New England* (Boston, 1702), 1.

Thus the conversations of the godly, the civil, and the profane continued through the Great Awakening. For many of the clergy, the standard for moral analysis of their society remained the Reforming Synod. For instance, in September 1748 the members of the Marlborough Association of pastors in central Massachusetts looked to the "Synod An 1679 pro Reform" as they considered the "degeneracy and Backsliding in Religion" that, they believed, beset their region in the aftermath of the revivals.[3] As in the past, "worldliness," or excessive concern for personal prosperity, generated "Temptations"; but the profane life created "Evils . . . which do need Reforming," including the usual themes of "Profanation of the Holy Sabbath . . . Tavern-haunting, Company-keeping, Chambering, Uncleanness, Profaneness."

The prescriptions too echoed those of the 1680s. The laity was urged "to consider the worth of their privileges" in the congregational order "and the Danger of being deprived of them" by "evil doctrines" and "by the conduct of too many persons toward their ministers." Anticlericalism and lay religiosity of dubious orthodoxy remained problems. More than preaching was called for. "Let us Endeavor to revive good customs & practices among them, particularly the antient good practices of Catechizing, Family Order, Worship, and Gov't, Religious Societies under good regulations; godly Conference & Conversation." In short, "Church Discipline should be reviv'd" as "Brotherly Watch and Admonition." Equally essential was the warning "to take special Care of the Children & Youth," another perennial concern of the Reformation of Manners. After calling on "all Persons of Distinction & Influence to unite with us in this work of Reformation," the members called on the churches to consider "Solemn Renewal of Covenant . . . , as very useful upon these occasions." As they considered their problems and tactics, these pastors did not believe that they faced a radically new situation but rather a recurrent cycle in the lives of their churches and towns. The elements of continuity in the Reformation of Manners were obvious. Yet however strong their sense of precedent, the members of the Marlborough Association in 1748 were invoking not tired formulas but a vibrant, evolving tradition of moral and religious reform.

Much of the adaptability of the tradition in the eighteenth century derived from changes in the role of civility in both moral theory and conduct. In effect, civility was becoming—even more pronouncedly than in the previous century—a bridge between the profane and the godly and a means of altering

3. Marlborough Association of Ministers, Records 1725–1802, AAS, 65–69.

both, sometimes in subtle ways. As godly reformers incorporated more of the style and content of Augustan civility into their social ethos, they provided themselves with new means of influencing not only the "merely civil" but also the profane.[4] For their part, the profane too maintained their traditions, as the Marlborough Association claimed; but also, many found more opportunities and benefits in the stress on "Civil Liberties," which made them less inclined to disaffection and overt criminality.[5]

There were, however, contradictions and ambiguities in the reformers' attempts to reconcile godly standards with Augustan civility. The bulk of them revolved around the question of the effectiveness of a system of manners and morals not necessarily grounded in saving grace. The potential disconnecting of piety from morality aggravated the tendencies toward "enthusiasm" and "Arminianism" inherent in English Puritanism. These tensions, of course, played an important role in the Great Awakening.[6] Other related issues concerned the role of the passions or affections in religion and morality, the dangers of hypocrisy and "wit" in social relations, and the possibility that gentility was more apt to be used as a mark of social distinction than as a means to moral reform.

The style and content of Augustan civility, of course, largely determined its usefulness and limitations in the continuing Reformation of Manners. In terms of style, the direct, even confrontational, mode of moral address was passing out of fashion. John Dunton remembered "a blunt, honest Christian" of Boston who in the 1680s went to visit a "Lady." She said that "she was glad to see him, but sorry that he came at such a time when her house was dirty." His response was, "Why, pr'ythee, when was it otherwise?" The woman took the remark "as a great affront; but it was all one" to the pious layman, "who still spake as he thought, let his friends take it how they

4. A recent excellent study of Augustan civility, interpreted as "catholic" broadness, among New England ministers is John Corrigan, *The Prism of Piety: Catholick Congregational Clergy at the Beginning of the Enlightenment* (New York, 1991). See also Richard P. Gildrie, "Civility, Piety, and the Reformation of Manners in Augustan New England," *Studies in Puritan American Spirituality* 2 (1991): 107–28.

5. David H. Flaherty, "Crime and Social Control in Provincial Massachusetts," *Historical Journal* 24 (1981): 339–60, documents a generally declining "crime rate" in Massachusetts from the 1690s to the 1750s, the only exception being the 1710s.

6. Stephen Foster, *The Long Argument: English Puritanism and the Shaping of New England Culture, 1570–1700* (Chapel Hill, 1991), esp. 3–28, 287–311; David S. Lovejoy, *Religious Enthusiasm in the New World: Heresy to Revolution* (Cambridge, Mass., 1985), 178–214; John Corrigan, *The Hidden Balance: Religion and Social Theories of Charles Cauncey and Jonathan Mayhew* (New York, 1987).

pleased." To Dunton such conduct may have been admirable, but it was also amusingly quaint.[7]

The differences between the elder and younger Mather also illustrated the change. Increase Mather, as Michael Hall has noted, "was stubbornly, ideologically plain, severe, ascetic," while his son "was flamboyant and exhibitionistic." Dunton found an "abundance of freedom and familiarity in the humour of this Gentleman." Nor was this difference solely a matter of personality. Cotton Mather cultivated his manner as both a moral imperative and a mode of ethical instruction. "There is," he explained in 1701, "a Civil, Genteel, Handsome Carriage which we are to treat men withal, though we may see much Folly in them." In 1726 in his advice to young ministers he reasserted the reformist goals of etiquette. "And, When I propose to *Ingratiate* myself unto any People by the Civilities of Conversation, it shall be, that I may gain thereby the better *Advantages* to prosecute *Good Purposes* upon them."[8]

Linking affability and moral earnestness, Cotton Mather became (as Kenneth Silverman observed) "the most noted conversationalist of his time much admired and sought after by contemporaries for his erudite and beguiling wit." In the cultivation of this talent he was participating in a major cultural trend. Among English moral reformers "wit" was seen as "a sharp Weapon as apt for Mischief as for good Purposes, if it be not well manag'd." But properly used, it was not merely amusing but also instructive—able, in Archbishop Tillotson's words, "to season Conversation, to represent what is Praise-worthy to the greatest Advantage, and to expose the Vices and Follies of Men, such things as are in themselves truly ridiculous." Out of this sense of the uses of wit evolved the era's penchant for satire—a continuing effort, as a recent scholar put it, "to force the irrational world of experience into the ordered perspective of hope."[9]

Part of the appeal and impact of this form of moral commentary was that it paralleled, even appropriated, the parodic strain in traditional popular culture. Satire was a learned stylistic adaptation of folk practice, much as the political settlement rooted in liberty and property signaled some accommo-

7. John Dunton, *Life and Errors* (London, 1705), 1:94.

8. Ibid., 1:98–99; Michael Hall, *The Last American Puritan: The Life of Increase Mather, 1639–1723* (Middletown, Conn., 1988), 176; Cotton Mather, *The Young Man's Preservative* (Boston, 1701), 20; Cotton Mather, *Manuductio ad Ministerium* (Boston, 1726), 11.

9. Kenneth Silverman, *The Life and Times of Cotton Mather* (New York, 1984), 36; Sir Richard Blackmore, "An Essay upon Wit," in his *Essays on Several Subjects* (London, 1716), reprinted in Augustan Reprint Society *Publications,* 1st ser. (1946, 1967), 206; David Nokes, *Raillery and Rage: A Study of Eighteenth-Century Satire* (New York, 1987), 14.

dation to popular aspirations. Wit and satire functioned on the same moral principle of humorous juxtaposition of the real and the ideal, of practice and theory, that animated rough ridings, the Feast of Fools, and picaresque tales.[10]

The "Augustan literary charivari," as one critic has called it, shared the potential for ambiguity inherent in the popular form. It was not always clear whether satire was a spur to reform or a substitute for it. Its overt tone was usually one of amused hope based on clarity of moral conviction. Yet it seemed at times to express despair at intractable human perversity or even uncertainties of moral judgment amid conflicting values. On occasion, not only the purpose but even the targets of ridicule were imprecise or multiple. Elaborate jokes in skillful satire as in popular mockery could turn on the author or audience as well as the overt target.[11]

In Boston in the 1720s, for instance, the rage for voluntary associations became a source of humor. Young Ben Franklin in his Silence Dogood letters suggested "Friendly Societies" for widows and spinsters, including "a very proper proposal" that "every single Woman, upon full Proof given of her continuing a Virgin for the Space of Eighteen Years, (dating her Virginity from the Age of Twelve), should be entitled to 500 pounds ready cash." Besides associationism, possible points of the joke included prevalent attitudes toward women and marriage, women themselves, the demographic impact of continuing warfare, and the commercialization of social relations. Even the tensions between communalism and individualism were deftly exposed when he claimed "that the Country is ripe for many such *Friendly Societies,* whereby every Man might help another, without any Disservice to himself." At the same time he may well have thought that there was merit beyond humorous plausibility in the proposals. Despite apparent contradictions, he could have intended all these possibilities.[12]

The proclivity to satire and its ambiguities were not restricted to literary figures. In September 1728 a group of Harvard students formed a "Philomusarian Club" ostensibly because "the Honourable & Laudable Designs (viz. The Promotion of Learning & Good Manners) for which this Illustrious

---

10. Anonymous, "A Letter to A. H. Esq. concerning the Stage" (London, 1698), in *Augustan Reprint Society Publications,* 3d ser. (1946, 1967), 15–16; Pat Rogers, *Literature and Popular Culture in Eighteenth-Century England* (Brighton, England, 1985); Ronald Paulson, *Popular and Polite Art in the Age of Hogarth and Fielding* (Notre Dame, Ind., 1979); Pat Rogers, *The Augustan Vision* (New York, 1974), esp. 180.

11. Margaret Anne Doody, *The Daring Muse: Augustan Poetry Reconsidered* (Cambridge, 1985), 123.

12. Leonard W. Labaree, ed., *The Papers of Benjamin Franklin* (New Haven, 1959–), 1:32–36, 38; Nokes, *Raillery and Rage,* 23.

Academy was founded Have Been of Late Subverted." Reform through a student society was necessary because "Conversation, which is the Basis of Friendship the Fundamental Principle of Society The Great Prerogative of Mankind & every Way adapted to the Dignity of Humanity, is Now att a very Low Ebb, the Necessary Consequence of which is the Decay of Learning and Civility." With deliberately excessive repetition, their preamble bewailed that "Vice & Folly are in their Zenith & Meridian & Gild the Hemispheres of the Muses with Meteors whose false Glare is by many Mistaken for the refulgent Stars of Wisdom & Virtue." The passage concluded, "To be Brief, Vice is now Become a la Mode & Rant Riot & Excess Accounted the Height of Good Breeding & Learning." In a good-hearted sophomoric way the "Philomusarians" struck at the rhetoric, assumptions, and solutions of Augustan moral reform. Judging by the fact that at least one of the members, Samuel Curwen, later became an embodiment of Augustan civility in his Salem ministry, this satire was not a rejection but an ironic embrace of the ideal.[13]

The ambiguities of wit and satire were, of course, a possible source of "Mischief," to use Archbishop's Tillotson's word. John Barnard, the witty and modish Marblehead pastor, tried in 1727 to clarify the uses and abuses of humor in a sermon, *The Nature and Danger of Sinful Mirth*, delivered to a young men's society. There was, he was certain, "a clownish sort of Mirth" that can "transgress the Laws of Good Manners" rather than forward them. He objected to humor directed at "those who are defective in their understanding, or labour under Bodily Imperfections" as demonstrating a lack of compassion and a denial of shared flawed humanity. He also denounced mirth that made light of sin rather than exposing its perils. There were some, he said, who "make themselves merry with the Rehearsal of their past Follies" and others who "divert themselves by recounting their Neighbour's Failings." Similarly, he criticized those who "flout at Religion . . . and make themselves mighty pleasant with all that is *sacred* and *serious*." He regarded all such conduct as not only "rude and unmannerly" but also morally dangerous. To be of "good humour" was to affirm the ties among people and to further moral and religious commitments.[14]

Barnard's attempt to define the limits of "mirth" illustrated both the problems and opportunities presented by fashionable wit. Its protean character reflected the complexities of the larger construct, Augustan civility, of

13. "The Articles of Association of the Philomusarian Club," Curwen Family Manuscript Collection, AAS, box 2, folder 3.

14. John Barnard, *The Nature and Danger of Sinful Mirth* (Boston, 1727), esp. 105–11.

which it was an expression. A powerful social ideal, eighteenth-century gentility was described in a vocabulary indicative of its style. Good conduct was "polite," "polished," "refined," "genteel," "graceful," "affable," and "urbane." It reflected "taste," a respect for "fashion" among the "beau monde." This "ethic of good humor," as Edmund Leites has termed it, required self-restraint and sensitivity to the interests and feelings of others, two traits that were deeply appreciated by the moral reformers. Indeed, the advocates of this ethic often thought of themselves as reformers. Sir Richard Steele, whose essays in the *Tatler* and the *Spectator* did much to shape the ideal, was also an active member of the London Society for the Reformation of Manners. Cotton Mather had no doubt that the *Spectator* and the *Guardian,* which he read avidly, served "the best Interests in the Nation." Harvard students and Boston intellectuals, including leading ministers, produced periodicals and wrote articles in the 1720s imitating those of Steele and Joseph Addison in the belief that such work forwarded moral as well as cultural improvement.[15]

In the 1720s Daniel Defoe defined a gentleman as "a Man of Honour, Virtue, Sense, Integrity, Honesty and Religion." Henry Fielding in 1743 summarized the moral content of the ideal. "Good Breeding, then," he wrote, "or the Art of pleasing in Conversation, is expressed two different Ways, viz. in our Actions and our Words, and our Conduct in both may be reduced to that concise, comprehensive Rule in Scripture: Do unto all Men as you would they should do unto you."[16] Interpreted in such terms, Augustan civility was fully congruent with the Puritan traditions of New England.

Also, the reformers believed that gentility could be taught and that its benefits, potentially available to all, could raise the moral tone of the whole society. Jonathan Swift in 1710 thought of "Good Manners, or Breeding" as "a Sort of artificial good Sense adapted to the meanest capacities; and introduced to make Mankind easy in their Commerce with each other." Without "some Rules of this Kind," persons of "Low and little Understandings" would "in their ordinary Conversation fall into the same bois-

---

15. Edmund Leites, *The Puritan Conscience and Modern Sexuality* (New York, 1986), 67–68; Richard L. Bushman, "American High-Style and Vernacular Cultures," in Jack P. Greene and J. R. Pole, eds., *Colonial British America: Essays in the New History of the Early Modern Era* (Baltimore, 1984), 358, 362; Edward J. Bristow, *Vice and Vigilance: Purity Movements in Britain since 1700* (Dublin, 1977), 19; Worthington C. Ford, ed., *The Diary of Cotton Mather* (New York, 1916), 2:227.

16. R. W. Harris, *Reason and Nature in the Eighteenth Century* (London, 1969), 119–20; S. J. Sackett, Introduction to Fielding's "Voyages of Mr. Job Vinegar from the *Champion* (1740)," in Augustan Reprint Society *Publications* 12 (1958), ii.

terous Familiarities that one observes amongst them when a Debauch has quite taken away the Use of their Reason."[17]

In practice, however, gentility was often used as a sign of social distinction not to be shared with the populace. The more elaborate expressions of personal refinement and fashionable living required levels of wealth and leisure most people found unattainable. Persons of the requisite social bearing, familiar with the polite arts and letters, met together to display and further develop those accomplishments in private settings such as dinner parties and balls and on public occasions such as court days and church services. A resulting element of competition in clothing, for instance, seemed to Cotton Mather an opening to "Vanity and Luxury" amid the "Immoderate and Exorbitant Gaieties" of such genteel gatherings.[18]

Contempt for the "vulgar" rather than concern for their improvement seemed endemic. Samuel Moody, a Maine pastor, denounced in 1710 those "Proud and Haughty Spirits, if they make Some Figure in the World" who found it fashionable to "scorn God's Chosen and Precious Ones, because, for the most part, they are Poor in the World." In Massachusetts even some of the ministers amused themselves early in the eighteenth century with "pleasant stories" at the expense of those who lived "up to the knees in Piggs." The wisest of the reformers, however, believed that a competitive and complacent civility, like some forms of Separatist piety, created invidious distinctions that subverted the ideal itself.[19]

The ambiguities of civility extended beyond social usage into content. Reformers in England and Massachusetts hoped that "fashion" might recast "habits." Expressing a commonplace of the era, John Locke observed in 1690 that most people "govern themselves chiefly, if not solely, by this Law of Fashion; and so they do that, which keeps them in Reputation with their Company." The problem was that fashion, like wit, was fickle. Indeed, the moral relativism suggested by attention to fashion seemed implicit in the social contract theories of such writers as Thomas Hobbes and John Locke. Intended in part as philosophic underpinnings for civility, the theories partook of and deepened the ambiguities of this ethic. Cotton Mather in 1718 directly attacked the idea "That all the Differences between Good and Evil, Right and Wrong, lies in the Agreement of Humane Society thereupon." He

17. Jonathan Swift, *Bickerstaff Papers and Pamphlets on the Church,* ed. Herbert Davis (Oxford, 1966), 184.

18. Cotton Mather, *Grace Defended* (Boston, 1712), 13; Swift, *Bickerstaff Papers,* 184.

19. Samuel Moody, *Doleful State of the Damned* (Boston, 1710, 1739), 103; Curwen Family Manuscripts, box 2, folder 1.

argued that "these Wicked Sons of [Hobbes's] Leviathan do confute themselves" in that they were forced to hold "That antecedently unto all Compact, it is Good & Right that a Compact should be kept." In other words, Mather asserted that there were moral absolutes that undergirded and found expression in social relations. This insistence was fundamental to the reformers' version of civility; and yet it seemed at hazard in Locke's political and psychological theories, which helps explain why his work, often so congenial to Puritan thought, provoked such a mixed response among colonial moralists.[20]

While conceding that "customs" varied, the reformers insisted that the fundamentals of good and evil were embedded in the natural as well as the social order. "The Follies of Sin," Cotton Mather argued in 1700, "are so many, so obvious, and so very *Brutish,* as abundantly to convict those of not acting *Reasonably* who do not live Religiously." Was it not true, he asked sinners, that they found "thy *Health* decayed, thy *Name* disgraced, thy *Purse* wasted?" Sin not only resulted in personal disaster but also provoked social calamity, which came as much by a sort of natural law of evil as by God's direct punishment. "There is a natural Tendency in Vice," wrote a pamphleteer for the Society for the Reformation of Manners, "to ruin any Person, Family, City, or Nation that harbours it. It engenders Sloth, Variance, Profuseness, Pride, Falsehood, Violence, and a Neglect, and a Betraying of the Publick Good." Both reason and experience, claimed a Connecticut minister in 1714, combine "to recommend Religion to us, as tending to promote the Welfare & Happiness of a People; and to dissuade from Sin, Vice, and Immorality, as having a contrary tendency."[21]

This overt appeal to reason, natural law, and the temporal benefits to individuals and societies was an effective response to the increasingly diverse and latitudinarian assumptions of the reformers and their audience. The

20. Nokes, *Raillery and Rage,* 94–95; J.G.A. Pocock, "The Varieties of Whiggism from the Exclusion to Reform: A History of Ideology and Discourse," in his *Virtue, Commerce, and History: Essays in Political Thought and History Chiefly in the Eighteenth Century* (Cambridge, 1985), esp. 236; Locke quoted in Thomas L. Pangle, *The Spirit of Modern Republicanism: The Moral Vision of the American Founders and the Philosophy of John Locke* (Chicago, 1988), 215; Ford, ed., *Diary of Cotton Mather,* 2:142; Norman Fiering, *Moral Philosophy at Seventeenth-Century Harvard: A Discipline in Transition* (Chapel Hill, 1981), 240n.–41n.; John Dunn, *The Political Thought of John Locke* (Cambridge, 1969), 7.

21. J. C. Curtis and W. A. Speck, "The Societies for the Reformation of Manners," *Literature and History* 3 (1976): 49–52; Cotton Mather, *Reasonable Religion* (Boston, 1700), 25, 48; Josiah Woodward, *An Account of the Rise and Progress of the Religious Societies in the City of London and of Their Endeavours for Reformation of Manners,* 4th ed. (London, 1712), A7; Samuel Whitman, *Practical Godliness the Way to Prosperity* (New London, 1714), 3.

danger, however, was a conflation of etiquette, custom, manners, morality, and religion that would prove rigid and simplistic. Daniel Defoe in 1727 illustrated the temptation. "Modesty, then," he wrote, "is nothing but a strict regard to Decency, as Decency is a strict regard to Virtue, and Virtue is a strict regard to Religion; indeed, they seem all, in some Sense, to be synonymous, and to mean the same thing." In this climate, as Harry Stout has observed, "natural theology and the light of reason threatened not to augment revelation but to displace it."[22]

For orthodox New Englanders this sort of moralism raised the specter of Arminianism, the belief that human effort as reflected in proper conduct rather than divine grace led to redemption. Cotton Mather—in the same sermon in which he appealed to sinners to consider their "Health," "Name," and "Purse"—also asserted that ultimately these were "Lying Vanities" and "miserable Comforters." The godly life required more than that "Men pursue after nothing but that they may have their *Senses* Gratified, and their *Estates* Flourishing, and their *Neighbours* putting a value upon them." The problem for orthodox thinkers such as Mather was to reconcile Puritan tradition, Enlightenment thought, and popular aspirations in order to evangelize and reform society without succumbing to what they perceived as dangers inherent in such a course.[23]

Civility to the reformers was a worthy and necessary goal, but not an end in itself. Increase Mather's observation in 1673 that "There is a Moral Sobriety which is not saving, and yet even that is lovely and commendable" was still relevant. However, proper civility not perverted by the winds of fashion or subverted by hypocrisy had to be rooted, as Samuel Moody explained in 1701, in "the great End for which we are Made, Preserved, and Redeemed," the sincere worship of God. Civility, then, was an element of, rather than a substitute for, worship in the formation of reformed human character. As Cotton Mather formulated the relation: "Hence, Whatever contributes unto the *Welfare of Mankind,* and such a *Relief* of their Miseries, as may give the Children of Men better *Opportunities* to *Glorify* Him, *this* also is to Glorify Him."[24]

Yet despite its virtual dominance within the Church of England and its popularity among many English Nonconformists, Arminianism did not seem

---

22. Daniel Defoe, *Conjugal Lewdness* (London, 1727), 4; Stout, *New England Soul,* 135.
23. C. Mather, *Reasonable Religion,* 55.
24. Increase Mather, *Wo to Drunkards* (Boston, 1673), 15; Samuel Moody, *The Vain Youth Summoned* [preached 1701 in York, Maine] (Boston, 1707), 22; C. Mather, *Manuductio,* 8; Stout, *New England Soul,* 158.

to Cotton Mather to be a serious threat to the orthodoxy of New England's clerics. As he observed to an English correspondent in 1726, "I cannot learn, That among all the Pastors of Two Hundred Churches, there is one Arminian; much less an Arian." But he did detect it as a tendency among the populace.[25]

In 1704 he published a remarkable analysis of those "Wiles of the Devil" intended "to hinder all Men from a Godly Conversation."[26] In essence, the sermon was a critique of the weaknesses of popular piety. In order of frequency, the first flaw was complacency, "persuading the Unconverted that they are already and really Converted." One form of this error was a sort of Arminian moralism, tempting them "when they turn from their Sinfulness with some semblance and shadow of Conversion, to stop in their own Righteousness." The second was a more complete form of Arminianism infecting "the Unconverted with a loose and vile Opinion, that there is no Need of any Conversion at all." Morality was sufficient to gain salvation. To counter that notion Mather reiterated the orthodox position that "A Man may be very fair and strict in his Morality, and yet very Defective in his Christianity." The third was despair at "the Desperateness of their Condition," which had a less virulent variation (based on a misreading of orthodox dependence on grace) encouraging the "Unconverted to neglect their own Conversion to God, under pretence that they cannot convert themselves." Mather reminded his readers that preparation, at least to the extent of avoiding "those Wretches that Scoff at Serious Religion," was always possible. Finally there was the tendency, related to Arminian belief in human initiative, "to put off their Conversion, and promise of future Conversion."

Supplementing these doctrinal errors were satanic distractions, including "involving them in the Hurries of the World" and "deluding them to place their whole Religion in one private Opinion, and swallow up all Duties in a Zeal of Parties." Apparently the eclecticism of popular piety did not automatically lead to tolerance. Mather clearly did not believe that there was a popular religious consensus in Massachusetts, regardless of how close the orthodox ministers may have come to it early in the eighteenth century, and one of the tendencies among the folk that worried him was Arminianism.

Mather was not alone in his concern. A Long Island pastor in 1722 thought that "of all the engines that ever the devil formed against the salvation of men,

25. Conrad Wright, *The Beginnings of Unitarianism in America* (Boston, 1955, 1966), 9; Richard Warch, *School of the Prophets: Yale College, 1701–1740* (New Haven, 1973), 99–100.

26. Cotton Mather, *The Armour of Christianity* (Boston, 1704), 102, 108, 111, 114–15, 125, 141, 144, 146, 162, 166; Ford, ed., *Diary of Cotton Mather,* 1:298–99, for this and subsequent paragraphs on this sermon.

Arminianism seems the most effectual." It seemed particularly "mischievous" in his experience because "it goes less feared and mistrusted . . . under the specious colours of vindicating God's Justice, encouraging Virtue, and the like." In a notable execution sermon of 1733, Thomas Foxcroft of Boston's First Church complained of youths in particular "resting in a dead Faith, a legal Repentance, & unregenerate Morality." He did not denounce "open profaneness" as much as a form of Arminianism reflected "in a partial Reformation of Manners; in a formal Round of Religious Duties; in a Spirit of Bigotry for certain Superstitions, or in empty noisy Zeal for Divine Institutions: as if such things intitled you to the favour of God."[27]

The apparent spread of popular Arminianism even among the traditionally turbulent youth indicated to some clergymen that the long campaign for moral reform was succeeding. Of course, those seeking to inculcate the godly life were unwilling to settle for a mere civility unrooted in sincere piety. As John Norton explained in a 1708 election sermon on "Reformation," it was not enough "to cease to do evil, to learn to do well" if "our Malady viz. Unbelief" continued.[28] Yet "a partial Reformation of Manners" was apparent to him, as was the continuing strength of "a Spirit of Bigotry for certain Superstitions," a clerical depiction of the passionate eclectic and individualistic piety of folk religion. During the Great Awakening these two tendencies—"Arminianism" and "Enthusiasm"—collided, provoking the ministers to champion one or the other and then leading some of the wisest, such as Jonathan Edwards, to seek a way of reconciling them within a tolerably orthodox framework.

Another sign of partial success of the Reformation of Manners and of the tendency to accommodate elements of popular tradition was a trend toward a more favorable assessment of the role of the "passions." From at least the time of Erasmus the major goal of the reformers had been to discipline what Edmund Leites has called the "oscillating temperament" of popular culture. From the classical era into the late seventeenth century moral philosophers generally regarded the "will" as an instrument of "reason" to control the "passions." But then there was a shift in theory as, in Norman Fiering's words, "the lowly and dangerous passions were tempered, transformed, and elevated to become in some cases not only themselves the auxiliaries of reason, but often also the actual and proper leaders of the soul, the very beacons for reason to follow." An argument that "The Passions of the Soul are in themselves

27. Joseph Morgan to Cotton Mather, 31 October 1722, Curwen Family Manuscripts, box 2, folder 2; Thomas Foxcroft, *Lessons of Caution to Young Sinners* (Boston, 1733), 48–49.
28. John Norton, *An Essay Tending to Promote Reformation* (Boston, 1708), 16–17.

naturally good" at the Harvard commencement in 1689, a nicely symbolic date, was the first sign of public discussion of the shift among New England's intellectual elite. The terminology also changed to reflect the new attitude as "sentiments" and "affections" tended to replace "passions" in learned discourse.[29] While never universally adopted during the colonial period, this revolution in theory could only have seemed credible to the careful pastoral psychologists among the orthodox clergy if popular mores had indeed appeared more "tempered, transformed, and elevated" than they had in the 1670s.

This shift also meant that Anglo-American moralists became increasingly apt to try to harness the passions or sentiments to further the Reformation of Manners. The most profound of the passions was, as Increase Mather observed in 1702, "a sinful self-love which is the root of many and great evils."[30] In classic Christian terms it was Original Sin or pride. However basic to human nature, "self-love" was also fundamental to the quest for personal autonomy or honor, which motivated many of the populace. One tactic was to legitimate some forms of self-love as a matter of personal right and then define their proper characteristics so as to encourage communal or social responsibility.

In this context the Whig discourse on liberty in Augustan England and America took on rich personal and social as well as religious and civic significance. "Liberty, which exempts one man from subjection to another," Joseph Addison argued, "should reach every individual of a people, as they all share one common nature"—an affirmation of the egalitarian impulse. This judgment had for many the compulsion of natural law. As a Yale thesis of 1733 held, "The necessity of pursuing Happiness is the foundation of Liberty." Hence for orthodox Calvinists as well as Arminians, "Liberty is essential to the moral agent" even in the face of Predestination because "Divine Foreknowledge does not abolish human liberty." Yet its proper exercise, as Addison added, had to be "consistent with public peace and tranquillity."[31]

In 1726 Cotton Mather thought it a "Maxim without Controversy" that "a free Indulgence of Civil Rights" accrued "unto all that approve themselves

29. Leites, *Puritan Conscience,* 51–54; Norbert Elias, *The History of Manners* (1939; reprint, New York, 1978), 198–200; Fiering, *Moral Philosophy,* 148, 165; Ernest Tuveson, "The Origins of the 'Moral Sense,'" *Huntingdon Library Quarterly* 9 (1947–48): 241–59; Stanley Green, *Shaftesbury's Philosophy of Religion and Ethics: A Study in Enthusiasm* (Athens, Ohio, 1967), 137–83.

30. Increase Mather, *The Excellency of a Publick Spirit Discoursed* (Boston, 1702), 25.

31. Harris, *Reason and Nature,* 107; Warch, *School of the Prophets,* 224–25.

Faithful Subjects and Honest *Neighbours,* and such Inoffensive Livers, that *Humane Society* cannot complain of Disturbance from them." The fundamental constraint, in other words, was in civility itself, leading to the conclusion embodied in a Yale thesis of 1737 that "The only cause of misery is abuse of liberty." Abuse here meant both licentious excess by the person and tyranny by the society or government. In this context it is not surprising that in 1733 another Yale thesis would make the explicitly reformist point that "To moderate the passions is the correct exercise of liberty." When properly understood, liberty, the right to express the passions and pursue individual interests in a social setting, was not the enemy of moral reform but its necessary agent.[32]

Personal autonomy, grounded in natural law as evinced through the "sentiment" of happiness, had become the central motif of moral thought in England and America. Many of the orthodox continued to tie that conclusion back into earlier Puritan formulations. They asserted that "The highest liberty consists in extending obedience to the laws of the Omnipotent," but those laws were generally interpreted to confirm the trend. At the level of the "sentiments" now seen as controlling conduct "the passion towards self-good" remained "vicious" in any man until limited by "the natural affection for his kind." Sentiment controlled sentiment with reason or revelation as mediator. For the English moralists Shaftesbury, Joseph Butler, and even David Hume the sentiment "Benevolence" was as "natural" as "self-love"—and even related to it—and could be harnessed to moral reform.[33]

In the 1730s the great American philosopher of Calvinist orthodoxy, Jonathan Edwards, tied the argument back into traditional Christian interpretations. He insisted on the power of love or charity, "affections" whose right understanding and use can come only by divine grace. "Some, although they love their own happiness," preached Edwards in 1738, "do not place that happiness in their own confined good . . . but more in the common good." Indeed, the essential "nature of love is good-will." Conversely, "there are many principles contrary to love, that make this world like a temptuous sea. Selfishness, and envy, and revenge, and jealousy, and kindred passions keep life on earth in a constant tumult." These evil passions erupted in Adam's

32. Warch, *School of the Prophets,* 233; C. Mather, *Manuductio,* 119.
33. J. A. Passmore, "The Malleability of Man in Eighteenth-Century Thought," in Earl R. Wasserman, ed., *Aspects of the Eighteenth Century* (Baltimore, 1965), esp. 34; John Radner, "The Art of Sympathy in Eighteenth-Century British Moral Thought," *Studies in Eighteenth-Century Culture* 9 (1979): 189–210.

Original Sin as "Self-love became the absolute master of his soul, and the more noble and spiritual principles of his being took wings and flew away."[34]

The method provided by God to counter this disaster was not an outward "obedience" to natural or revealed law. Nor was it faith seen merely as rational assent to doctrine. Self-control evinced as "good-will" in Edwards's usage had to become an interior emotional reality responding voluntarily to the love of God. This inner state resembled the Augustan sense of happiness as "a quiet contentment equally removed from the strife of desires and the ecstasy of enthusiasm."[35]

Civility, interpreted as rules of conduct reflecting an inner emotional stability rather than conformity to authority, was closely related to the Whig sense of liberty. Civility and liberty seemed interdependent. Of course, the congruence between inner disposition and outward conduct was not always clear. These "mysteries of the heart" raised the issue of hypocrisy for the advocates of civility just as it had been raised earlier among Puritans searching for the evidences of conversion.

Jonathan Swift in 1709 argued that "Hypocrisy is much more eligible than open Infidelity and Vice," for "it wears the Livery of Religion, it acknowledgeth her Authority, and is cautious of giving Scandal." The merit of hypocrisy was that it at least encouraged acceptable public conduct. There was also the chance that outward conformity might lead to inner conviction in much the way Solomon Stoddard saw the sacraments as a means of grace. As Swift observed, "And I believe, it is often with Religion as it is with Love; which, by much Dissembling at last grows real." Cotton Mather too believed that "Custome shortly becomes a Second Nature," whether good or bad, and thus the correct formation of habit was primary in moral reform. On the other hand, Benjamin Franklin among others argued that honesty was at the core of civility and that therefore the hypocrite would not only slip on occasion but also inevitably subvert civility into corrupt forms while misleading those who regarded him or her as a model of virtue. In 1722 the young Franklin, asking "Whether a Commonwealth suffers more by hypocritical Pretenders to Religion, or by the openly Profane," concluded "that the Hypocrite is the more dangerous Person of the Two."[36] Never resolved, the issue was raised often in criticisms of the "formalities" of gentility and in debates over the

34. Jonathan Edwards, *Charity and Its Fruits* [1738 sermon series] (Carlisle, Pa., 1969), 158, 164, 196, 350.

35. Conrad Cherry, *The Theology of Jonathan Edwards: A Reappraisal* (Garden City, N.Y., 1966), 71–88; Harris, *Reason and Nature,* 103.

36. Swift, *Bickerstaff Papers,* 57; Cotton Mather, *Advice from the Watchtower: In a Testimony against Evil Customs* (Boston, 1713), 9–10; Labaree, ed., *Franklin Papers,* 1:30–32.

necessity and characteristics of "a converted ministry" during the Great Awakening.

Compounded by the ideal of liberty, the ambiguity of civility thus incorporated not only the popular culture's emphasis on personal autonomy but also its respect for the emotions. This complexity also affected ideas about property, that crucial sibling of liberty in the Whig lexicon. From the beginning of settlement, Puritan moralists praised efforts "to further our more comfortable subsistence" both by "a way of Trade and Commerce" and agricultural expansion.[37] Personal economic autonomy and security were aspirations and rights deeply embedded in English folk mores. Given the fragility of familial and communal order in late medieval and early modern Europe, this drive for personal independence may well have been rooted in economic necessity among the common people. But quickly economic autonomy and relative success became an important way of asserting personal honor as well. Thus it became a "passion."

New England reformers tried to balance their respect for the populace's "due concern about their Temporal Affairs" with their worry over incipient moral anarchy through definitions of "covetousness." "This sin discovers itself," wrote Joseph Sewall in 1718, "in an Excessive Esteem of Worldly Riches, in an immoderate Love to it, and delight in it when gotten; and a criminal backwardness and unwillingness to part with it to Pious, Publick, and Charitable Uses."[38] As Cotton Mather explained in 1707, "To Desire Wealth, To Pursue Wealth, to be Thankful for Wealth, will not fix upon us the Brand of Covetousness; while we keep within the Rules prescribed unto us, by the God who gives us power to get Wealth." The "Rules" were clear to the reformers, and indeed Mather's description of improper conduct showed a rather sophisticated appreciation of the moral perils of the developing capitalist ethos:

> When a man, to carry on a Greater Stroke of Business, will defraud his *Creditors,* decline timely and honestly to pay his *Debts,* break multitudes of *Promises,* care not how many *Debts* he Contracts, detains the *Wages* of the Hireling, utter *Falsehoods* without number, use a *Shuffling* and *Sharping* sort of Conduct with almost all that he has to deal withal and care not whom he may *Hurt;* if he may but *Serve* himself; Tis *Covetousness* that has debauched him.[39]

37. William Hubbard, *The Benefit of a Well-Ordered Conversation* (Boston, 1684), 97–98.
38. Joseph Sewall, *A Caveat Against Covetousness* (Boston, 1718), 3, 5.
39. Cotton Mather, *A Very Needful Caution* (Boston, 1707), 9–10, 14.

These were some of the obviously adverse results of "Idolatry"—that is, regarding wealth as an end in itself rather than as an instrumental good. With enforcement depending largely on conscience and reputation, ambiguities arose once the more overt forms of misconduct were set aside. A major problem was that the same self-discipline sought by the Reformation of Manners also contributed to economic success. Once again the moral tests seemed inadequate guides to inner or spiritual states. Thus, according to Cotton Mather, "the Covetous Man often sleeps in Profound Security" and "Dreams of no Danger attending him," for "he is a man of a very *Unblemished Conversation* before the World." He "does not Stagger with the Drunkard, . . . Wallow in Unchastity," nor "Curse and Swear Profanely." He may even be a "consistent Attender on the Ordinances of God." In good conscience "He takes all to be Safe." And so did his neighbors. The Arminian tendency to deem decent conduct as sufficient applied here as in other realms of civility.[40]

Indeed, the prestige of economic power was strong enough to lead Mather to complain that many "do not count the Righteous Man more Excellent than his Neighbour," even if "a wealthy Wretch," and that the "great Concern of Parents is, How to make the Children Rich? They are not concerned so much, How to make them *Good,* and *Wise unto Salvation?*" He was certain that "Worldliness" was "eminently the Sin of my own Countrey" largely because "multitudes . . . are not in any measure sensible of their Danger by that Sin." Nor was the problem restricted to the wealthy or mercantile sectors of society. In 1733 Samuel Wigglesworth thought that "the Powerful Love of the World" had become "the reigning Temper in Persons of all Ranks in our Land."[41]

By the early eighteenth century Anglo-American moral reformers were encountering a culture whose dominant aspiration seemed "a refined materialism," another ironic sign of their partial success. New England portraiture reflected, as one recent art historian observed, "a moderate brand of elegance, sophistication, self-esteem and prosperity, a gentlemanly and ladylike decorum, a strong dose of individualism, pragmatism, and self-confidence, a representation of frugality and of materialistic taste, and a refer-

40. J. E. Crowley, *This Sheba, Self: The Conceptualization of Economic Life in Eighteenth-Century America* (Baltimore, 1974), esp. 50–53; C. Mather, *A Very Needful Caution,* 16–17.

41. C. Mather, *A Very Needful Caution,* 32–33; Ford, ed., *Diary of Cotton Mather* 1:584; Samuel Wigglesworth, "An Essay for Reviving Religion" (Boston, 1733), in Alan Heimert and Perry Miller, eds., *The Great Awakening: Documents Illustrating the Crisis and Its Consequences* (Indianapolis, 1967), 6.

ence to one's beneficial relationship with God."[42] In other words, Cotton Mather and his colleagues now found more to worry about in the proclivities of the "merely civil" than in the "openly profane" in the realm of economic thought and conduct just as they had in more general realms of morals.

To some extent they continued to contribute to the problem by pitting the virtues of possessive individualism against the vices of hedonism. As John Webb of Boston preached in a 1721 lecture aimed at youths, "There is not only a Moral but Natural Tendency in the Exercise of many Christian virtues to get and secure to ourselves as much of the World as our State and Circumstances in it may call for" because "by moderate Expenses, Temperance, Frugality, and the like, the Virtuous Man keeps what the Idle Spendthrift prodigally throws away." Reputation, prosperity, and religion were closely linked. "By being Religious betimes you take the most proper and direct Course you can to get and establish a good Name, Credit, and Reputation in the World, among all those whose Value and Esteem is worth having."[43]

It became a commonplace among English moral and economic thinkers that one set of passions could be pitted against another to gain "harmony." Acquisitiveness could discipline lust, violence, idleness, or rebelliousness. As Samuel Johnson summarized, "There are few ways in which a man can be more innocently employed than in getting money." John Evelyn rhapsodized a century earlier that "the miracles of commerce taught us Religion, instructed us in Polity, cultivated our Manners, and furnished us with the Delicacies of virtuous and happy Living." One of the cornerstones of Whig thought was the belief that social and political order could be better based on disciplined self-interest than on the need for purely external constraints. Under the right conditions individualism and communal order were mutually reinforcing.[44]

Of course the New England thinkers, not immune to this logic, used it from the beginning. But as they had in the related discussions over hypoc-

42. Wayne Craven, *Colonial American Portraiture: The Economic, Religious, Social, Cultural, Philosophical, Scientific, and Aesthetic Foundations* (Cambridge, 1986), 177.

43. John Webb, *The Advantages of Early Piety* (Boston, 1721), 8, 10, 12; Crowley, *This Sheba, Self,* 2–3; J. William T. Youngs, *God's Messengers: Religious Leadership in Colonial New England, 1700–1750* (Baltimore, 1976), 8.

44. Joyce O. Appleby, *Economic Thought and Ideology in Seventeenth-Century England* (Princeton, 1978), 114–15; Albert O. Hirschman, *The Passions and the Interests: Political Arguments for Capitalism before Its Triumph* (Princeton, 1977), 31–44, 58; D. C. Coleman, *History and the Economic Past: An Account of the Rise and Decline of Economic History* (Oxford, 1987), 6, for Evelyn quote; Crowley, *This Sheba, Self,* 31.

risy, they tried to maintain the tension between "civil" and "godly" modes of thought and conduct and to assert the superiority of the latter not only in religious but also in moral terms. The danger was "corruption" of both the individual and the society. As Wigglesworth noted, the pursuit of wealth "takes up our Time, seizes our Affections, and governs our Views." There was, he thought, a narrowing of perspective and sensibility that could only be remedied in the "abandon'd, slighted and forgotten Religion." Ebenezer Parkman of Westborough encountered this decline of "practical godliness" in 1739 when one of his deacons objected to a consideration of a church member's economic plight, "judging it unfit to be mentioned on the Lords Day." Decorum endangered charity even among the godly. The reformers tried to make charity fashionable, but fashion proved at least as fickle as conscience had in the seventeenth century.[45]

Augustan civility, an appreciation of decorum and harmony based on an ordered sense of liberty and property, had deeply imbued New England culture by the 1720s. The process of anglicization toward these Augustan modes in law, political practices, consumer preferences, and the region's sense of identity as provinces within British culture continued apace. Predictably, the prestige of the Church of England as a paramount expression of that ethos also increased. The defection of several Yale students and tutors to Anglicanism in the 1720s was the culmination of a trend reaching back into the 1680s. The orthodox Puritan reemphasis on a general Protestant reform coalition inadvertently encouraged questions as to whether "all the pastoral Acts done by those who have not episcopal Ordination are Invalid." In 1712 twenty-two Newbury townsmen, in requesting a priest of the Bishop of London, asserted that they "would no longer persist with their mistaken dissenting Brethren in the Separation." By 1713 Cotton Mather feared that Anglicans in Marblehead could "prove a mischievous Majority."[46]

Some of the clergy who took Anglican orders, such as Stratford's Samuel Johnson, did so in part because they felt that Congregationalism was "a way so entirely popular" that it "must from the nature of it crumble to pieces as

---

45. Wigglesworth, *Essay for Reviving Religion*, 6; Francis G. Walett, ed., *The Diary of Ebenezer Parkman, 1703–1782* (Worcester, Mass., 1974), 66.

46. John M. Murrin, "The Legal Transformation: The Bench and Bar of Eighteenth-Century Massachusetts," in Stanley N. Katz and John M. Murrin, eds., *Colonial America: Essays in Politics and Social Development* (New York, 1983), 540–72; Richard L. Bushman, *King and People in Provincial Massachusetts* (Chapel Hill, 1985), esp. "Part 1: Political Culture, 1691–1763"; Ford, ed., *Diary of Cotton Mather*, 2:88–89, 147–48, 221; M. Halsey Thomas, ed., *Diary of Samuel Sewall, 1674–1719* (New York, 1973), 2:681.

every individual seems to think himself infallible." Yet, oddly, the most common charge against the Anglicans was their reputed appeal to the more flamboyantly individualistic churchgoers, providing "a Sanctuary to the contentious, refractory, and ungovernable." The prestige of Anglicanism, seconded by the orthodox clergy's latitudinarianism, made it a respectable form of dissent. Ebenezer Parkman discovered in 1745 that one of his deacons, "Shaken in Mind," was "dispos'd to listen to any Defence of the Church of England, or Opinions of the Baptists," apparently indifferently. Some months later Parkman feared that the "dissatisfy'd party" to one of the perennial factional squabbles within orthodox churches was "in Danger of turning to the Church of England."[47] In New England's religious culture Anglicanism was not so much a threat to individualism as another possible and increasingly acceptable mode of expressing it among both the elite and the common folk.[48]

These conflicts reached a climax during the Great Awakening. The members of the Marlborough Association, as they considered the impact of the revivals on the churches, warned their colleagues in 1748 to "beware of dangerous Errors which many have run into; particularly the *Arminian* and *Neonomian* on the one hand, and the *Antinomian* and *Enthusiastical* on the other." Rooted in New England's popular religiosity but separating both clergy and laity, these were extremes along a spectrum of opinion, style of discourse, and conduct that scholars have termed "rationalist" and "evangelical." Harry Stout distinguished them in terms of sermonic style within social contexts. "As rationalist essays were geared to the understanding and appreciation of informed audiences, evangelical notes were aimed at public arousal and the inspiration of the moment."[49]

The Great Awakening was indeed a decisive event. Yet equally impressive was the degree of institutional and intellectual continuity the godly were able to preserve. Reinforced by a deliberately irenic latitudinarianism at both Yale and Harvard after 1743, clerical associations such as the Marlborough group

47. Stout, *New England Soul,* 187; Warch, *School of the Prophets,* 123; Walett, ed., *Diary of Ebenezer Parkman,* 114–15, 124; Bruce E. Steiner, "New England Anglicanism: A Genteel Faith?" *WMQ* 27 (1970): 122–35. See also John Frederick Woolverton, *Colonial Anglicanism in North America* (Detroit, 1984), 113–34, 173–88, and Carl Bridenbaugh, *Mitre and Sceptre: Transatlantic Faiths, Ideas, Personalities, and Politics, 1689–1775* (New York, 1962).

48. A similar set of tensions animated the "Singing Controversy" over psalmic hymnody. See Laura L. Beckler, "Ministers vs. Laymen: The Singing Controversy in Puritan New England, 1720–1740," *NEQ* 55 (1982): 79–96; Gilbert Chase, *America's Music from the Pilgrims to the Present* (Chicago, 1987), 19–34; A. L. Lloyd, *Folk Song in England* (London, 1967, 1968), 15–17.

49. Marlborough Association, 69; Stout, *New England Soul,* 221.

worked to avoid the extremes and to reconcile both persons and positions so as to maintain and revitalize the heritage. They were remarkably successful. Of the seventy-seven "Separate" congregations born of schisms within the churches between 1742 and 1750, only twenty-three persisted after 1765. The more determined of these groups headed in a Separate Baptist direction and remained, together with the Quakers and the slowly growing Anglican presence, as alternatives to the still-dominant orthodox congregational ethos.[50]

Out of the long conversations among the profane, the civil, and the godly, three major themes had emerged that helped preserve unity among the orthodox in the aftermath of the Awakening. The first was a reaffirmation of the notion that "common Christians" could serve as "good judges" in both doctrinal and ecclesiastical matters, an idea inherent in Congregationalism from the beginning but put at hazard before and during the Awakening. The second point was the relevance of civility as a moral criterion for evaluating the personal and social impacts of the revivals. If these events seemed to encourage a stronger sense of mutual responsibility among participants, then they were judged godly rather than narrowly "enthusiastical." The third was an agreement that the Reformation of Manners, particularly the effort to discipline and convert the profane, had to continue. A religious and moral climate which undermined that campaign or encouraged the profane was intolerable to a majority of both Old and New Lights who remained committed to New England's traditional covenantal mission.

From its inception in the Connecticut Valley in the 1730s through its eruption more generally in the wake of George Whitfield's New England tour in 1740, the Great Awakening was in large part a popular challenge to clerical authority. Laymen withdrew from churches whose ministers they believed were either "unconverted" or "enthusiastical." They formed new congregations or removed pastors whom they disliked with aplomb. Some insisted on "lay prophecizing" or relied more heavily on itinerants than on "settled" pastors for religious guidance.

An underlying theme was the right, indeed the obligation, of individual judgment rather than acceptance of authority. These "awakened" lay folk regarded their activities as a recovery, not a repudiation, of tradition. As one Separatist deacon asserted, "every Man has a Right of judging for himself, of trying Doctrine by the inspired Scriptures, and of Worshipping according to

50. Stout, *New England Soul,* 212–17; C. C. Goen, *Revivalism and Separatism in New England, 1740–1800: Strict Congregationalists and Separate Baptists in the Great Awakening* (New Haven, 1962, 1969), 258–82.

his Apprehension of the Meaning of them." Although Old Light or conservative pastors initially resisted many of the applications of this right,
which led to schisms and divisions, many found themselves bound by their
own principles not only to acquiesce but also to appeal to the same standard.
In 1743 William Rand, an embattled Old Light minister at Sunderland,
writing in response to one of Jonathan Edwards's defenses of revivalism,
urged his readers, "Believe *no* Man, however knowing, pious or zealous;
however peremptory or popular . . . Prove *all Things* by the Standard of
Scripture. . . . You have a *right* to do this; it is your *Duty:* It is your
Interest."[51]

There emerged a crucial consensus among both Old and New Lights that
church order rested on the independent judgment of "common Christians,"
bound only by their understanding of the Bible. If true in religion, a matter
of eternal importance, then it was even more true of the ephemeral realms
of society, economy, and politics. Guided only by Scripture, Natural Law, or
statutes created in some consensual form, the independent common man
was now both theoretically and practically the basis of the New England
social order.

Another source of reconciliation was agreement on moral criteria for
evaluating the character and results of the Great Awakening. Indeed, among
these heirs to and advocates of the Reformation of Manners this understanding was fundamental to the consensus on relying upon the judgment of the
"common Christian." As early as 1735 Eliphalet Adams, pastor at New
London and a Yale trustee, defended the valley's spate of revivals as a "divine
work." He defined "a divine work" among a people as that which not only
"makes them serious, watchful, prayerful & heavenly minded" but also
"helps them to govern better their thoughts, words, & Actions, their appetites & inclinations, passions & affections, disposeth them to be just &
righteous, kind and charitable to all that are about them and finally fills them
with Love to God."[52]

In 1738 Jonathan Edwards told his Northampton congregation that
proper conversion led to "a right spirit." "A man of a right spirit," he

51. Stout, *New England Soul,* 188–89, 208–9, 211 (deacon's quote), 216–18; Gregory W.
Nobles, *Divisions throughout the Whole: Politics and Society in Hampshire County, Massachu-
setts, 1740–1800* (New York, 1983), 10–11, 36–74; Youngs, *God's Messengers,* esp. 10;
Kenneth Lockridge, *Settlement and Unsettlement in Early America: The Crisis of Political
Legitimacy before the Revolution* (New York, 1981), 43–45; William Rand, *The Late Religious
Commotions in New England* (Boston, 1743), 19.

52. Eliphalet Adams's introduction to Eleazer Williams, *Sensible Sinners Invited to Come to
Christ* (New Haven, 1735), iii–iv.

observed, "is not a man of narrow and private views but is greatly interested and concerned for the good of the community to which he belongs, and particularly of the city or village in which he resides, and for the true welfare of the society of which he is a member." Old Light thinkers such as William Rand concurred that the converted should "live better Lives than they did before." If revivals helped "the People" become "*more* honest, and just, and kind, and merciful, more punctual to their Words, *better* Neighbours, *better* Relatives, that they bridled their Tongues *better*, and in general were more circumspect in their Behaviour; this would have made the Face of things *beautiful indeed.*" In Scotland, also experiencing an awakening, similar criteria emerged. As one Scottish moralist observed at the end of their cycle of revivals, "Christianity not only sanctifies our souls, but refines our manners; and while it gives the promise of the next life, it improves and adorns the present."[53]

Initially, of course, there had been some dispute among the godly as to whether revivalism actually improved morality. Particularly worrisome were the "bodily effects" of the experience "such as *falling down* and *crying out* in the Time of Worship, *Faintings, Swoonings, Twitches, Trances, Visions,* etc." encouraged by some itinerants and others. To Old Light critics these events did not seem harmless passing phenomena unrelated to doctrine or social conduct. Rather, they appeared to be an eruption of some of the worst features of popular piety. Those liable to "Violent Agitations of Body" were often "pretending to extraordinary Communications from the Spirit of God—*The Light Within,* Revelations, Trances," which implied a depreciating of "the Word of God, and setting up the *Light Within* or some other Rule above it." This "extreme passion" encouraged "censoriousness," the tendency to condemn "all others, though never so wise, and good, and thought they have given the brightest Evidence of their true Piety by an holy, wise, heavenly unblemished Conversation; yet all this passes for nothing at all with an Enthusiast."[54]

According to Northfield's Old Light pastor, Benjamin Doolittle, the moral consequence was that the antinomian impulse would "freely sentence such to Heaven as live in Drunkenness, Whoredom, Lying, Cheating, Deceiving, Envy, Contention, and Strife, if they are but warm Enthusiasts." The social danger was that "they begin to transgress Order and Regularity in

53. Edwards, *Charity and Its Fruits,* 169; Rand, *Late Religious Commotions,* 14, 21–22; Richard B. Shea, *Church and University in the Scottish Enlightenment: The Moderate Literati of Edinburgh* (Princeton, 1985), 31, Scots quote on 65.
54. Rand, *Late Religious Commotions,* 34, 38.

Church and State, and pretend Conscience for so doing; and that nothing is Order but their own Fancies and Imaginations." Rampant individualism meant moral and social anarchy, a fear at least as old as the Reformation of Manners itself. To reinforce the point Old Light theorists such as Charles Chauncey also issued historical polemics reminding New Englanders of the long struggles against such heretics.[55]

The Old Light emphasis on continuity was not misplaced. Yet there were significant differences that suggest important cultural changes since the seventeenth century. Not even the most virulent critics found more than a suggestion of violence or rebellion among the New Lights. Absent as well, even amid the flood of denunciatory self-righteousness, was subversion by mockery. Rather, the "Disorders" that the critics feared were those which undermined "*Family Order, Family Religion,* and *Closet Devotions*" so beloved by the reformers. The country was beset "by the Rise of so many *weak, illiterate,* lay-preachers" claiming "that *strange Liberty* . . . of going about from *Parish* to *Parish,* calling the People off from their necessary secular business" and possession of "that *Spirit of Discerning* . . . a Method of judging and censuring their Brethren." There was a "Faction and schism, and general Confusion" but no violence. "A Spirit of Censoriousness, Reviling, Clamour, Insolence, Spite, and Malice" was loosed in the society, but the egalitarian and anticlerical impulses had found relatively tame modes of expression. In a brilliant aside David Hall recently observed that the converts in the Great Awakening "reaffirmed the liberating impact of the Holy Spirit, the true 'carnival' for godly people." This group of the godly reasserted their freedom and challenged authority but without some of the excesses of their "profane" predecessors.[56]

Comparison with the witchcraft crisis of the 1690s provides another perspective on cultural changes. During the seventeenth century persons whose "Passions have been in a *violent commotion . . . seeing Visions* and *falling into Trances,*" disrupting worship or daily activities, were generally suspected of being under demonic possession. During the Great Awakening these same symptoms were interpreted by vast numbers of New Englanders as signs of God's grace. Indeed, not even the "opposers" of reviv-

55. Benjamin Doolittle, *An Enquiry into Enthusiasm* (Boston, 1743), 33, 35; Anti-Enthusiasticus [Charles Chauncey], *The Wonderful Narrative: Or, a Faithful Account of the French Prophets . . . To which are added Several other Remarkable Instances of Persons of the like Spirit in various Parts of the World, particularly in New England* (Boston, 1743).

56. Anti-Enthusiasticus, *Wonderful Narrative,* 103–4; Rand, *Late Religious Commotions,* 13; David D. Hall, *Worlds of Wonder, Days of Judgment: Popular Religious Belief in Early New England* (New York, 1989), 244.

alism suggested demonism. Signs of satanic subversion had become intimations of the Kingdom of God or of mental illness. In popular imagination, apparently, Satan was now largely restricted to his own domain in hell and no longer stalked the earth directly and personally confronting people with the temptation to indulge moral and political chaos.[57]

This difference partially reflected changed social circumstances. The wars and economic troubles of the 1730s and 1740s were not so severe as the pressures of the 1680s and 1690s. At least as important, however, were the cultural changes. For the intense purgation of the tensions between godly standards and folk mores to be viewed as personally and communally beneficial rather than catastrophic, the conflicts must not have seemed so dangerous. That argues that the traditional conversations were more nearly congruent than they had been in the late seventeenth century but not yet identical. The aspirations of the Reformation of Manners were more widely accepted among the populace, while the advocates of reform had morally legitimized more elements of popular tradition. The old theme of "a world turned upside down" was now both internalized by more people and even ritualized by the society into what David Hall has termed a "rhythm of alternations of purity and corruption" in the long run more apt to bridge social and moral conflicts than exacerbate them.[58]

Orthodox New England in the 1740s was generally a more "orderly and decent" society than it had been in the late seventeenth century, as was much of the rest of the English-speaking world.[59]

"In vain did ministers preach against those things before, and in vain were laws made to restrain them, and in vain was all the vigilance of magistrates and civil officers; but now they have almost everywhere dropped them as it

57. Anti-Enthusiasticus, *Wonderful Narrative*, 103–4; Paul Boyer and Stephen Nissenbaum, *Salem Possessed: The Social Origins of Witchcraft* (Cambridge, Mass., 1974), 29–30, 215–16.

58. Laurel Thatcher Ulrich, *Good Wives: Image and Reality in the Lives of Women in Northern New England, 1650–1750* (New York, 1982), 225; David D. Hall, "Religion and Society: Problems and Reconsiderations," in Greene and Pole, eds., *Colonial British America,* 337–38. I would argue that this "rhythm of alternations of purity and corruption" remains characteristic of American politics, religious life, and popular culture.

59. Flaherty, "Crime and Social Control," esp. 357–60; Christine Leigh Heyrman, *Commerce and Culture: The Maritime Communities of Colonial Massachusetts, 1690–1750* (New York, 1984); Paul Donald Marsella, "Criminal Cases at the Essex County, Massachusetts, Court of General Sessions, 1700–1785" (Ph.D. diss., University of New Hampshire, 1982); Allan Kulikoff, *Tobacco and Slaves: The Development of Southern Cultures in the Chesapeake, 1680–1800* (Chapel Hill, 1986); Jack P. Greene, *Pursuits of Happiness: The Social Development of Early Modern British Colonies and the Formation of American Culture* (Chapel Hill, 1988), esp. 170–206.

were of themselves. And there is a great alteration amongst old and young as to drinking, tavern-haunting, profane speaking, and extravagant apparel." As Edwards's supporter William Cooper observed, "'tis certain these fruits do not grow on Arminian ground."[60]

Edwards got the best of the argument among most of his peers, once the excitement abated. For instance, the members of the Marlborough Association, made up largely of moderate Old Lights, wondered publicly in 1748 "whether we have not given Strength & Boldness to the Ungodly when we have been testifying against the Extravagancies and Excesses of the late Times." Even Charles Chauncey at the height of the controversy in 1742 was willing to concede that "if, when their Passions are subsided, and their Imaginations cooled, they now continue to discover a truly Christian *Temper* and *Conduct*, there is reason to hope well concerning them."[61] Thus it was that even the "Extravagancies and Excesses" of popular piety could be baptized into the Reformation of Manners.

The two generations between the Reforming Synod of 1679 and the Great Awakening marked a vital phase in the larger Reformation of Manners that was fundamental to shaping the regional ethos. Following in part a sophisticated theory of cultural interaction among the godly, civil, and profane conversations, New England's clerical and intellectual leadership maintained the vitality of the Puritan tradition while absorbing and refining elements of folk aspiration and expression. The tradition offered the people of New England the chance to incorporate self-discipline and communal responsibility with the drive for personal autonomy and individual dignity. As the American Revolution approached, the notion of "independence" was redolent with immediate social and personal implications for the folk of New England.[62]

In eighteenth-century Massachusetts both liberalism, with its stress on personal autonomy, and republicanism, with its belief in communal virtue as essential to human dignity, were integral to the region's ethos. These commitments, while apparently contradictory, were also complementary.[63] They

60. Jonathan Edwards, *The Distinguishing Marks,* in C. C. Goen, ed., *Works of Jonathan Edwards: Great Awakening* (New Haven, 1972), 223, 230, 241, 244.

61. Marlborough Association, 67; Anti-Enthusiasticus, *Wonderful Narrative,* 103.

62. Noble E. Cunningham, *In Pursuit of Reason: The Life of Thomas Jefferson* (Baton Rouge, La., 1987), 79; Richard L. Bushman, "'This New Man': Dependence and Independence, 1776," in Richard L. Bushman et al., eds., *Uprooted Americans: Essays to Honor Oscar Handlin* (Boston, 1979), 77–96.

63. John L. Brooke, *The Heart of the Commonwealth: Society and Political Culture in*

marked zones on an old spectrum of reform opinion sharing a common language, set of problems, and moral basis in the themes of the Reformation of Manners. The culture of early New England was never a monologue; it was always at least a dialogue.

Worcester County, Massachusetts, 1718–1861 (New York, 1989), 17–128, is the best description of this ethos.

Index